D1564554

The Waltz He Was Born For

An Introduction to the Writing of Walt McDonald

The Waltz He Was Born For

An Introduction to the Writing of Walt McDonald

Edited by

Janice Whittington

and

Andrew Hudgins

Texas Tech University Press

The paper used in this book meets the minimum requirements of ANSI/NISO Z39.48-1992 (R1997). ∞

Design by Brandi Price

Printed in the United States of America

Library of Congress Cataloging-in-Publication Data

The waltz he was born for : an introduction to the writing of Walt McDonald / edited by Janice Whittington and Andrew Hudgins.
     p.   cm.
Includes bibliographical references and index.
ISBN 0-89672-487-5 (cloth : alk. paper)
1. McDonald, Walter—Criticism and interpretation. 2. Texas—In literature. I. Whittington, Janice. II. Hudgins, Andrew.
PS3563.A2914 Z97 2002
811'.54—dc21

                                        2002001767

02 03 04 05 06 07 08 09 10 / 9 8 7 6 5 4 3 2 1

Texas Tech University Press
Box 41037
Lubbock, Texas 79409-1037 USA
1-800-832-4042
ttup@ttu.edu
www.ttup.ttu.edu

Contents

Acknowledgments   vii

Transcending Hardscrabble: The Evolving Vision of
Walt McDonald   1
   An Introduction by Andrew Hudgins

I. Overview of Works
All His Hands Can Do: The Poetry of Walt McDonald   16
   Henry Taylor

II. War and the Return of the Veteran
Domestic Tranquillity and National Defense: The Personal
History of Walt McDonald   30
   Jerry Bradley

Reclaiming the Homefront: Walt McDonald's
Peacekeeping Soldiers   37
   Barbara Rodman

McDonald's *A Band of Brothers*: A Plea for a
Deeper Understanding   48
   Clay Reynolds

III. The Southwest in McDonald's Poems
Walt McDonald's Beautiful Wasteland   62
   Michael Hobbs

Unignored Plunder: The Texas Poems of
Walt McDonald   80
   Dave Oliphant

An Uneasy Truce: Wildness and Domesticity
in the Poems of Walt McDonald   92
   April Lindner

Walt McDonald, Poet of the Southwest   100
    Nick Norwood

Poetry to Trespass For   111
    Dan Flores

IV. Aesthetic Strategies

Walt McDonald's Poetry: Images of Man's Acceptance of
His Place in Time   122
    LaVerne Popelka

Angel and Mirage: Concerns of Imagination in Walt
McDonald and Wallace Stevens   134
    William Wenthe

How to Spin Rightly: Walt McDonald's Vision
of the Artist   148
    Janice Whittington

V. Religious Imagery, Thought, and Implications

"Dark Pearls": An Introduction to Walter McDonald's
Poetic Journey of Faith   162
    Darryl Tippens

Intimations of Higher Matters: Anagogical Closure in
Walter McDonald's *Burning the Fence*   175
    William Jolliff

Perseverance in Walt McDonald's Poetry   185
    Chris Willerton

Forms of Incarnation in the Recent Poetry of
Walter McDonald   195
    Helen Maxson

VI. In McDonald's Own Words

An Interview with Walt McDonald, April 2000   216
    Phyllis Bridges

Notes   227

Works Cited   232

Works by Walt McDonald   240

Works about Walt McDonald   241

Contributor's Notes   246

Index   249

Acknowledgments

Grateful acknowledgment is made for permission to print the following:

Hudgins, Andrew. "Transcending Hardscrabble: The Evolving Vision of Walt McDonald." *Southern Humanities Review* 35.3 (2001): 209–23.

Jolliff, William. "'Intimations of Higher Matters': Anagogical Closure in Walter McDonald's *Burning the Fence*." *Christianity and Literature* 49 (2000): 205–14.

Maxson, Helen F. "Forms of Incarnation in the Recent Poetry of Walter McDonald." *Christianity and Literature* 49 (2000): 225–44.

Oliphant, Dave. "Unignored Plunder: The Texas Poems of Walt McDonald." *Concho River Review* 10.1 (1996): 50–62.

Tippens, Darryl L. "'Dark Pearls': An Introduction to Walter McDonald's Poetic Journey of Faith." *Christianity and Literature* 49 (2000): 189–203.

Willerton, Chris. "Perseverance in Walter McDonald's Poetry." *Christianity and Literature* 49 (2000): 215–24.

Transcending Hardscrabble: The Evolving Vision of Walt McDonald

An Introduction by Andrew Hudgins

Over the last three decades, Walt McDonald has emerged as a unique and significant voice in contemporary literature. He first came to national prominence writing, in both poetry and fiction, about the Vietnam War, and the war is a subject that he has continued to explore in some of his darkest and most troubling poems.

Readers and critics next began to focus on McDonald as an important poetic voice of the West. In particular, his is the voice of Texas, a landscape that has inspired countless pages of fine prose, but had lacked its defining poet before McDonald, with what seems in retrospect like astonishing ease, filled the role.

Recently, the critical focus has expanded again to examine and appreciate McDonald's significance as one of the country's best religious poets—not a devotional poet by any means, but an important poet in the great Christian tradition of a spiritual search that is hesitant, modest, skeptical, and joyous. And I would contend that all these ways of understanding McDonald's work are inextricably wound around each other, each contributing to the strength of the others.

What a body count there must be in Walt McDonald's eighteen books. Consider *Witching on Hardscrabble*. In that book alone—a book that probably contains fewer deaths than most—Kline crashes into a swamp in the Mekong delta, Barnes is killed by a rocket at Da Nang, and Durwood drowns on a childhood rafting trip. The number goes up exponentially if we count livestock slaughtered in the course of business or put out of its misery on the range—not to mention the natural depredations of eagles, wolves, coyotes, and cougars, or the thousand snakes captured at a rattlesnake roundup and cooked into chili with "green / sweet relish, jalapeno" ("Chili at the Rattlesnake Roundup" 52). In the pages of Walt McDonald's world, men die in combat in the twentieth century's wars, including Vietnam, where McDonald served with the U.S. Air Force. Home is safer but not safe. Scratching a life from the hardscrabble of West Texas, men lose digits, limbs, and their lives. It's a man's world in all the old senses of that phrase. Though the poems change speakers and perspectives, the voice that speaks these poems is remarkably consistent: it's the voice of a man who has seen a lot of violence, suffered it and inflicted it—and is haunted by it.

Far from glorifying, exploiting, or sensationalizing violence, the speaker is quietly horrified as he struggles to make sense of it. He knows that some violence is pointless and some necessary. He is a man who, with complicated feelings, teaches his son to shoot a shotgun, a skill that can be misused. "Clipped in place, the target / waits like a child" (3), McDonald tells us in "On Teaching David to Shoot," the first poem in *Anything Anything*. He knows that his son could use the weapon to kill an innocent child just as surely as he is killing his own innocence as he takes on the power and the dangerousness of manhood. The father would prefer to raise his boy in a safer world, some Eden where there is no danger to be met and where one does not have to be dangerous to meet it:

> This son I would with choice
> raise in another country
> where the only trajectories
> are flights of bees to the moist
> dilating cups of tulips
> yellowed with pollen. (3)

But Eden is unattainable, and since his son must live in the treacherous fallen world, he would be endangering the boy if he didn't teach him how to defend himself. He's been a boy himself, though, and he knows how attractive the destructive power of the weapon can be. In "Loading a Shotgun" from *After the Noise of Saigon*, the speaker remembers the power he felt holding the loaded weapon while "my father stands / above me, and watches": "Now I can kill / whatever I point at // like a wand" (39).

The knowledge that what saves can also destroy and that what protects can also murder is a guilty knowledge which runs throughout Walt McDonald's poetry, suffusing it with a sad and savage wisdom. "On Teaching David to Shoot" ends with simple acceptance:

> Together we crunch back
> to our positions, and reload.
> I tell him ready, aim.
> And he takes aim. And fires. (4)

Sorrow hovers between the words, and if the tone is rueful, haunted, grieving, another note is also struck: pride. The father does what he must, though he doesn't want to. But he is proud of his son for moving on to adult responsibilities, and he is proud of himself for not shirking a duty that he would rather avoid.

In "Making a Living" from *Witching on Hardscrabble*, we get the same lesson from another angle, the angle of the boy who is learning it:

> My father was killing pigs again,
> another thing to make a living.
> I heard little kids sing to their mothers
> Pig man's coming. (49)

Like the father in "On Teaching David to Shoot," the boy, embarrassed by his father's job, also wants to run away, "join the navy, / see something in the world / that didn't squeal and bleed." He doesn't understand the irony of his own desire, but the man the boy has grown into clearly comprehends necessity.

With the boy standing beside him, the father makes arrangements with a widow to slaughter her hog:

> The widow listened, pushing
> strands of wild hair in her eyes.
> He sighed and thumped my head.
>
> Then with his levis stiff
> from the day's first slaughter,
> he took a wire noose to the pen,
> pigs grunting, huddled in the corner,
> and gave that first sharp knife to me. (49)

The scene precisely captures the boy's horror—and the understanding of the grown man meditating on the squeamish innocence he once entertained. The boy is horrified by the butchering and by the fact that his father is "the pig man," a title that conflates the father with the pig he kills. Now, remembering, he acknowledges his father's sigh, which implies that the father at least partially hoped to be spared the job he had sought. The father's stiff blue jeans let us know that the father is not making the boy do the job because he's too lazy to do it himself, and the phrase "that first sharp knife" tells us there have been many other sharp knives since.

Though the actions in McDonald's poems are often violent, the language seldom is. It's usually laconic, giving us the facts, the terse voice letting us know that this is the way things are and that, while a man will almost certainly regret what he has to do to survive, there is no shirking necessity. In other poems the sadness shows through, and the language is, in its rueful, laconic, Western way, thoughtful, meditative, haunted.

What is one to make out of living on this hardscrabble that is the world? That is the question that McDonald's books ask over and over again. With the opening lines of the opening poem, almost every book presents a violent world, laying it out as a wound to be probed, a sad fact that the book attempts to find a way around.

Witching on Hardscrabble begins with "Black Wings Wheeling":

> The danger more than wolves
> is hardpan caving in,
> tumbling down an arroyo
> alone and bawling, bone snapped,
> stumbling, unable to stand. (3)

Soon, "black wings" begin "to wheel / down a slow whirlpool of air" to feed on the dead calf.

The Flying Dutchman opens with a different poem, also titled "Black Wings Wheeling":

> Every drought, we find buzzards
> stacked in a spiraling cylinder,
> red heads and fanned black wings,
> tip feathers pronged like knives,
> coasting, waiting for something to lie down
>
> under a black circling mobile
> and close its eyes. (3)

After the Noise of Saigon starts by introducing two predators, man and wolf, and the wolf is man's superior:

> Living on hardscrabble, a man is less
> than a wolf and knows it, carries a rifle
> in season or not. Out here, killing's
> always in season, time enough for scruples
> sweating in bed with the windows raised.
>   ("When Children Think You Can Do Anything" 3)

The opening poem in *Night Landings* expands the violence from the natural to the human world. Pennington, "a nice kid / eager for everything," crashes on his third solo flight, and dies (11).

Once this harsh world has been established, the books spiral out, charting the violence—its causes, manifestations, and effects—but also searching for the joys that balance it, palliate it, make life worth living. What are they? There are small, equivocal ones, like language and song. When the Quaker ancestors of the speaker in "Estacado" arrive in West Texas from Iowa, they found one comfort: "The only milk here flowed in the cow / roped to their wagon, / their only honey, words in a book" (*After the Noise of Saigon* 14). The speaker's bitter tone implies he does not completely share his ancestor's comfort in the words of the Bible, though he also grants that there is honey to be found in words. In "Sweet Nothings" from *The Digs in Escondido Canyon*, the speaker also finds some solace in words and music, even if it's only temporary solace:

> The same old songs keep twanging back,
> slurred by steel guitars and a fiddle,
> tear honey for the heart. They make me young
>
> and vulnerable again, for three minutes,
> as if Saigon never happened. (16)

A larger, more philosophical comfort is the existential code the speakers have developed to deal with a world that makes only partial sense and in which law and society have at least partially failed. It's the old chivalric code of medieval romances refracted through the code of the West and refracted again through the existentialist Hemingway code of Jake Barnes and Robert Jordan. In a world that has no intrinsic order, a man orders himself and lives true to his own sense of integrity. A man is true to his commitments to friends—commitments that trump law. He does what he has to do in the face of necessity, and he observes a tight-lipped reticence about his suffering. "Between the Moon and Me" from *After the Noise of Saigon* represents a good if slightly romanticized example of the code in action. On land that he has inherited from his grandfather, the speaker finds, hidden in cactus, a board that says "*J. W. McCall & son, rustlers, 1899*" (19). Knowing what he will find, he digs beneath the makeshift grave marker and unearths "their bones, the skulls // and buckles of their belts." Before he calls "the deputy I shot pool with in Dickens" to report the body, the speaker takes

> . . . that long Winchester down
> from the mantel and oiled it, and wound it
> over and over in oilcloth, and buried it
> under the moon, deep down. (20)

By burying the rifle, an act that parallels his grandfather's burying the rustlers he shot, the speaker protects the family name. Ballistic evidence could connect the inherited rifle to the crime, and in modern eyes his grandfather would be a murderer rather than an upright citizen who was protecting his property in a way that was considered proper at the time. The grandson calls the law but frustrates the investigation before it begins. He knows where his true loyalty lies. And by wrapping the rifle so carefully, he is in one sense rejecting the violence in his family's past, while preserving his valued link to that past and reserving the right to use the weapon in the future, if he has to.

In a hostile world, and especially in combat, the cohesion of comrades in arms is an obligation of the code, and a life-or-death matter. It's also a real comfort against fear, and the fear makes the camaraderie even more intense. In "War Games" from *After the Noise of Saigon*, men crouch in a "sandbagged bunker, / lights out, listening for rockets" while they play craps:

> We rolled till our luck ran out,
>
> passed the empty handful
> to the next man kneeling
> in the dark, bunkered down,
> having the time of our lives.
>
> We never knew the color of scrip
> we lost, not caring
> what was at stake in night games,
> not daring to think. (54)

In "For Friends Missing in Action," also from *After the Noise of Saigon*, the speaker lifts a toast in memory of "a flier / missing since Saigon / fell in the seventies." Whether he "cratered deep in a swamp" or "languished, / chained to a bamboo cesspool,"

> [h]e's gone.
> Lift up your savage mugs
> and let the truth ring
> like a gong: he's gone. (66)

Remembering fallen comrades with a toast is an obligation that runs deep into history, well past the Vikings, the Romans, and the Greeks into the phalanxes of prehistory. McDonald's poem honors both fallen warriors and the act of honoring them.

But loyalty to comrades in arms is not an unchallenged good, as we see in "My Father Quits Another Job" from *After the Noise of Saigon*—though the speaker's father celebrates its virtues loudly.

He's staggered home drunk and bloody from a fight, bringing "his best friend home again," a best friend who the poem implies is a stranger "passing through from somewhere":

> My father had it again—
> one guy doing for the other, he announced.
> His moustache quivered. That's all
> makes this pigsty of a world
> worth living in. His grin
> could have swallowed the house. (32)

The son, though, sees the hollowness of the romantic gesture by his drunken father, who is clearly searching out "best friends" to stand up for, and he is worried and frightened by the risks his father is taking with his body and his job. But he also sees that his father's need to manufacture situations to prove his manly loyalty comes at the expense of his own family, whom he is driving out of the house, both literally and figuratively. Outside in the snow, away from his father who is "roaring ballads to my mother," the son remembers another time when he himself came home in tears. His father held him "tight, / like the heavy coat that seemed now, outside, / the only thing between me and freezing" (33). It's a deft and complex scene, the boy remembering the comfort of his father's love that stood between him and the cold like a coat. But now the deeper human warmth of the metaphor "like a heavy coat" has given way to the thing itself, the heavy coat, which is like nothing but itself.

The speakers in these poems learn to depend on themselves in a harsh world. But if they possess a lineage that extends to Hemingway's Jake Barnes and Robert Jordan, it's a Robert Jordan who works a ranch and teaches his son to shoot, a Jake Barnes who has returned to America and married happily. In this sense Walt McDonald's voice is the voice of a Nick Adams who loves his wife and, at least in part because of her, keeps trying to find a way through his despair. For all the violence in his poetry, few poets write better and more deeply about married love than Walt McDonald.

What pleasures are deep enough to sustain the man returned home from combat, the man scratching a living from the hardscrabble of West Texas? Love, marriage, family. And in McDonald's poetry, it is love that lets him begin to understand the uses of adversity. "A Woman Acquainted with the Night" from *The Flying Dutchman* begins "My wife is not afraid of dark" (22). Climbing in caverns or camping in dark forests, she is perfectly at ease with darkness. Why? Because

> [w]hen she was six a fat man
> digging a storm cellar

shut her and a friend inside,
and stood on the black steel door

and stomped like thunder.
Frozen, too frightened to reach
for Becky screaming in her ears,
she felt nothing could ever

be that dark again. In time
the door clanged open and light
baptized her with perhaps
too deep a trust of saviors.

Living through her fear has taught her the limits of her fear, and the
experience has taught her to believe that she will be delivered from
whatever darkness she finds herself in:

She lies down now in darkness
with no human hand but mine
to cling to, nothing but faith
in the moment to let her sleep.

And she knows "how many steps to the candles / so if our children
wake and cry / for light, there will be light" (23). The husband does
not yet share his wife's faith, but he longs to. The trust of saviors that
she has been baptized into is only "perhaps" too deep. The fact that
she clings to "no human hand but mine" implies that she also clings
to a more-than-human hand. And as the speaker takes comfort in his
wife's faith, he is already beginning, without quite acknowledging
it, to share her belief.

This spiritual progress continues in "The Middle Years" from *After the Noise of Saigon*. Camping in the mountains with his wife, the
speaker notices that the campfire's embers "wink like mountain
lions" (74). Life is still dangerous and fleeting, but there's an increasing acceptance of death as natural and inevitable—and perhaps, in
fact, not an end:

The last sparks

fling away from this spinning planet
and burn up in the only air there is.
All those years to make a roof for children,
gone from us faster than sparks.

Now we are back to beginnings
deep in the mountains, one fire at a time.
Stars are our comfort, and ferns that sough
and hover over us all through the night.

We lie in eiderdown and hold each other
a long time, silent. Later, I wake
and listen. The quick cry of a coyote
rises in the distance, the sound

of wings lifting, eagle or owl.
Nothing else for minutes, only your
steady breathing, asleep, believing
nothing's out there that shouldn't be. (74–5)

The natural processes of our planet and the natural processes outside our solar system—the stars—are evoked as a comfort. To live
and die is to be a part of something larger than one's self. But don't
those stars hint at something timeless, like God, and don't those hov-
ering ferns have some of the sense of a protective God? The ending is
deeply ambivalent. After all, the wife's belief that "nothing's out
there that shouldn't be" could be a false belief. And the something
that should be out there could still be dangerous, like a cougar. But
the line also hints at the preacher's pulpit assurance that God will
not send the believer any more of a trial than he can handle. The
wife's faith is the husband's hope. But only by first having her state it
can he state it even to challenge it—a challenge that allows the hope
into his mind and into the poems. Finally, hesitantly, he comes to accept it and affirm it, as we will see.

I did not hear these spiritual hints as anything more than vague
spiritualism when I first read *After the Noise of Saigon,* as I did not
fully see the possibilities of salvation at the end of *The Waste Land* until I had read *Four Quartets.* But in McDonald's next book, the stars in
"The Middle Years" return in "The Waltz We Were Born For," the final poem in *Blessings the Body Gave,* and here the poet's vision extends beyond them:

My hands find the face of my bride.
I stretch her skin smooth and see bone.
Our children bring children to bless her, her face
more weathered than mine. What matters
is timeless, dazzling devotion—not rain,
not Eden gardenias, but cactus in drought,
not just moons of deep sleep, not sunlight or stars,
not the blue, but the darkness beyond. (109)

Walt McDonald, as Eliot said of John Webster, sees the skull beneath
the skin, an echo that must be intended. Here again he searches for
something timeless, a devotion that lasts forever—something that
the flesh is incapable of. Even the bone, which endures more than
flesh, does not last as long as the devotion it inspires. But that human

devotion, limited by the flesh, suggests something eternal. The search, then, is spiritual, and it is balanced on what we interpret the darkness in the last line to mean. Is it God or nothing? Traditionally, we associate darkness with absence, emptiness, nothing. But here the statement, with the "nots" stripped out, is that timeless, dazzling devotion *is* the darkness beyond the stars—and that is what matters, not the physical facts of the universe. One is reminded of Marianne Moore's saying in "He 'Digesteth Harde Yron'": "the power of the visible / is the invisible" (430).

These ideas are similar to the Platonism of Pauline Christianity, but is the vision Christian? McDonald's language doesn't become unequivocally Christian until the last poem in the *After the Noise of Saigon*. "The Rodeo Fool" presents a Christ-like figure in explicitly Christian terms. The rodeo clown is perceived by the crowd as

> some kind
> of saint, a fool holy enough to do what
> they'd like to do, nightly to save someone
> from death and make believe it's fun. (87)

The rodeo clown is a holy fool who makes a spectacle of himself for a greater good; he suffers so others may live. The reference is to I Corinthians 4:9–10, in which Paul admonishes the believers not to worry about the derision of the worldly:

> 9 For I think that God hath set forth us the apostles last, as it were appointed to death: for we are made a spectacle unto the world, and to angels, and to men.
> 10 We are fools for Christ's sake, but ye are wise in Christ; we are weak, but ye are strong; ye are honourable, but we are despised.

A secular version of Christ, the rodeo clown intercedes between the fallen bull rider and death. He gives people hope that, though "all fall down, get gored and trampled on," they will, because of his sacrifice of his own body, defy death and walk again: "all men are able to rise with the help / of clowns, able to look death in the eye, / to wear a clown's face, laughing, and walk again" (87).

Despite its use of the language and imagery of the Gospels, and the direct allusion to Paul's epistles, the poem remains at least slightly equivocal. The rodeo clown is not Christ; he's merely Christ-like—a man who sacrifices his body for other men, not a god who dies for them. But in *All Occasions* the vision becomes openly Christian, and that vision is made explicit by the title. The book's epigraph (and its title) comes from John Donne's Christmas Day sermon in 1624: "All occasions invite his mercies, and all times are his seasons." One section of the book takes its epigraph from Gerard

Manley Hopkins's "Carrion Comfort": "That night, that year / Of now done darkness I wretch lay wrestling with (my God!) my God." But the epigraph for the last section, quoting John Berryman's "Eleven Addresses to the Lord," makes an even stronger statement about how that wrestling match turned out: "Under new management, Your Majesty: Thine." Though the book as a whole returns to familiar material—Vietnam and the harshness of life on the West Texas plains—the context now is different. The spiritual challenges and doubts are those of someone inside the faith, not those of a doubter rejecting or longing to leave his doubts behind. Before, the blessings existed as moments of light, peace, solace in the overall harshness of life. Now grace is paramount, and suffering is seen in the context of grace.

Uncharacteristically, the book starts with the blessings before moving onto the trials. The opening section of the book is titled "The Midas Touch," and it presents a checklist of blessings: the pleasure of watching a granddaughter whose father has returned alive from the Gulf War, the speaker's abiding love for his wife, the beauties of the natural world, the love shown by tending to the old and dying, the pleasure taken in instructing the young. These individual blessings are not only individual blessings, as in McDonald's earlier work, but also evidence of God's overarching grace. A crucial and brilliant poem in this first section is "At Dawn with the Blinds Raised," its title hinting at the biblical story of the apostle Paul, blinded by his vision of Christ, having the scales lifted from his eyes in Damascus. It begins with a question Paul must have pondered:

> How does faith come—like a hummingbird darting by,
> or a pair of elk cows clipping our grass at dawn,
> sniffing the picnic table while we wait
> with the blinds raised. Soon, beams will splash
> the mountain peak, lights will come on,
>
> a cabin door will close, the elk will lift their heads
> and stare, and trot with eyes wide, back to the tree line.
> Suddenly, others come, almost glowing in their blond,
> thick, winter coats, bowing to grass we've watered
> and not mowed, hoping for this moment—four,
>
> fourteen, the whole herd here on our lawn,
> sisters and mothers on our green slope,
> cougars and coyotes a thousand yards behind them,
> calves on their way within weeks—but all that's later,
> and the best grass since last summer is right now.

Cannily, the poem leaps ahead to the full panoply of the vision, of which the hummingbird is harbinger, and then withdraws, saying "Let's not get ahead of ourselves. Let's return to that single hummingbird, those first two elk cows, that first summer grass" (13). Everything after the opening question—"How does faith come?"— is metaphor: "Faith comes *like this.*" But the metaphor is also specific events in the real world, and the poet holds them in his mind as pleasures in their own right. The poet claims the fullness of his vision and the beginning, before its fullness was known. He lingers in the moment—and the moment is both utterly itself and at the same time a metaphor for something larger. The poet lingers in that first arrival of both spring and faith—*carpe diem* and *carpe Deum.*

It's tempting to think that the hummingbird from "At Dawn with the Blinds Raised" is the same one that turns up later in the book in "Faith Is a Radical Master." This poem also begins with a question, one to which the answer is obvious: "Can that hummingbird / that slammed against the glass / believe invisible facts?" Yes, the invisible is real. The hummingbird can tell it is because he's knocked himself cockeyed against the glass he can't see, as the speaker, the poem implies, has also been clobbered by the invisible reality of God in the world, and within himself. Here, at last, the language and imagery of the Gospels is embraced without reservation and without mediation through the wife's belief:

> Is God in the clear, after all,
>
> not beyond, not hidden in clouds
> I've stared at, but here
> in my heart where I rise
>
> like a blind man leaping
> and shouting *Look!*
> look, I can see! (94)

In the last poem in the book, "Watching Dawn on Padre Island," a man recovering from heart surgery lounges, "lazy as Lazarus," beside his wife on the deck of a condo. Together, they watch the sun rise over the Gulf, which "glistens like a highway paved with gold." The symbolism could hardly be clearer. The gulf between the resurrected man, who literally has a changed heart, and the sun (Son) is a highway paved with gold that emanates from the sun and leads toward it. A good surgeon with the "touch of a master's hand" has brought him back from the dead. The poem ends with the patient waking in the recovery room, confused:

> I remember counting back, then odd confusion

in a recovery room, like waking dazed in a cave
or casket, bright light and voices, but whose?
And what were they saying, what happened
and where was this, wondering why can't I rise
and throw off these winding sheets and walk. (101)

But of course, from the way the poem begins we know that the speaker has in fact, with time, done just that: he's thrown off his winding sheets and walked. This is the sustaining vision that all Walt McDonald's work has been leading to: "the way to be immortall is to die daily," as Sir Thomas Browne says in *Religio Medici* (1678). We wake every day in Plato's cave of the visible world, the casket from which, confused, we must arise every dawn.

In the fine essays that follow, most of them written expressly for this book, Walt McDonald's impressive and increasingly important body of work is considered from many different angles. With subtle discrimination, the poet and critic Henry Taylor addresses the issue of McDonald's vast productivity. Barbara Rodman and Jerry Bradley analyze McDonald's writings about war and the return of the veteran to civilian life, while Clay Reynolds takes a close and incisive look at how McDonald writes about the war in his fiction. Dave Oliphant, April Lindner, Nick Norwood, Michael Hobbs, and Dan Flores turn their critical attention to the work about Texas and to the fascinating question of what it means to be a regional writer. William Wenthe, LaVerne Popelka, and Janice Whittington examine McDonald's aesthetic strategies and thoughtfully place him in the context of other writers. Looking beyond the aesthetic, or perhaps into another aspect of it, Darryl Tippens, William Jolliff, Chris Willerton, and Helen Maxson contemplate the religious imagery, thought, and implications of the poetry with a bracing depth of scholarly and theological knowledge. Finally, in a fine interview with Phyllis Bridges, Walt McDonald himself has the last word.

This book owes its existence to the poet Janice Whittington. Her vision and hard, smart work took it from concept to fact with a dedication I marvel at. Though I have been a longtime admirer of Walt McDonald's poetry, I admire it more—and understand it better—after reading the fine essays gathered here. I hope you will too.

I. Overview of Works

All His Hands Can Do:
The Poetry of Walt McDonald

Henry Taylor

A note on his website says that Walt McDonald has published over 1,900 poems in periodicals. That is more poems than Emily Dickinson preserved. The great bulk of this overwhelming production has been in the past twenty-five years, which is to say that McDonald has for a considerable time averaged about seventy-five periodical publications a year. In this circumstance, a general discussion of his poetry will most likely be based on a partial reading of the work, and on a tentative distinction between modes of productiveness among poets. It has been fashionable for some time to regard immense productivity as a mistake. "He writes too much." All right, he writes more than I have read or will get around to reading. To cut a little nearer the bone, he writes more than I do, and you, too, probably. Wouldn't he be more manageable if he were more like us?

Well, he isn't, nor will he be.

It might be argued that some of McDonald's poems would be better if he had spent more time on them instead of on several others. But this is to assume that McDonald's way of working is amenable to the kind of patience that regards each poem in progress as having the potential to be a finished product of some importance. What if, instead, McDonald is being truest to his talent when he is writing something he has not seen before? What if he thinks of a poem as the brief record of an even briefer moment, a way of taking notice, of being fully alive? And finally, what if it happens to be fairly easy for him to get from the initial impulse to the finished poem? In these instances, which add up to the present one, the terrific individual poem will come along when it feels like it, and no amount of wheedling and whittling will bring it about more often or more regularly. The product of the labor is not so much the cumulative effect of poems one at a time, but the combined effect of a great many of them—the works, not a work.

None of this is to suggest that McDonald is a careless craftsman or that his poems lack finish. Over the years, in fact, he has become increasingly secure in a potentially treacherous mode, the irregular use of meter. When it doesn't work, the poem seems indecisive in its lineation; when it works, the lines and sentences seem to take turns being measurably iambic. At its best, it is a way for a very capable poet to both join and enlarge the tradition.

Consider the situation of the athlete, for example a high or long jumper. Through practice, training, and coaching, he (or she, assuredly; I briefly lost my heart to the televised splendor of Stefka Kostadinova) gains the strength and the technique to be dependably competitive up to a certain height or distance. But now and then come days when the usual practiced moves—the slight rocking back and forth at the start, the settling in, the attempts to shake off the earthbound self—all work just right, and great jumps come with what seems little effort. If they were poems, these would be the anthology pieces. But they are individual jumps—videotaped, maybe, entered in record books more rarely; but they count only once and then are gone. Why not write poems in that spirit?

True, the poems are there to be revisited, like videotaped leaps. For many years following Bob Beamon's mysterious and epochmaking long jump in Mexico City in 1968, his filmed technique was analyzed and pronounced upon. He had jumped more than twenty-nine feet when the world record was well short of twenty-eight. How did it happen? Study of the films is useless. Technically, by the conventional wisdom, it was a somewhat wasteful jump, inclusive of a few moves the coach might deplore, maybe even a slightly chopped landing. Yet he broke the previous world record by twenty-one and a half inches. The things he got right were immense in comparison to whatever he may have gotten wrong.

In his (at this writing) latest book, *All Occasions,* McDonald works ground he knows well. He goes back over it because he knows that familiar ground need not lose its capacity to surprise. He has written often and well of the Vietnam War, during which he was a pilot, and of the Texas hardscrabble, which produced him and upon which he has ranched, and of his family, both forebears and offspring. Jet planes, motor vehicles, horses, cattle, firearms, children, and a beloved woman have all responded in various ways to his touch, and he has pursued a distinguished professorial career. He has had many opportunities to consider the margin between expectation and outcome, between hope and experience. That gap has rarely brought him to despair, though he is no stranger to grief. It is his fate to have nurtured some realistic hopes, to have seen a few of them tragically dashed, and to have lived with passionate attention.

Thus it is that "Facing It" (*All Occasions*) can open with calm opacity, its first three lines addressing, in all likelihood, the speaker's parents, though it will take a while to reach that preliminary conclusion:

> I suppose you turn on the horizon,
> expecting me, both of you on tiptoe,
> others bumping past like pilgrims.

Then an instant cinematic cut, not even a stanza break:

> That time when I was five at the Royal Gorge
> comes back to haunt me, wandering off
> across that swaying bridge a thousand feet
> over the fast, white-water Arkansas. (57)

The sentence is slightly loose syntactically, so "that time" may briefly be seen to have "wander[ed] off," before we see how the "me" that is "wandering off" is at once a five-year-old and an adult haunted by a moment long past. There follows one of those offhand moments some poets live for: to put "white-water" and "Arkansas" together apolitically in the year 2000 is a little like the passage in which Robert Louis Stevenson ends a paragraph "nevertheless" and starts the next one "All the more."

The next two stanzas evoke the years of World War II, when people in passing cars called out "Don't fall!" and meant it, adding a kind of spiritual web of community to the steel cables supporting the narrow bridge. In this passage, two of the figures are "my father" and "Mother," helpless at the end of the bridge, but when the poem skips ahead, it also reverts to addressing the second person:

> Two decades later, I banked an Air Force jet
> at 20,000' and snapped the camera at that bridge
> an inch long at arm's length to show you
> it was nothing.
> Then the war, and the return from it:
> I flew to Saigon a decade later
> and came back to the scramble of surviving,
> to children running and tumbling
> over dangerous bridges I'd never crossed,
> and to my aging father and mother almost gone,
> the drawbridge rising while I stood
> helpless and waving a few yards away. (58)

The shift between second and third person slightly clouds one's certainty that "you" addresses the speaker's parents, or mother, but that confusion is not so great as to outweigh its advantage, which is that "you" could also be the woman addressed in many other poems, the mother of children who have frightened the poet's fatherly persona as he frightened his parents.

Though in one view McDonald has made a habit of working quickly, he has come somewhat gradually to the quiet, inclusive vision that characterizes his poems from the past decade. His first book was called *Caliban in Blue*, a title that among other things suggests one sort of person who can find himself in an Air Force uniform, a temporary occupant of the sky. His second (not counting a chapbook), *Anything Anything*, reveals at times a wounded man on a slow road to recovery. It takes its title from a passage in Faulkner's *The Unvanquished*, placed as the book's epigraph: "And this was it—the regret and grief, the despair out of which the tragic mute insensitive bones stand up that can bear anything, anything." The first poem in the book is about helping a twelve-year-old son with target practice. "On Teaching David to Shoot" balances fatherly pride and an awareness of the dark side of what is going on. The fourth stanza ends, "Cockleburs yellowed by sun /stab my legs like old regrets." The fifth enlarges on what seems a new regret:

> This son I would with choice
> raise in another country
> where the only trajectories
> are flights of bees to the moist
> dilating cups of tulips
> yellowed with pollen. (3)

The sentence does not quite say that the father has no choice but to teach his son to shoot, but it comes close to encouraging a careless reading to that effect. The final stanza opens with a frightening image:

> Clipped in place, the target
> waits like a child.
> Together we crunch back
> to our positions, and reload.
> I tell him ready, aim.
> And he takes aim. And fires. (4)

If this poem is close to the edge of a dangerous state of mind, there are other poems in this book that are closer, or even over it. A couple of examples will be enough to establish the place from which McDonald has been able to emerge, though with no loss of power.

"The Girl in the Mackinaw and Panties" is one of those titles that
has to be read as the first line; the poem opens:

> thumbs at you staring at her
> legs, gives you the finger
> as you hesitate. Backing up
>
> you see her waiting, a passive
> bitch after all. (19)

Here, then, we have a hitchhiking woman covering near-nakedness
in a raincoat, and a speaker willing to make rapid judgments that
seem harsh even in these weird circumstances. The promise of hard
times ahead is not long in being—I almost said "fulfilled," but perhaps that promise is only strengthened. This is the end of the poem,
following a brief exchange between them about origins and
destinations:

> Lose something
> in a poker game? you try
>
> to joke. Listen is all she says,
> shut up and drive. She keeps
> looking back. Faster, she says. (19)

This brings to mind Robert Creeley's miniature classic, "As I sd,"
but does not compete with it; it is an echo, a swift connection with
the poetic community. McDonald does this from time to time with
extraordinary economy, probably more often than one reader will be
able to recognize.

In fact, my second example from the dark side of *Anything Anything* has a paranoiac flavor reminiscent of a period in Mark Strand's
work, though it seems unlikely that McDonald thought of that as he
was writing. "Signs and Warnings" is in the first person and the
present tense. On his front porch the speaker finds a dead cat. Its
throat has been cut. He recalls four earlier vague threats, the best of
which is "A postcard / from Death Valley: no message, / no return
address." At last he drags the newspaper with his foot and gets it
inside:

> I scan the classified ads. My name
> is there. And Greetings.
> I dial the newsroom again. Still
> no one remembers who placed
> the ad. I decide to take the cat
> to the alley. I open the door.
> Only its head is there. (21)

That last detail lifts the story out of the remotely plausible into the highly unlikely, and the entire poem comes under suspicion, if it wasn't already. Is this something that we are to take as having happened, if only fictionally, or is it something projected by a troubled, vengeful imagination? There is no way to answer the question definitively, and that turns out to be one source of the poem's power.

Another twenty-five pages into the book, we encounter this woeful mentality again in "Especially at Night." Creatures of some sort are besieging the speaker's house and grounds, frightening the dog, making noises that stop as soon as they gain attention. Then the speaker lets himself go just a little farther around the bend, to the fear of not knowing, which is nearly primal:

> We watch our fifth-grade son play
> football. The other team are
> not from this town. They crouch
> as if they know what to do.
>
> Driving home we skid to avoid the fool
> who whips into the intersection.
> Car doors open suddenly at dusk;
> we swerve to miss them; their owners smile
> as if they knew something we don't. (46)

This exhausting exercise of willpower on the brink of lunacy is an emotional situation that McDonald begins to forsake soon after the publication of his second book. He does not shrink from the thought or sight of violence, and he is quite candid about fear. But in most of his later poems on the subject, his speaker's fears are for others, not for himself.

After the Noise of Saigon (1988), however, reveals a transitional period, when the speaker knows what the matter is, and what might be good for him. The title poem is a powerful merging of meditation and narrative, as the speaker hunts high country, trying for cougar with a bow and arrow. The poem's first line is "If where we hunt defines us," and that "If" is a bold stroke, inviting the rejoinder, "Well, maybe it doesn't." Consideration, not assent, is elicited here, and the poem is thereby stronger than some of James Dickey's more insistent poems on similar topics. Eventually we might recall the various classifications of animals and tribes that are based on just that point. The poem concludes with a hard look at the way up to these evergreens:

> These blue trees have nothing
> and all to do with what I'm here for
> after the noise of Saigon,
>
> the simple bitter sap that rises in me

> like bad blood I need to spill
> out here alone in the silence
> of deep woods, far from people I know
> who see me as a friend, not some damned
> madman stumbling for his life. (65)

Years later, the weight of those earlier post-Vietnam anxieties can still trigger some fresh recollection or re-creation, as in "The First Months Home," collected in *Blessings the Body Gave* (1998). Yet, though the poem is set during those first months and is in the present tense, it is mitigated by its surroundings, recent poems of a gentler and wider-ranging consciousness that remind us of how long ago this was.

It is not quite coincidental that *Blessings the Body Gave* is the first of McDonald's books to be signed "Walt McDonald" instead of "Walter McDonald." This is not a matter of aligning himself with major Walts of our culture; it is rather an acknowledgment that certain levels of formality are no longer true to his sense of who he is, even as a poet. There are areas of endeavor in which a higher level of seriousness is most readily achieved by way of certain kinds of relaxation.

A year before *After the Noise of Saigon,* McDonald published *The Flying Dutchman,* which falls not quite halfway down the list of his books (its position depending on whether the list includes chapbooks). Here he has taken up more strongly than before the conversation with other poets, without which meaningful poetic composition is perhaps impossible. A vigorous nod to Frost in the title of "An Old Dog's Winter Nights" may have helped make the opening through which comes, fleetingly, a muted echo of Arnold's "The sea is calm to-night," as well as the speaker's own familiar sense of something trying to get in:

> Face to the moon, the old dog tells it
> all there is to know of grief,
> sirens that woke him already far away.
> Red digits of the clock say four,
> time to shift from dream
> to dream. The wind is wild tonight.
> Limbs heavy with pears
> bump like something trying to get in. (12)

It may be that the poem becomes a touch overburdened with echo at the end of the third stanza, the ingenuity perhaps too visibly pleased with itself as Dylan Thomas's great villanelle is invoked:

> Old dog, Father would say,
> his slow voice banked with ash,
> his terrier snarling,

    hovering on his tail
    near Father's chair. Old dog,
    he'd say again, and laugh
    as teeth the size of pearls
    attacked his cuff and shook like rage
    against the dying of the game. (12)

Here, too, however, McDonald continues to deepen his facility with the image that is exact because it cannot be paraphrased: "his slow voice banked with ash."

The line has some of the qualities of a superior moment in a country-and-western song. It happens that this music is a recurring source of image and feeling in McDonald's poetry, most recently in *All Occasions*, where "The Songs of Country Girls" decries the overlay of glitz that Nashville often gives us:

    They pinch the mikes with scarlet nails,
    balancing diamond rings like birds.
    Bring back the days of faithful girls
    so homely they hurt.
    .   .   .   .
                        When their hearts broke,
    we swayed and held them close, humming softly
    to ourselves and waltzing to the grave. (62)

The several earlier poems arising from this music all manage a delicate balance between complete allegiance to it and a sophisticated awareness that the melodies and accompanying lyrics may sometimes oversimplify and distort the way its adherents really live and die. All in all, the poems lean toward loyalty to the music, even as they detail the extremes it glorifies. *Rafting the Brazos*, another collection that appeared in 1988, includes "The Songs We Fought For," a poem that veers between humor and pathos with amazingly deft quickness. The speaker recalls ranching, riding the range during the week and on weekends descending on a bar called Rusty's. The singers there had their artificialities:

                Their innocent, wicked faces
    were safe behind the same thick makeup,
    their nests of sprayed hair floated yellow-blue

    in spotlights and smoke of local men and women
    groping for their lives. . . . (39)

That last phrase is brilliantly double-toned. In the midst of all this, there is the occasional young woman who comes out from behind her protective shield and reveals herself as someone with feelings, but such people can't last long in a place like that:

Those hard-voiced untouchable women
gave us the tunes we wanted, the same old wailing
on stage that made fist-fights and a dance

enough to dream about all week in the saddle,
roping another bawling calf to castrate and burn
with a branding iron, touching our own bruised ribs
and teeth, wincing and spitting blood. (40)

An unusual combination of sincerity and self-conscious posturing characterizes a great many country songs, in which the honestly
plaintive melody is sometimes undercut by the extravagant ingenuity of the lyrics. *When you leave me, walk out backwards, so I'll think
you're coming in.* This poem manages that same seductive oscillation
between taking itself seriously and making fun of itself.

Less humorously but just as deftly, the title poem of *Where Skies
Are Not Cloudy* (1993) makes sensitive and well-timed use of departure from, and arrival at, iambic pentameter. The first stanza sets up
a few rhythmical expectations:

I hear old heartache often on the plains.
The whine of steel guitars
and songs of lonely blondes escape
from pickup windows passing by.
Whoever's driving waves, and I wave back.

In the middle of the poem, the speaker's dogs putter about him, then
seek shade, and another set of tires whines on the road. Meanwhile
the meter roughens, encompassing an alexandrine, then draws
through two heavily trochaic lines toward metrical resolution, but
holding to initial trochees even at the end:

Soon I'll hear the song, the same old fiddles
sobbing in a neighbor's truck, some singer
swearing a stranger's arms are all she owns,
pleading as if these plains are all she needs. (52)

"Voices on Jukebox Wax," from *Blessings the Body Gave,* gathers
into a relatively small poem a sweeping embrace of most of the years
when dancing to this music meant something. It begins with recol-
lections of dancing as respite from the war. Years pass, and here
some of them are, in a time when statement of raw fact can be a way
of getting at deeper mysteries:

Long after a war no one we cared for
survived without scars, Earl and I are here
with wives as old as country songs and guitars,

our children older than all of us that fall.
Don's a name on a wall in Washington.
I hear his name sometimes in questions
at class reunions. I haven't heard from Carl. (74)

The recognition that he has been recalling a time when he was
younger than his children brings him up short. McDonald is a poet
for whom living is in itself a great blessing, a fact he can acknowledge at moments when it seems almost inhumane to do so. "Rocket
Attack" from *Blessings the Body Gave* is direct in its surprised recognition that surviving seems better than the alternative. It starts with
the noise and chaos of the attack, then a lull, and the aftermath, men
sifting dirt for bones amidst blood "splattered like motor oil":

> I remember breakfast was lard
> and runny eggs with ketchup and burned toast
> butter-soaked, and bacon fried soggy
> in a tent reeking of greasy smoke and wood.
> It seemed insane—*but the fragile body*
> *was hungry, and it was good, it tasted good.* (24)

"Soggy" and "body" do not rhyme as closely as "wood" and
"good," but they are closer than some of the other expertly disposed
near-rhymes and assonances in this poem, which opens with this
progression at the line-ends: "slammed," "explosion," "down,"
"run." "Slammed" is unpaired. To some ears, so might be "dawn"
and "taught," "slept" and "dead," or "bones" and "toast," but Mc-
Donald is drawing the rhyme a little tighter with each stanza, and
making more witty end-word connections than are usually encountered in twenty lines. In the middle stanza, the end-words are "slept,"
"skull," "dead," and "blood"—an *abab* scheme by pure assonance,
but the sounds of *l* and *d* make other connections, and help fore-
shadow the sounds of the last stanza.

The insanity of war, recalled at increasing distance from the
event, continues to be among McDonald's most persistent sources of
strong poems. In the years of increasing calm, he has gained a firm
control over a kind of direct factual statement that still has the mysterious precision of poetry, the quality of being impossible to para-
phrase without great loss of effect. This quality is nowhere more
evident in his work than when he faces the horrendous fact of the
death of a son in an automobile crash.

All Occasions includes the most recent of these poems, "I Still
Can't Say the Word," a near-rant the speaker addresses to his wife
and to himself at once, about the need to scream, to hit the table hard
enough to break a hand, simultaneously to contemplate and reject

terrible vengeance on a drunk driver. At the end of the poem, though, there is a turn in the direction of acceptance by way of recognizing a complex and difficult truth:

> I'd skin him
> like a deer and stitch it like a shield, if that
> would bring back our boy, leap arm-locked with him
>
> into the fire myself, if our son could live.
> I've said it again and I mean it, but it's bald
> as a lie. The facts are we are home, like this
> together, grieving, and our son is gone. (87)

The next-to-last sentence is a small miracle of dense clarity: it embodies the realization that however deeply he means what he says, these things he has imagined doing are beyond possibility. The realm of the possible is where he is constrained to exist, no matter how overwhelming the circumstance. It is a signal characteristic of McDonald's poetry that it has steadily exhibited acknowledgment— sometimes grateful, sometimes stoic—of that fact.

A poem slightly earlier, and therefore even closer to the event, is "Cataracts" from *Blessings the Body Gave*. The first half of the thirty-two-line poem contains a series of images arising from failing vision: clouds that disappear when the speaker looks away and then back, distant herds of deer "like TV reception in the fifties." His gaze tightens down to the river in front of him, and he recalls the many times he watched his son and his friends going by in a rubber raft, through a passage of pure roaring into "a shimmer twisting away downhill." The sixth of the eight stanzas ends, "I've helped my wife / tidy his room, storing trophies, giving away good clothes" (75). In this particular printing, the page ends below that line. The last two stanzas make matters clearer, but one of those matters is the unbearable difficulty of saying directly what has happened:

> I watched the car towed back, glass and metal
> mangled out of focus, a scarred blur almost a car
> that didn't burn. I've been to the scene, walked down
> the ledge and lowered myself by roots and boulders
>
> where his car careened. I've stood there where it crashed.
> I've turned my eyes as far as I could see downstream,
> even twisted in my chair, thinking I heard
> his voice behind me, not merely the river's roar. (76)

"Fathers and Sons," a poem just a few pages beyond "Cataracts," recounts a restless dawn on the farmhouse porch, the speaker walking softly so as not to wake his wife, trying to establish e-mail connection with a son who is with U.S. forces in Bosnia. The second stanza introduces a rich confusion between two kinds of screen: "hunched at the screen still blue, waiting like me / for words that shoved me out of bed at three. Outside, / I hear crickets as if there's not a screen between us" (82).

The poem is a strange convergence of relatively traditional semi-formality in its verse and up-to-date technology in its topic. It reports the son's having been beyond reach during Desert Storm, when "nothing, not even a phone call or a fax, / could find him." Held between the death of his own father during World War II and his son's peril, he remembers his own service in Vietnam, and begins to write a message in which he embellishes the facts, making up jets about to land, coyotes howling, his wife there on the porch with him:

> I ask *How are you,* but delete that,
> add something about the crops, the herd bull's shoulder
> he hurt butting the barn. I go back inside for a cup,
> and pace the porch until the sun is up. I close
> with *Love,* and sign it, all my hand can do. (83)

These remarks arise from admiration for the excellences in McDonald's poems. That there are poems in his work that fall short of excellence is obvious. I myself once caught him saying that oxen were "bull-necked," but I was watching very closely at the time. To return to the athletic analogy, McDonald may have less in common with the once-outlandish Beamon than with Carl Lewis, whose greatest disappointment may be that it was not he, but Mike Powell, who finally broke Beamon's world record. During the years when he approached the record, Lewis made eleven of the twenty-five best jumps on the books. Walt McDonald has made a few observations lately concerning his advancing age, but his pace shows no sign of slackening, and his poems are getting better all the time.

II. War and the Return of the Veteran

Domestic Tranquillity and National Defense: The Personal History of Walt McDonald

Jerry Bradley

By my count Walt McDonald has issued eighteen volumes of poetry. His first volume, *Caliban in Blue,* won the Texas Institute of Letters award for poetry in 1977; *Whatever the Wind Delivers: Celebrating West Texas and the Near Southwest* earned the same honor in 2000. Both books were published by Texas Tech University, the institution where McDonald has spent the bulk of his academic career, a school located in the very town where he was reared.

A quarter-century is time enough to do some stock-taking. I reviewed *Caliban in Blue* in *New Mexico Humanities Review* (1:3) in September 1978, one of the first considerations of McDonald's verse. It seemed to me then that *Caliban in Blue*'s lean verses formed a kind of non-linear McDonald biography that without naïveté and sentimentality focused upon the universal concerns of sex, death, patriotism, parenthood, and religion. They were affirmative poems that counseled, as in "Making Time," to "do the earth good" (49). I heard echoes of Jarrell and Kunitz in McDonald's Air Force poems, and in the book's second section, "Tribute Poems," he openly acknowledged some of his literary influences—Hemingway, Homer, the Bible, Joyce, and especially Shakespeare and Conrad. Though the poems themselves were not tentative, McDonald's attitude then may have been, and, by echoing famous literary artists, he could grant his poems an importance and seriousness he feared they lacked.

Whatever tentativeness McDonald once had has given way with the years. There is increased confidence in his newer work, but it is more poetic than thematic. Whatever has been wrought between his first book and his latest, *All Occasions*, McDonald still seems as caught (if not poised) between his double lives of soldier and family man—between loving husband and military assassin—as he was in *Caliban in Blue*. His poems still equivocate between the lush jungles of Southeast Asia and the arid flatlands of West Texas, between organized warfare sanctioned by governments and the savage justice of the natural world, between the need to believe in fathers and the desire to believe in God. After two and a half decades, he is still wondering how much to hold onto and what to let go.

McDonald remains a man desperate not to feel lost between wars. Though he may be uncertain about what will keep the next cataclysm at bay, he tries not to be the tool of unwitting reaction. He wonders what he should do when all around him nothing happens (nothing happens much of the time in West Texas). Stony silence is, after all, still stony silence. Despite the passing decades and his ruminations, he has not deconstructed war and his part in it because he knows that such deconstruction would have no point beyond itself. He has not repudiated the disappointments and defects of history, even though he might like to turn his back on them from time to time. Instead, what he has done is to replace history with something more akin to sociology—or at least to cancel history and its false empiricist allure in favor of personal history.

In "That Silence When a Mountain Lion Attacks" from *All Occasions*, for example, McDonald argues the superiority of personal to official history:

> Those puffy clouds in the Rocky Mountains
> could be gunfire, another time and place.
> Before this planet spins us back home to the plains,
> dozens will die by rockets or cannon fire,
>
> puffs like clouds the last skies they will see.
> I heard explosions often in Saigon
> and the rapid pop of rifles, but high over jungles
> I saw only distant puffs and fire, silence
>
> except my own breath and chatter in my headset.
> Even when Kelly exploded in mid-air, no others heard,
> only a blip that disappeared on radar screens
> back at Da Nang. The earth turns green again,
>
> no matter what. Outside our cabin, magpies clown
> and crazy hop for worms and lazy bugs, sluggish
> under a thawing, Colorado sun. Last week,

two campers had their throats slit in their tent

not ten miles east. We never heard a scream.
The world will be the world, springtime or not.
Our oldest daughter's forty and a day, and we are wiser
only by repute. The cost of living past a war

bankrupts the heart. Feelings are cash stashed in cigar boxes
and not invested, no access by the Internet.
Only an elk calf knows how its neck feels
pierced by a puma, how nothing matters when fangs

bend it staggering back, unable to scream
or breathe. Others don't need to know, but if they could,
they'd trade—nobody's pain has been shared
anywhere, no other's loss is ever this severe. (32–3)

What McDonald does—has always done—is to offer a modest proposal for stemming what he eloquently depicts as an unconscionable moment in life. He knows that the race is not always to the swift nor the battle to the strong, so he pleads for a sort of cosmic compassion, even if the compassion is unearned and the cosmos fundamentally merciless. The main difference in the world of this later poem and that in *Caliban in Blue* is that his children are older, but McDonald has measured the long odds of eternity and made them his own. He contrasts the mystery of the past—remote objects and faraway places—with the palpability of objects in life's foreground. "History doesn't always repeat" ("Instant Replay" 53) or may be forgotten, so he treasures keepsakes from the days before Saigon and wears dog tags his Uncle Carl wore when he was killed in Okinawa ("Killing Nothing but Time" *All Occasions* 83).

In the concluding stanza of "The Winter Our Grandson Turned Thirteen," McDonald beseeches protection for those close to him now:

Held wide, the fingers tremble, the fist
I pitched with, that held the stick
in Air Force jets, that slipped the ring
on my wife's finger, fists that held
three babies up to the world as if to beg
Be good, be careful with these kids. (11)

The ex-pilot who flew solo seeks duality (even plurality) at home; his love for his wife, their children, and their children's children surpasses whatever patriotism may have fueled his military missions. What demands his attention in the poem is what is at hand, what is literally in his hands—family. What he would prefer, of course, is to return to "where Eden was—that ranch before the war" ("Choco-late" 42), that unrecoverable time before knowledge and experience forced his expulsion. Alive yet in the fallen world, about all McDon-ald's poetic personas can hope for is to have someone to waltz with to the grave, even though as in "To the Tribe" he calls everyone a jerk who like him

> . . . sweated in jungle boots
> and trudged with buddies,
> all of us jerks
> who wanted only
> the love of someone
> and the grace of breath. (34)

It is women for whom men fight. It is their healing touch, their magic and grace, their promise of continuity through family that men yearn for. All he ever needed, he affirms in "The Midas Touch in Texas," is

> a lovely woman who nibbles my ear
> and then says *Please, hubby, love me*
>
> . . . I'm healed
> wholly by her touch, amazed each time. (14)

To McDonald, women are alchemists who forge emotional gold from the baseness of male experience ("In the Alchemist's House-hold"). They are the antidote to man's solitariness, whether, as in "Marching through Georgia" they are local girls, centerfolds the flyboys tape to lockers, or "schoolmarms or farm girls / wild to cou-ple with anything with wings" (21). And if modern men occasionally prove faithless, it is because, in the absence of women, they have parted company with what gives them substance. Though they fly missions for their Uncle Sam, he is at best a distant relation—God is even more remote—but they learn "how to die" for something more intimately familial. In a world lacking cohesion, without heroes and gods, only women, impermanent and earthly themselves, offer a stay against chaos.

There is, to be sure, a large measure of nostalgia in McDonald's verses. They have always been full of lost comrades, lost joy, lost time. Their poignancy derives in part from the fact that over the years McDonald's writing and life have become increasingly con-gruent and conterminous (a fact that may also explain his amazing productivity). However, there is a problem inherent in evoking lost friends and family, for by the time they are recalled and reflected in verse, the poetic mirror has been largely obscured by something more dissembling than the West Texas sand. What results is lyrical poetry in a laconic context. McDonald's nostalgia, like most, is an expression of something essentially inexplicable, the passions that produced it having already been traduced by both the verse itself and the interval between his experience and his writing about it.

The techniques McDonald uses as a poet to interpret the world are not the same ones he uses as a scholar to interpret texts. Rather, his poems are a pleasurable dislocation between what he knows intellectually and what he loves, and he emphasizes this distinction by making virtues of reticence and inarticulateness. (One of his new poems is appropriately called "I Still Can't Say the Word" [*All Occasions* 87].) In his work there are no recognitions of poetry as a useful creative outlet or a diversion forced on him by life's lonely situations. It is the poem he has not written, not the memory at hand, that is more likely to bring peace. Furthermore, his capacity for survival is more than a heroic act of memorialization in verse, even if it is an effort ultimately doomed to failure, for his poems carry density and force, the brunt of human doing, the slow, painful culmination of suffering and human possibility. In them are an eagerness and concentration, almost childlike in their single-mindedness sometimes, though these are not poems written by a wounded child, a baffled survivor of trauma, or an ingenuous naïf. McDonald is no Candide, for his persistence has both thematic and formal significance. His is an aesthetic of patience delivered in the same voice day after day, poem after poem. Over time there has been no marked shift in his characteristic tone, and any failure of nerve to answer the "big questions" of life over the years has certainly been tempered by his sincerity. McDonald's poems are verbally tactful; every poem contains its small revelations. Many of them are structured by departures, to war and back again home, comings and goings that frame an essentially unsettled life against which the rhythms of nature sound. Hawks fly sorties; prairie dogs dig in like embattled infantry; herds of cattle plod like armored battalions. Anything more universal would sound hollow.

Some might argue that by emphasizing the familiar McDonald has been wasting his talents on West Texas, but his poems, like those of any writer, are made out of cultural circumstance beyond his control. Indeed home is home wherever it is, but it is McDonald's scrupulous regard for what lives beyond him—geographically and genealogically—that drives the moral force of his poetry, a force inseparable from his poetic style. His poems have no ulterior intentions, for he knows that words, as difficult as they are to fashion, are the most fitting way to make reality known. What one hears in his poetry these days is a clear human voice, one that is not disembodied, one that we recognize and probably love. His writing is the realization of a detailed attention to and love of the world. If it lacks linguistic radicalism, it is because he has not succumbed over the years to the tyranny of poetic fashion. His poems are the genuine article. Through his relentless adherence to linguistic honesty, he has produced an extraordinarily ambitious body of work that eschews abstraction and through its plain-spoken but sonorous style puts old ideas about the nature of poetic language into question.

Whatever irony one finds in McDonald's verse results from the contrast between the world of learning and its fostered intelligence that has all too often been forced to witness violence without meaning. He has peered into the fissures of society, its fragmented culture; he has walked with its low and mean-spirited detractors and, having done so, challenges the rhetoric of authority, the internal crevasses of blind obedience, and the quicksand upon which raw power stands. For these reasons, it is difficult to read McDonald's poems with pleasure; they are often profoundly unsettling. However, it is not difficult to read them with admiration. No disinterested party, he is not deaf to echoes of the dispossessed; his poetry belongs to them, but there is no anger or estranged feelings. His technique is to describe ordinary things or lost things with fresh significance so that they become a universe in themselves. His fine sense of prosody and syntax—precise imagery, natural rhythms, and clean, uncluttered lines—overcome his lack of elaborate linguistic flourishes. His epiphanies give the sensation of wholeness restored. The "windmill / spinning fast" and "the far-off roar of stars" ("A Thousand Miles of Stars" 75) offer comfort and consolation; the world ravels back into place, the self and the things of the world come together as they belong (or nearly so), and for a moment meaning is perceived in the everyday scene.

McDonald's poetry encourages illusions, but it also challenges their use. His evocative vignettes are ways of finding accommodation in the world. His subjects hover between presence and absence. By his remembering them, McDonald's dead relatives and lost companions assert their immortality in the world of language, a sort of beguiling family discourse, a conversation that negotiates its way through the commonplace, refusing innovation in favor of intimacy and immediacy. The reader needn't know anything in particular in order to read them and be moved.

McDonald defies being read through any lens of history except a personal one. Although he finds resonances in history, his poems are both passive and active—like memory. His goal is to make life available, to establish coherence in the absence of life's narrative thread. His burden, therefore, is not to let the poem break down. Life, he reminds, is continual improvisation; public duties and private are inseparable; domestic tranquillity and national defense are not mutually exclusive objectives. But without God, everything gets measured against seasonal change and daily weather. His poems carry the recurrent atmosphere of menace, a violence of feeling that is part of life's natural processes. His poetry knows how to go outdoors; it is full of open spaces, a world a West Texan can recognize.

McDonald's great-grandfather "believed God was plain as prairies / after Eden" ("Reading *Ecclesiastes* at Sixty" 72). There is rectitude in something so plain, something so evident as to be almost unseen. If God can be as meandering and anecdotal as a poem about West Texas, then His catechism may teach one to kill "nothing / but time, riding home to our wives after dark" ("Killing Nothing but Time" 84). Given the inaccessibility of ultimate truth and beauty, McDonald's poetry gives itself over to the valor of remembering. It is the rendering of life and not life itself that may last, a conundrum that leaves McDonald wondering, as he does in "Watching Dawn on Padre Island," "why can't I rise / and throw off these winding sheets and walk" (*All Occasions* 101).

Reclaiming the Homefront:
Walt McDonald's Peacekeeping Soldiers

Barbara Rodman

This year the news on Veteran's Day is of Texas National Guard troops returning home from several months of what we euphemistically call "peacekeeping" assignments in Bosnia. The images of these faces, mostly young, lighting up as they de-plane and catch sight of a loved one waving from behind the roped-off waiting area are familiar to anyone who's read the poems of Walt McDonald, though his war was the one in Vietnam. Like these teachers, computer programmers, technicians, bus drivers, and other "volunteer" soldiers, McDonald's pilots are not military careerists but ordinary men who heed duty's call, who go to war reluctantly and necessarily. The voice which summons them is not the abstract one which preaches political doctrines or geographical objectives, but one embodied by family members and friends, the whispered voice summoned in lonely places by men who open a wallet to stare at a snapshot, the sweet voice unfolding from the well-creased squares of a letter opened and closed and re-opened so many times that it's begun to soften, the almost-forgotten voice of a child climbing onto a parent's knee and begging for one more story.

Most of Walt McDonald's work focuses on the lives of fighter pilots, dryland farmers and ranchers, long-haul truck drivers, West Texas pioneers, bad-luck uncles, and even the occasional oil field roughneck, but, paradoxically, the major theme of his poetry, a tenacious thread that links unlikely voices and backgrounds to each other, is the theme of domestic life and love. McDonald's characters live in the landscapes of Vietnam, of Colorado, and of the Southwest, but all of those seem included in a landscape that is much larger and more inclusive than any of them, the internalized plain on which the quotidian dramas of families are played out with real intensity. He writes about the travails of raising children, the responsibility of supporting a family, the difficulty of remaining faithful to an absent spouse. McDonald understands that the lives of men, no matter what calls them from their homes—war, work, nature—are inextricably tied up with the lives of their parents, wives, friends, lovers, cousins, and next-door neighbors. The most significant and powerful moments in many poems take place in imagination or memory and may link even the most warlike of maneuvers with a child or wife, a father's loving or angry gesture, the desire to plant a tree or teach a child to swim or chop a stack of wood into usable pieces.

This is true not only in those poems which take marriage, child-rearing, and aging as their subjects directly, but in many of those which seem at first glance to be far removed from such topics. McDonald does not sentimentalize or trivialize, but juxtaposes images of death or the fear of dying with tender, nurturing moments. The men who appear in his poems are presented always with compassion and affection, even when they are misguided or mistaken.

Only a few of McDonald's poems are written in female voices; roughhousing boys, pilots at war, farmers and ranchers fighting for their lives in inhospitable environments, roughnecks and drillers, truck drivers, hitchhikers, and drifters are more common. Yet McDonald evokes not only women and the feminine pursuits usually associated with wives and daughters, but stakes a claim to the life of the family that is both masculine and original.

Even the poems about pilots and cowboys lack the machismo and posturing one usually associates with such characters, the strutting and bragging of men living in a "man's world." McDonald's men are sons and husbands before all else, carrying the love of family and home into all the lonely corners of the world where their commitments lead them. What he manages to convey is the heartbreaking reality of men who are capable of acting with great courage and loyalty while remaining tender and reflective. These are not academicians, but blue-collar workers, sons of farmers, boys who can shoot and fish and chop wood. While I do not believe that such men are rare, poetry that honors and evokes them is. What's more, McDonald's portraits do not romanticize or condescend to their subjects, but lift them up with respect and honest appreciation.

In "Night Landings" and "Ejecting from Jets," the deaths of other pilots are presented not with bombastic melodrama, but with humility, regret, and the recognition of the "luck" of the observer who lives to tell the tale. The narrator's compassion is shaded by a kind of wonder, an awareness of how quickly death can come to a man—and how inexplicably. In the first poem, one young pilot's successful solo flight is juxtaposed to the death of another:

> The night I soloed,
> red lights rolled flashing into the woods,
> searching for Pennington . . . a nice kid
> eager for everything. . . . (*Night Landings* 11)

Pennington has apparently become confused, "up" literally seeming to be "down," so that his attempts to correct his course do the opposite of what he intends. The successful pilot imagines "the god in his ears / pleading *pull up*, and Pennington [obeys] / with all his soul" (12). The tone of this poem belies the violence of the death of the young pilot, evoking a sort of meditative wonder focused intently on the innocence of the man of who dies and the luck of those who live, a recurring theme in McDonald's work.

"Ejecting from Jets" makes the same point more bluntly ("Practice saves no one / but the blessed") and invokes a litany of names of those lost to dangerous, if inexplicable, lapses or ordinary miscalculations. Davis, Jones, and Kirk all have gone down in accidents the narrator understands as being no one's fault or the result of a mistake any one could have made. "I stuck thumb's up / down at my buddies, all of us / amazed to be alive," this pilot concludes (14).

Another survivor, in "For Friends Missing in Action," reflects without bitterness that

> [w]e studied gauges and codes
> like prayer beads, believing
> nothing that big could kill us,
> those wings would hold us up. (*Counting Survivors* 6)

The irony is that the wings did hold the pilots up; what failed them was something else, something random yet miraculous. The motif, and the irony, is repeated in "Principles of Flight" by a narrator who says, "I believed wings could save us / and wore them on the chest / / . . . where we were told the heart was" (*Witching on Hardscrabble* 31).

The same sense of connection between the dead and the living, the understanding that both are participating in some larger drama is expressed also in "The Digs at Escondido" in which an archeologist comes across the skull of a girl who apparently died quickly from a violent blow to her head. "She fell down, bowing / under the same tornado sky / we worship," he says. And then he wonders, "What did she see, / those last few / days?" Ultimately, he conjectures, those earlier residents of the plains whose lives he is reconstructing surely felt more reassurance than fear, experiencing something like the gift of grace:

> if they wondered about gods,
> when they stumbled on this canyon,
> they believed: a spring-fed stream,
> rabbits and quail, enough flint
>
> for fire and arrows. (42)

What is noticeably lacking in these poems is machismo, bravado, or the emphasis on skill and achievement that such masculine subjects usually engender. Instead, there is a sense of being undeservedly "blessed" (blessings being inherently unearned) or saved by some power which can't be explained. For example, the pilot in "First Solo in Thunderstorms" says:

> Better jets
> than mine had crashed in weather,
> or by the heart's confusion. . . .
> . . . I kept the stick
> and throttle steady by faith. (*Night Landings* 16)

The "faith" invoked here and which underpins much of McDonald's work is seldom described in religious words or embodied by the commonplace religious symbols. The only winged beings—aside from airplanes—in his poems are the birds any observant person might learn to recognize and name—owls, herons, hawks. Still, McDonald's narrators all seem to hold this steady faith which is represented by frequent references to absent wives and children, aging parents, death, and the struggle to make a living in unwelcoming environments. Fidelity is not an empty slogan for these men but the "stick and throttle" to which they cling.

"Marriage," a lovely tribute to a long-term relationship, makes this clear with its visions of a wife whose "fingers know the dark / corners of my mind" (19), but many other poems subtly, even indirectly, lay claim to the same territory, quietly asserting the power of love to heal, the importance of fidelity even when a lapse might be forgiven, and the power of love expressed in endurance and duration though it might not be given breath in words. His narrators are often silent, voicing in the poem the sentiments that are not spoken otherwise.

In "Wildcatting" an oil field worker jolts across a landscape so lonely he must follow "hunch and arroyos more than maps." Yet he observes

> [n]othing is there until we find it.
> We believe in steel bits and stone
>
> and twist our wrenches tight,
> cursing the constant spinning, each twist
> of the bit like love, trying it over and over. (*Night Landings* 45)

This is the same faith of "Charts" whose aging narrator, a man "this side of fifty," studies the night sky and muses:

> With luck we survived a war, the raising
> of children and monthly debts, so far. . . .
> . . . a puzzled hunter stiff in the joints
> and faithful wife stumbling somewhere under a maze
> of stars. . . .
>
> . . . Father of light,
> we can't dread outer darkness when burning stars
> hurtle outward, a gallery of myths,
> but beg for more light in this created world. (*Counting Survivors* 60)

A similar connection is made in "Living on the Plains" when the speaker compares learning the landmarks of the desert to learning "the hollows of each other's flesh" (*Night Landings* 37). Likewise, in "Taking Each Breath," a couple watches a storm move in, blotting out their view of their own nearby barn, but they are not frightened, believing in:

> . . . only this porch swing
> dry in the downpour, an ark we rock on,
> gliding under the crack of thunder,
> taking each deep breath to let it go. (*All That Matters* 23)

In all these poems, a seemingly masculine place or situation is domesticated, made familiar and comforting by usage and daily life. The love here is mutual, shared, evidence of partnership. The narrator, a man who values relationship and family life, seems to see his world almost as a housewife would, pleased to live not only for his own reasons, but to share another day with someone loved by him. This ideal of shared space is expressed with clarity in "Nights in the San Juans" in a description of a rustic cabin:

> Bed and chairs, table and stove,
> home for a week in the mountains.
> Because the logs are stacked

> we love them, two rooms
> that would be a shanty
> on the plains. (*Rafting the Brazos* 13)

Such domestic spaces are not seen as confining so much as defining the sites of mutual pleasures, from which the dangers of the outside world are excluded. Similarly, in "Fences," barbed wire "cinched tight from post to post" is cast as something desirable, closing out danger, closing in love. "Nothing not tied down / stays home," the speaker says, adding, "Even our children // rise up like owls and fly away." But the speaker does not wish to follow them. His wife turns in bed "for me to hold [her]." And though each day's dust erases the previous night's "love notes," the speaker equates the never-ending film of grit with "the earth we live on, the dust our fingers / string new fences on, holding each other / one more night with loving words" (*Night Landings* 36). Even after describing the hectic life of a couple "[d]rowning in bills / and children, in bed too often with a disease / called dread," the narrator of "The Golden Bowl" acknowledges the pleasures of "brief encounters" over dinner dishes and "rendezvous" at the dumpster, recognizing in these humble moments "the answer to all loss." In this poem's conclusion, the couple, "[h]ands locked," re-enters their home—"the shining house" —together, closing out intruders both physical and metaphysical (*Rafting the Brazos* 16).

Birds appear in many poems, often signaling another kind of blessing, though they cannot be translated as "angels" or anything like mystic symbols; they remain entirely creatures of nature, symbolizing the cyclic and concrete world of which humans are a part. In McDonald's understanding of this world, birds may sometimes be an emblem for the domestic life, which he sees as both natural and good. "The Wild Swans of Da Lat" clearly associates the monogamous mating of the swans with the longings of the soldier for his home, juxtaposing the brutalized landscape of war-torn Vietnam with a sweet, almost paradisiacal vision:

> Near Da Lat that winter
> I often saw wild swans
> graceful on bomb craters
> filled by the monsoons. . . .

As the poem progresses, the speaker says that the jungle hid the swans from view most of the time, "unless we hovered overhead." Even in the midst of a destructive war, one which devastates the earth, the landscape McDonald frames is one being healed by nature and love, and the poem concludes with a vision of

> . . . the cratered clearings
>
> tangled with vines growing back,
> the swans somehow able
> to find their way down
> under tiered trees to breed. (*Night Landings* 20)

A similar (if more heartbreaking) scene is evoked in "The Children of Saigon" in which a soldier comes upon children scavenging for food and plunder in the "piles of junk burning / on the base." He says, "Children / climbed those bulldozed heaps // for food, for clothes, for trash" (22), and yet the image with which the poem leaves us is not the ugly futility of the scene (which haunts the speaker), but that of the compassionate soldier attempting to feed them, remembering

> how many nights
>
> I went without supper,
> how many leftovers I begged
> and carried in darkness
> out past the tarmac and bleachers
> passing it all to the children
> who grabbed it and backed away. (23)

The suffering children, whose lives have become a waking nightmare, follow the soldier home so that even when he is living again with his own well-fed family, "watching [his] wife / make breakfast for children / who weren't born overseas," he is haunted by memories of them ("Learning to Live with Nightmares"). "No one's responsible / for tricks the mind plays," he says. He dreams that he died in Saigon, and though he's alive and home, now observes his family as a ghost might, a disembodied observer, not a full participant yet in the life of his family. Like a child, he must relearn the most basic of life skills and invokes the image of a young child "reaching / to lace my shoes, / my own shoes" (*Night Landings* 28).

Another soldier, recently returned home, tries to make sense of his survival in "After the Rains of Saigon" as he lies beside his wife, his daughters close enough at hand for him to know that they "sigh / and kick the sheets." He mistakes the rumble of distant thunder for bombs, and sees "lightning flashes in the east like flares" while he tries "to piece together why I'm here" and, presumably, why others are not. Life and death are bound together in one moment, as are memories of war and awareness of domestic tranquillity. Interestingly, the former soldier ends the poem wondering not which of his comrades will die in the next few hours, but

> how many calves will die tonight
> by drowning, how many angels dance
> in a flash flood, how many years
> we'll live out here in a desert? (*Night Landings* 29)

The final image of the poem is that of the man standing sentinel on his porch, still a soldier keeping watch, a barrier between his family's ruin and their survival—a fragile, fallible barrier, but a barrier nonetheless.

In "Splitting Wood for Winter," another man passes along to his sons his own father's art of chopping firewood. There is irony in the poem, both in the contrast between the force and violence of the chopping and the conclusion that "[a]ll logs are anyway is smoke," and in the contrast between the domestic purpose of the task and the masculine effort employed. The speaker in this poem is aware of himself as a link between two other generations, those of his father and his sons. The imagery is gentle and sweet: "One by one they lift my father's ax / and raise it back and try to guide it / like a kite" (*Night Landings* 33).

McDonald does not ignore or underestimate the power of the female, however. He frequently acknowledges its existence as something prior (and perhaps superior) to more masculine arts. In "Witching," he compares the scientific doubts of men about the "priesthood / of dowsers" to the understanding of women:

> But wives
> who've felt children come from nothing
>
> . . . confirm this faith
> in witches. They believe at night,
> almost asleep, release themselves
> less consciously than prayer to dreams
> all through the night. (34)

And in "First Solo," it is the wife learning to fly. Aware of his limitations, the male narrator (a pilot) wants his wife to be able to land "[i]f something should ever happen to me" (68). Now, their roles reversed, he is watching from the sidelines as she flies alone, with nothing to do "but curse the pheasants / . . . and pray they have grain enough / to stay clear of traffic." At the end of the poem, the woman moves "faster and faster, she's off again / into the sun, the wild blue" (*Night Landings* 69). Here is a man able not only to envision his wife living without him, but to take pride in her competence, to admire her independence and strength. There is nothing patronizing or paternalistic in this poem; in fact, it expresses the mutuality of love and loyalty that is the hallmark of McDonald's domestic imagery.

Many poems deal with aging, but they focus not only on what is lost, but also on what is found, the homegrown comforts of family and adult relationship. In "After Years in the Mountains," a couple returns to the plains of their origin "To ease our parents' / last years. To be with friends / who never left. To take a job." The narrator says that in the mountain wilderness they had "tried // to get lost" but "[a]llways we found / another trail or others like us / . . . climbing for Eden." Settled in their new/old home, they both understand that "Something has been lost. / Some things remain" (*Burning the Fence* 10), and the poem ends with an image that lies at the heart of much of McDonald's work, the marital (companionable) embrace:

> We hold each other
> a long while,
> unload another box,
> and start to settle in. (11)

Though the speaker in many poems seems to have grown up in an environment in which men seldom spoke to each other about love, McDonald's men are not emotional cripples. They struggle to be fathers, husbands, friends who are capable of more than empty repetition of their own fathers' lives. One says, "Never in my life // had I heard my father mention / love," but by the age of forty, "after a war and another child," he wants both to speak and to hear this affirmation ("Never In My Life" 48). He finally manages his end of the exchange just moments before the old man's death and thinks for a moment, "*I've killed him*" with what he calls the "dim, disturbing news" (49). But the older man revives long enough for the son to imagine his father's inner gaze traveling "down maybe to his childhood / and his own dead father's doors." In this imagined reconciliation, even death is not a barrier to the expression of love, and, implicitly, forgiveness. The speaker concludes:

> It was enough,
> was all I could receive or ever give
> to him. Even in that glaze
> that stared toward death,
> I had seen him take me in,
> been blessed by what I needed all my life. (50)

This moment is similar in many ways to that in "Finding My Father's Hands in Midlife" when the speaker recognizes in his own hand "the fist of my father, the fist / he struck me with," but also the hand of a man who worked hard to support his family. The memory includes not only the fist of discipline and anger, but the hand which could offer its thumb to a child for support and guidance. The speaker says,

[w]hen I make a fist, I see his
half-moon thumb fold over four
tight fingers, a picture of family,

that big thigh-muscle shank
of his thumb something we closed on,
muscle we loved. (*Night Landings* 67)

In "Saying the Blessing," a man muses about his adult children, who
have grown up and are out of his sway: "I can't say anything new to
children / on their own. They need my blessing as I / wanted my
own father's love" (*Counting Survivors* 76). Fathers are complex, contradictory, and even cruel in poems such as "My Brother and the
Golden Gloves" (24) and "Father's Mail-Order Rifles" (25), or portrayed as an unpredictable drunkard feared by his sons in "Life with
Father" (18). But the sons in these poems seem to grow into the fathers they never had, men who can stand, as one does, before the
Vietnam Memorial wall beside his own soldier son, reflected together in the polished stone, connected in a wordless image despite
all their implied differences. Similarly, another father can good-
humoredly pass along family lore and advice to his sons in "Teaching
Our Sons Old Chores" (12).

Fathers must sometimes leave their families in these poems, but
they never abandon them. They go to find work, to perform the duties demanded by democracy, to prepare a place for the others who
will follow. In a real sense, the family is never left behind but present
always in the father's thoughts and memories, as well as his longings. In "Faraway Places," a father strokes his daughter's golden
hair, thinking that she "knows / nothing of Vietnam" or the coming
separation (7). "Night Before My Father Went to War" reverses these
roles, however, and a son follows his father "past every picnic
ground and play fort of my life" for a final conversation before the
father's departure. The son is aware that his father can no longer
keep him from grief in the landscape of an outgrown childhood, and
the poem ends with the father turning to his son, showing "the deso-
lation of his face" in an implicit coming-of-age moment for the
young man (*Caliban in Blue* 8)

In "Embarkation" (9) and "Night at Cam Ranh Bay" (13), parents
poised between peaceful domesticity and the dangers to be faced
during their separation try to keep news of the father's imminent departure from their children. A father-son reunion in "With Steve at
Lake Raven" seems to herald the homecoming from war. The man
and child swim to a buoy and the father thinks, "no matter what, we
are together now" (*Burning the Fence* 54). The "now" acknowledges,
of course, all those irreversible separations that have and will come
between the two of them, not only while the father is at war, but the

more simple, predictable separations of aging, the child leaving home, the parents dying. In "When the Children Have Gone," a father similarly muses, "What could we say, for they heard rumors: / something was out there that shouldn't be, / futures only they must own" (*Counting Survivors* 77).

For McDonald, flying, ranching, roughnecking, fly-fishing, and all the pursuits of men and boys seem meaningful not as ends in and of themselves, but as metaphors for the more significant tasks of adult life—embodied by living in loving connection to family, community, and the earth itself. Even as his fighter pilots lift off, soar up, and lead the watcher's eye into the unbounded sky, the poems do just the opposite, moving under the skin into the reader's heart. McDonald suggests that the true measure of a man's life is less likely to be found in battle than it is in his kitchen or garage. Though the occasional dance hall girl or carnival strumpet is invoked, these women never undress or succeed in seducing either reader or lonely husband.

If McDonald occasionally seems old-fashioned, straitlaced, or even innocent, so be it, for he is also honest and forbearing. His heroes provide the ethic for a new generation of men who are trying to be something more than their fathers might have been—patient, tolerant, and capable of saying "I love you" to a child. They remain loyal and constant in a confusing world, and their values are not abstract but concretized in the daily tasks of diapering, cooking, and carrying out the trash.

In the town where I now live, a local church annually honors families that demonstrate the kind of love and loyalty we wish all children could live with, and in a gesture which reflects the shifting tides of sociological insights, one award goes to single-parent families. This year's prize was won by a young man raising two daughters. I doubt he's ever been a soldier, and he probably isn't given to the reading of poetry, but I wonder if he might not agree with McDonald's statement that "[h]ome is a casino / of chance and choice / four arms that hold each other" ("Luck of the Draw," *Counting Survivors* 74). In any event, the love of home and family is powerful and compelling in all of McDonald's books, and it is embodied quite literally in human lives and concerns. In "All That Aches and Blesses," we are told,

> All that aches and blesses lives in the skin,
> the thinnest organ. . . .
> . . . More than the heart, we give ourselves away
> in skin, the blessing over all we are. (*Night Landings* 74)

McDonald's *A Band of Brothers:*
A Plea for a Deeper Understanding

Clay Reynolds

In 1985—the tenth anniversary of the fall of Saigon—with my mind on an idea for a scholarly study, I conducted a bibliographic search to determine just how many fictional works on the Vietnam experience had been published by American writers. I anticipated that I would find a thousand or more titles. Instead, just over a hundred titles could be identified, and these included some (*The Ugly American, Land of 1000 Elephants, The Bamboo Bed,* and even Norman Mailer's and James Michener's writings on domestic reaction to the war) that were ancillary to American military involvement in the war in Southeast Asia.

I should have anticipated this result. Although the Vietnam War touched the lives of tens of millions of Americans in direct ways, it did not have the deep-rooted daily—in some cases, hourly—force that was carried by either of the two world wars of the twentieth century. I already knew from research that World Wars I and II produced a remarkably slim body of prose fiction in the first decades following their conclusions; even today, World War I, as a bibliographic rubric for fiction, yields only a comparative handful of titles when measured against the thousands of volumes based on the Civil War or even such relatively minor incidents as Custer's Last Stand or the fall of the Alamo. (A quick Internet search actually revealed more in-print books dedicated to the assassination of John Kennedy than to World War I.) It's fair to say that even taken together, both world wars produced far more memorable hit songs than they did memorable literary masterpieces.

Even so, I was astonished by the small number of books that came out of Vietnam because of two considerations that set that period apart from earlier generations and their wars. One was that no event in this century has so polarized the American public or has been the subject of such continuing acrimonious debates. Apart from the Civil War, few events in our national history have generated such emotionally charged and divisive reactions; none I can think of has ever done more to disabuse Americans of the notion that their government—and their military—was infallible, invincible, or, more significantly, honest. The real casualty of Vietnam, I think, was the American illusion of our own perfection. I'm not sure the wound was mortal, and that may be to our detriment.

The second consideration for my supposition that Vietnam would be, more than any other, our "literary war" was that the men and women directly involved in the war were far better educated and better read, generally, than any who were directly involved in any previous military conflict. Possibly the most literate and erudite soldiers, sailors, nurses, and airmen in history served in Vietnam. A plurality of them—even among the enlisted personnel—at least had earned high school diplomas, and many, many had college degrees. Moreover, thanks to television, the average combatant in Vietnam had a "world view" that was far broader and more sophisticated than soldiers who served in America's previous wars. Thanks to modern technological innovations involving satellites and advanced telecommunications, they were continually better informed about events on the home front as well as in their own theater of operations than have been any soldiers in history. (The ability to come in from a combat patrol and, after a shower and a shave, a hot meal, and maybe a drink at the club, to make a long-distance phone call to talk to one's family back in Illinois or New Hampshire in "real time" was just barely practical for some airmen during the Korean War and wasn't even dreamed of in World War II.) Combined with the emotionally charged atmosphere of those years of the United States' involvement in Southeast Asia, one would think that these well-read, well-informed and technologically sophisticated veterans would have been the source of a veritable flood of Vietnam-set fiction. But in the first decade following America's pull-out of Southeast Asia, only about seventy-five novels and short fiction collections were published by indexed publishing houses—including university presses and small publishers—and of that number, only a few achieved recognition for having literary quality.

At the time, I asked Joe Blades, senior editor for Random House, why he thought this was the case. He responded that there was no shortage of submissions of Vietnam-based material; however, the quality of most of the manuscripts was poor. He said that the writers generally fell into four categories. There were those who wanted either to apologize for or justify their role in the war as individuals or as soldiers in the army of what was now being characterized as an aggressor nation. Next, there were those who were still fighting the war in their minds and hearts and memories and who sought to exorcise the demons of their past through self-revelatory and psychologically therapeutic prose. Third, there were those who attempted to use the complex and colorful background of Vietnam and the war as a context for stories about other things—generally sex, crime, drugs, espionage, even romance and other "genre" paradigms. Finally, there were the "warmongering" works of the pulp writers, sensationalist authors who tend to use war—any war—as a backdrop for novels containing gratuitous violence against other people, other races, other national philosophies, and as a propagandistic platform for their own jingoistic, patriotic platitudes. Among these, Blades averred, the best quality generally came from the first category, but this was also the smallest of the four.

A year or so later, in early 1987, with my project ready to launch, I discovered to my dismay that the list of titles indexed or listed as "Vietnam—fiction" had veritably exploded. Indeed, the number had trebled. It trebled again by 1988. By 1989, I was able to discover more than a thousand titles, many of them of the "pulp fiction" variety, now relating to Vietnam, its history, the war, its aftermath, and its impact on individual Americans and our nation's psyche. I immediately abandoned my idea for a comprehensive scholarly survey of the titles. Merely culling the synopses of these books was too daunting in a pre-amazon.com world. Although by that time I had read a great number of books inspired by Vietnam, I realized that it was possibly too soon to offer a judgment on literary responses to the war; until there was some sort of "sifting" of the volumes of work that were flooding out of publishing houses, making any sort of selective judgment was a fool's errand.

It was during this period that I also first met Walt McDonald. As one of the most influential literary figures in Texas, McDonald instantly impressed me with his quiet sincerity, especially when he spoke of flying and combat. As a rule, his comments were couched in his poetic utterances, often obliquely revealing of something deeper in his own emotional makeup that had been touched by his Vietnam experience. We talked only briefly in that first conversation, but over the next several years, through his writing and mutual friends, I learned more about his personal combat involvement, his personal witness of the terror of war and the particular horror that was Vietnam. I soon deduced—possibly incorrectly—that he, like so many veterans, preferred not to discuss the particulars with a non-veteran such as myself. My inference was that he felt I could never understand what he had seen, had been through, and trying to explain it to me in any meaningful way was futile. This was hardly a unique position; over the years, I had learned to respect the same reluctance when I ran across it in those veterans whose combat experiences in any war had large emotional impacts and carried over to their civilian identities. Indeed, my own father refused to talk too specifically about his World War II combat experience, which was extensive and, from all I know about it, profoundly horrifying.

For many veterans, combat—in Vietnam or anywhere else—was an intensely personal experience that was only incidentally connected to the larger geopolitical issues swirling around the war. Ultimately, I think McDonald would agree that combat is about individuals who are killing, dying, and trying not to think too hard about their own chances for personal survival.

Thus, I was astonished when in 1988 I was presented with a manuscript of short fiction by Walt McDonald. My surprise was predicated on my limited association with Walt, as a friend and colleague, but it was also because prose and fiction seemed, somehow, well out of character for a writer whose gentle and sensitive poetry—mostly about the hard land of West Texas—had brought him to national attention and recognition. There is, I suppose, an unwarranted assumption in the world of letters that poets just shouldn't write fiction; there is a larger assumption that they shouldn't write war fiction. But then, there's a wider assumption that West Texas is hardly a proper subject for poetry. It was fitting, somehow, that Walt McDonald proved both theories to be wrong.

Walt McDonald is, of course, not the first poet in America to try his hand at fiction, but in his single collection of short stories about Vietnam, this highly celebrated and accomplished poet demonstrated that he had perhaps taken the road of poetry not because he lacked ability or talent in prose, but rather because of some deliberate decision based on what his personal muse demanded. Indeed, my impression of the volume, which I read in galley proofs, was that it stood up as well as or better than most of the best Vietnam fiction I had read; by that point, my list was longer than it was impressive in terms of memorable volumes of high quality.

There are ready and identifiable themes in most Vietnam fiction. These cannot be characterized as "subtexts" or any such postmodern claptrap. Indeed, these themes recur with such frequency and are often so important to the makeup of the work at hand that they sometimes overwhelm the characters and become more important than the stories the writers have to tell. These themes can be identified in works by Phillip Caputo, John M. Delveccio, and Anthony Gray, among others; even in works where they are sometimes sublimated, such as *Going after Cacciato* by Tim O'Brien or the brilliant short fiction of Robert Olen Butler, they still echo with a resonance that's difficult to ignore.

Although they might be identified in various ways and under various headings, they include the strain of emotions between those who found themselves "in country" and those who were left back in the World ("World" is always spelled with a capital "W" in this context). They also involve the tension that existed in individual soldiers who tried to reconcile the traditional image of American heroism and patriotic values with the grim and sometimes terrifying realities of an unconventional war that was controlled more by politics (national and international) and layers of ineffective and often inept and self-serving bureaucracy than by military minds and well-conceived combat strategies.

Another identifiable theme finds its working-out in the tension that develops in individuals who were reared in a society that doted on notions of fair play, honesty, and law-abiding behavior. Suddenly finding themselves thrust into a homicidal madness where all such bets were off, where corruption, chicanery, and illegality became the norm, where lies were told even when the truth would be easier, and where fear was often centered as much in the seen and known as in the shrouded and obscured, they discovered that personal morality was mercurial, capricious, and, alas, as elusive as final victory.

Other themes are commonplace to almost all Vietnam fiction: the cultural gulf that existed between the young, often idealistic American personnel and the fundamentally dedicated and often indecipherable Vietnamese; the mental and physical toughness (to say nothing of the self-sacrificial determination) of the "enemy" Americans were sent over to fight; the general disillusionment of many soldiers who arrived full of nationalistic zeal, only to find their comrades counting the days until they could go home and their leaders deliberately misleading the press and public about their accomplishments and failures. Added to these are redefinitions of such terms as "cowardice" and "compassion," "integrity" and "character," "democracy" and "freedom," and, of course, "love" and "hate," "friendship" and "loyalty." After scanning a few dozen novels and short story collections, many of these ideas and their demonstrations become virtual clichés, paths of fictional exploration that almost always lead the reader to the same point: utter despair over the grotesque, ugly, bloody waste that was the Vietnam War.

As a result, most fiction writers turned away from trying to explore the Vietnam conflict through the "big picture," the overall, sweeping examination on the order, for example, of Herman Wouk's

Winds of War and *War and Remembrance*. They also began to turn away from attempts to characterize the war by examples taken of single operations such as was done by Norman Mailer, Leon Uris, or James Jones. More in the manner of a John Hershey or Joseph Heller, many Vietnam writers chose to focus on an individual, or possibly a small group of individuals, and their comparatively brief (typically one year) encounter with Vietnam. Their fiction was based less on military operations and strategic accomplishments and failures, and more on the internal, psychological or even spiritual impact of the war on an average American's psyche. This is the method McDonald chooses in *A Band of Brothers*.

Truly more of a short picaresque novel than a collection of short stories, *A Band of Brothers* centers mostly on one Lieutenant Mosley, called "Little Moose" because of his tenacity and strength as a wrestling champion at Ball State University. Sent to Vietnam late in the war—on the very eve of the final American pullout—Little Moose is commissioned to write a piece for *SNOW*, "Successively Numbered Observations on War." He is under the direct control of Colonel Tydings, an Air Force officer, who seems, at the outset, genuinely interested in Mosley's reports and the truth they will reveal. The "truth" Tydings is mostly interested in, however, is to demonstrate that the Air Force is doing its job by providing close air support for ground operations. He tells Mosley to take his time—"There's no deadline for truth," he assures him (5)—but in an ominous note, he tells another officer in Little Moose's presence, "I want the last American on the last flight home to be a SNOW writer"(9).

In the opening chapters, Mosley is oriented to the world of a combat zone that is Bein Dien, a forward airbase from which Phantom F-4s are launched with the specific mission of holding back the anticipated surge of North Vietnamese regulars who are now pouring into the southern sectors in anticipation of the final U.S. withdrawal. The fresh troops from the north are threatening American radar stations, Special Forces bases, and other outposts; the Phantom pilots' job is to be on hand to discourage this until the final pullout is ordered.

What Mosely finds when he lands is not even a close match to what he anticipated from watching television news and studying both official and unofficial reports of the war. The base appears to be nearly deserted, with empty buildings and dusty open spaces, the remains of recreational areas and signs of active military engagement left to bake in the Southeast Asian heat. Discipline is relaxed, even borderline insubordinate. The casual nonchalance of the men he finds manning the base carries him into a surreal world of low expectation, tinted by a constant hint of their mortality found in the mortar craters and distant sounds of combat filtering through the forest. Most of those he meets focus completely on their individual DEROS (Date of Earliest Return from Overseas), counting down to the point when they can put Vietnam into their pasts when they are restored to the World.

As Little Moose is integrated into the community of airmen, he learns that these pilots and ground crewmen truly represent a kind of forlorn "rear guard," commissioned to do what they can to harass the enemy, protect the villages that have received direct support and aid from the American troops, and to ensure the safety of the remaining combat forces in Vietnam's northern sectors. Their missions are almost routine, workmanlike sorties where advanced spotters respond to pleas for air support and find targets for the huge, deadly F-4s that scream from the sky to lay down enormous amounts of ordnance on an unyielding jungle. In recompense, Little Moose learns to his horror, Vietcong sappers, now reinforced by a steady stream of munitions and regular troops from the north, assault the airbase with nightly mortar and rocket attacks and are gradually taking over the villages that have been friendly to the Americans.

McDonald's series of chapters move Little Moose quickly from his position of naïve expectations to veteran status. A first-night mortar and rocket attack sends him scurrying to a bunker where he encounters his future comrades, Lebowitz, Hooker, Shackler, Malatesta, Croom, and Randy Wayne. Each of these men has attempted to make his peace with the war and his role in it, and each is resigned to endure the remainder of his tour until he is DEROSed or the American withdrawal is complete.

At first terrified by the nightly attacks, Mosley rapidly adopts a soldier's stoicism and develops a capacity to withstand the noise and fear that comes with the successively closer explosions. He begins to accept the fatalistic philosophy of his comrades, who regard another's death as being as much a matter of rotten luck as anything else. He comes to admire the psychological toughness of these airmen, astonished by their ability to accept circumstances that would, in any other context, be regarded as little more than orchestrated insanity. Soon, especially after his first flight in the "back seat" behind the constantly humming Shackler, he feels completely acclimated. He discovers in himself a shocking ability to objectify the war and its participants, to reduce even a fellow American to a number or a jargon-inspired term that dehumanizes the individual and insulates the men from their natural compassion for others.

After a while, however, Mosley begins to notice cracks in the façades of courage and high morale surrounding him. Croom, a veteran of several combat tours, spends his nights unable to sleep, roaming the perimeter of the base, actively seeking to find and kill enemy soldiers in vicious hand-to-hand struggles. Hooker, whose background previously exposed him to the unbelievable (albeit theoretical) verities of nuclear warfare and the potential results of unbridled conflict, gradually descends into a quivering mass of fear, shell-shocked by the mortars and rockets, unable to function or even find coherency except when under the care of a pretty and sympathetic nurse. Mosley watches Lebowitz, a genuine hero and ace pilot, fall completely apart when he discovers that a rocket from his plane accidentally landed on a schoolyard, killing and maiming innocent children, many of whom he knew.

Through it all, Mosley notes the tightness of the men's mutual dependency, their commitments to one another, and their stony unification when they are confronted by seemingly idiotic commanders who have no sense of what they are doing, what they are asking their men to do.

Gradually, Mosley's education in Vietnam becomes the reader's education, as well. Because McDonald has chosen for his setting the closing days of the war when American involvement is winding down, there is a profound irony surrounding all the characters' actions. They are doing their duty, naturally. But there is no sense of national pride or purpose, no commitment to political necessity or even of a comprehensive military strategy. Rather, the men who fly the missions do so out of a numbed sense of personal loyalty and rote response to specific orders. Anything that does not touch them or one of their group personally is not important or even worthy of acknowledgment. While on a mission to deliver medical supplies to a village hospital, for example, they come across a G.I.'s severed head mounted on a pole, the lips sewn together to contain the victim's genitals. Hooker, already descending into a depth of paranoid madness from which he may never escape, refuses to leave their vehicle to investigate, but the others slog through the rain to confront the physical horror. When they return to the jeep, they respond to Hooker's terrified question of who it was with the impersonal and satisfactory explanation, "Nobody we know" (65).

As the days move on in their inexorable march toward individual DEROSes, Mosley observes that the men around him have become expert at burying personal or even humane feelings deep within their psyches. When the report comes of an attack on an American facility, they are quick to respond, going about their deadly work with methodical precision, casually discussing the effects of their bombs, napalm, and cannons on the enemy in the same tones they note "hits" they have taken in their aircrafts or the potential danger of flying so close to the enemy's ground fire. But beneath these outward shows of nonchalant bravado, Mosley discovers that passions build with ferocity. When they drink too much or let go in some unguarded moment, their inner feelings are revealed; then they seem exposed, almost embarrassed by them; yet they keep their personal closeness handy, like a talisman that might eventually save them, if it doesn't destroy them.

There is a *Catch-22* feeling about *A Band of Brothers*, an almost indistinguishable sense of chaotic absurdity about the entire war and those who are in charge of the fighting that runs like an undercurrent beneath the daily routine. Apart from the obvious jokes about the "*SNOW* job" commissioned by Colonel Tydings, who will rewrite Mosley's accounts to downplay the personal tragedies he has witnessed and to enhance the bromides and platitudes of official patriotic language, there is a sense that the war has no direct meaning to any of the men. They smirk their way through briefings and spend much of their time evading the scrutiny of their superiors, blithely going about their business with robotic efficiency. But they always keep one eye on their personal safety and the other on the well-being of their comrades. Their interest in the war has little to do with any sense of national purpose or military pride. The "enemy," a word used only rarely by any of them, has no meaning in a political or even a personal sense. Targets become "objectives," and the concern expressed by the pilots is more for the technical accuracy of their missions than for any sense of strategic accomplishment that might have any relationship to a larger plan or picture.

This point is driven home at the end of the volume when Shackler, grieving for his wing-comrade, Randy Wayne, who was shot down, goes out "hunting" for anti-aircraft targets. His mission has no military purpose or mandate; he merely seeks revenge for the death of his friend. As his "back-seat man," Little Moose is helplessly pulled along on the ill-fated exercise—one that will suddenly thrust him "into" the war in a way he cannot have imagined. He suddenly becomes aware that his life is now in the hands of forces that he cannot control and is powerless to divert. But these forces are not extensions of a government or high command; they are controlled almost completely by a fatalistic pilot, a man whose sole focus is on personal revenge, no longer connected to any geopolitical theory or nationalistic philosophy, and certainly not connected to any sense of self-preservation or life beyond the moment.

In that sense, this collection of tightly connected stories offers, by extension, a brilliant account of the emotional deterioration of an entire nation's psyche. These characters are not draftees, combat cannon fodder, who against their will are trussed up for slaughter on some altar of bombastic jargon and jingoistic rhetoric. They are top professionals, well-educated and sensitive men whose lives have been deliberately given over to the lunatic purposes of war and whose identities reside in their deadly jobs, not their individual personalities. Ironically, what they discover in the midst of war—

particularly in the midst of this almost useless combat in which they are engaged—is that the only worth in the world lies in their relationships to one another. As those connections are severed by death or strained by emotional or psychological breakdown, they are compelled to put aside other priorities and to deal with their emotions on a much more pragmatic level.

Little Moose comes to understand this, but the realization hamstrings him. Ultimately reduced to an inability to record his experiences in any believable (or acceptable) way, he falls back on poetic phrasing, metaphoric utterances that color the complete horror he witnesses with something resembling beauty and (he hopes) truth. But in keeping with the imbecility that informs and controls the entire war—and by extension, every war—he is ordered to delete the poetry, eliminate the flowery language, and stick to the concrete facts and, more importantly, to the banality of the point. In perhaps the most ironic passage in the book, Colonel Tydings chides him for his style: "Who cares if there was a rainbow contrail or not?" Tydings demands of him with regard to the death of one of his pilot friends. "What counts is that Captain Wayne and a lot of others were up there risking their lives. . . . Remember, it's not so much what happens that counts, but how we *feel* about it. That's the value of *SNOW*. . . . There's already been too much bad press" (137). Thus, Mosley learns that good press is more important than good memories, that good feelings are more important than truth, even when the memories and the truth are nobly etched.

As Mosley, wounded but alive, makes his way onto a transport for home, knowing that he faces a long bout of surgery to restore him to some semblance of normalcy, he realizes that the true scars of Vietnam lie well beneath the millions of wounds and graves that the war has produced. The deeper injuries have been rendered to the integrity of a nation, of a people who were afraid to admit their mistakes and own up to their costs, with the result that they paid a much higher price than military embarrassment or political defeat ever could have cost. They have risked their very souls, and they have lost them.

In his introduction to the published volume, Robert Flynn writes:

> . . . McDonald doesn't give us good guys and bad guys. He gives us human beings trying to remain humane despite inhuman demands. This is Vietnam. A piece of it. It's not clean. It's not heroic. It's not the war as seen in movies or TV. But it is real in a way they never will be. (xv)

Flynn, himself a combat veteran of the Korean Conflict who also served as a war correspondent in Vietnam, understands the difficulties of capturing the madness of that "dirty little war" in prose; his own novel, *The Last Klick,* attempts to define the meaning the war had to individuals who found themselves caught up in it. For McDonald, though, the measure of the war has to be reconciled against the impact it had on the people who lived through it and ultimately came to understand it, not as a historian or even as a military strategist might understand it. He wants to present it in the only way it can truly be explained or understood, as a life experience, one which shaped the future and the fate of an entire generation.

Since 1989, the production of Vietnam war novels has declined precipitously. Of the more than one thousand titles registered by 1990, only a few dozen remain in print, and many of these are in inexpensive paperback editions that will soon disappear from booksellers' shelves. Interest in the war, as a war, has also declined. Through the filter of the enormously successful—one supposes—Desert Storm affair and the emergence of a unified Vietnam into the family of world nations as a respected and increasingly important economic factor in Southeast Asia, the blistering days that formed the backdrop for what may well be the ugliest chapter in American history rapidly fade into the twilight of the past. Flower children and war protesters appear on old, faded footage along with combat soldiers involved in panic-stricken firefights and villages left smoldering against the rain forest's incredible green. Our reactions are now more nostalgic than horrified, more apt to bring an ironic comment about national naïveté than the recollection of a time when "activism" and "commitment" had powerful and altogether different meanings.

Although tens of thousands still suffer from wounds—some visible, some invisible—sustained during their tours of duty in Southeast Asia, and although some still bristle when the question of the "morality" of the war arises, the whole conflict has been demoted in the national consciousness, relegated to history, something to be studied for its curiosity, not for its lessons. Today's college students were born too late to remember it, and many of the veterans are finding what one pundit called "Winnebago Retirement" to be an adequate reward for the services they rendered a largely ungrateful nation.

But in such volumes as Walt McDonald's *A Band of Brothers,* it's possible yet to catch a glimpse of a time, not so long ago, when "the smell of napalm in the morning" was more than a clever movie line, when two nations—one giant and one tiny—were locked in mortal combat that would ultimately determine the course of the future, not only in Asia, but throughout the world. Vietnam was, to use the *patois* of the sixties, "a happening." It was not a pleasant happening. Far more than a historical event, a war, a political power-play gone wrong, Vietnam was a cultural watershed, one that molded and shaped our nation's course, one which left a legacy that we have not yet entirely realized, perhaps one we are reluctant to embrace and far too eager to forget. Writers such as Walt McDonald understand this, and it is through their work that we can attempt to understand it as well.

Hence, it is fitting that a poet should help us in this attempt toward national understanding. Because a poet can bring to the subject a deep appreciation of and sensitivity to language, an awareness of its vast flexibility and richness, perhaps we can learn to see, as through a glass darkly, the larger truths of "the happening" that was so important to our lives. Perhaps a poet's words and the way he uses them can help us all understand and appreciate and know why it is important that there were rainbow contrails on the morning that a brave man so uselessly died.

III. The Southwest in McDonald's Poems

Walt McDonald's Beautiful Wasteland

Michael Hobbs

To a great extent Walt McDonald's early work focuses on alienation and isolation. The poetry in *Caliban in Blue, Anything Anything,* and *Burning the Fence* portrays figures wrenched away from family, tormented by memories of war and violence, and struggling to re-accustom themselves to life in a world they feel at odds with and estranged from. "With Derek in the Dunes," a representative early poem, provides a frightening example of the catastrophically fragmented psyches found in these first three books. The speaker *seems* okay at first. He appears to be enjoying himself and to feel close to Derek, but the poem signals that there are fissures forming, especially when we encounter the sand dunes, which become a threatening terrain. Partly what makes them so is that the dunes look innocuous, inviting, even recreational. But sand shifts, bogs one down, and the dunes begin to look the same. Left alone in a desert of white, shifting sameness, the family absent, familiar plains gone, the speaker loses himself; indeed, the language hints that the two people of the poem (Derek and the speaker) are actually one person, one version of the self leaving the other behind:

> By the time I get there
> he is gone, of course.
>
> I find him far away, still running,
> two dunes higher up. He waves,
> and from there it's like goodbye. (*Anything Anything* 14)

This farewell suggests a frightening finality, as if the self's breaking apart may be permanent. The figure we are left with at the end is isolated and fully displaced in a wasteland without any signposts to lead him out of the shifting dunes.

Such fragmented, isolated figures lost in a confusing wasteland are the rule rather than the exception in the opening phase of McDonald's career. The poet himself has commented on the abundance of these voices in his early work:

> Even five years ago [1980], I had too many of those haunted [voices], written from about 1977–1980. In fiction, I had written about Vietnam, and thought I had exorcised the haunting tone through those stories. But when I turned more and more to poetry from 1977 on, I seemed to go through it all over again, but changed from Vietnam to Lubbock, from images of war to surreal images of ordinary situations turned bizarre, the nightmare possibilities of the inevitable. (Woods 10)

These haunted voices continue to appear even in McDonald's most recent work; however, with *Witching on Hardscrabble,* McDonald begins to shift away from a poetry dominated by voices of isolation and to turn instead toward a more affirmative poetry of human communion. Despite what McDonald says above about Lubbock, this shift mainly coincides with a turn toward a poetry ostensibly about Texas but, in a larger sense, about the mystery of beauty that abides (and provides the occasion for human communion) in a world that seems to be as spiritually desiccated as the landscape is physically parched in West Texas and on the South Plains around Lubbock. In fact, West Texas and the South Plains serve, in McDonald's work, as desertlike microcosms of the postmodern world in general, and the poetry's stark physical terrain often suggests humanity's psychic wasteland. In an interview with Chris Ellery, McDonald has commented that his hardscrabble poems, echoing T. S. Eliot, contain

> a lot of this waste land experience—not so much because of the physical landscape, but because of my having come back from Vietnam. The two just became a blend—West Texas, Vietnam. I didn't intend it to be that way. So can I say that *The Waste Land* by Eliot had an influence? I guess it did, though I never thought of it until you asked the question. (40)

Nevertheless, around the time of *Witching on Hardscrabble,* McDonald's personas begin to encounter a strange beauty in the midst of this bleak terrain, a beauty that is mysterious and inexplicable but which also helps counter their sense of loneliness and isolation. This shift toward a poetry about beauty in the midst of the wasteland was probably precipitated by a comment Donald Justice made to McDonald about the absence of Texas in his poetry. McDonald knew Justice from the University of Iowa and sent him a copy of *Caliban in Blue* after its publication. Justice responded enthusiastically but also asked, "Where's Texas in your poetry, Walt?" According to McDonald, Justice's question was

> *the* turning point in my writing life, for it made me open up from things I felt I needed to write about (friends killed in Vietnam, and my own time there) to things I could discover to write about with pleasure, including family and the tornadoes and drought, the splendors of those wide horizons at sundown and high noon, here in my native West Texas. (McDonald, letter to the author)

Instead of narrowing the scope of his poetry, McDonald's focusing on West Texas and the South Plains broadened its thematic significance. Somehow, writing about the mysteriously stark beauty of his native West Texas helped McDonald not so much to exorcise completely the haunted voices of isolation from his work but instead to blend paradoxically the necessary bleakness of those voices with his affirmative voices of human communion.

Three poems in *Witching on Hardscrabble*—"When the Wind Dies," "Night Skiing on Lake Buchanan," and "Midnight at Dillon"— demonstrate magnificently the beginning of this blending of the bleak and the mysteriously beautiful. "When the Wind Dies" opens with mystery, even if the mystery is comic in nature: "No wind, mystery enough in that / to last a lifetime." The joke is perhaps not readily apparent unless the reader has lived on the South Plains where the wind never seems to die. What *is* readily apparent from the poem is the tremendously bleak terrain through which this wind incessantly blows. The place is blisteringly hot in the summer, dangerously cold in winter, treeless, waterless, wracked either by sandstorms or blizzards that "bury cattle / caught in the fields." Despite this rugged setting, the couple of the poem manages well enough. In fact, the wind itself provides a means of surviving—the two claim they "stay sane by listening to the wind"—though the remark is as comically ironic as the opening joke about the lack of wind. While the poem is comic in tone, the absence of wind does provide an occasion for communion with the mysterious. As the final lines of the poem make clear, the silence that dominates when the wind dies provides an unwonted moment of mysterious beauty that awakens the couples' imaginations:

> When the wind dies,
> we catch ourselves leaning

> to hear jets in the distance,
> geese flying by like a babble
> of tongues, and train whistles
> blaring at distant crossings
> as if someone is stalled
> on the tracks and dreaming. (6)

The intriguing line here is "we catch ourselves leaning." Its collo-quial meaning suggests that the couple suddenly becomes aware of imagining things and feels either embarrassed or ashamed about let-ting their minds wander. Their imaginations lean away from the ab-sence of the wind (and the unwonted silence accompanying that absence) and toward hoped-for sounds. Conceding to the actuality of the barren terrain, the couple refrains from imagining sounds, be-lieving such fantasies merely evade the fact of the wind's absence and the silence that replaces it. However, "we catch ourselves" also suggests that the couple has captured some fleeting or ineffable idea of themselves or even of their relationship to each other. They hear something beautiful in the absence of the wind—jets, geese, train whistles, or even the silence itself that has stimulated their act of imagination, in this case a communal imagining.

While the idea of catching ourselves contrasts affirmatively with the loss of self portrayed in "With Derek in the Dunes," "When the Wind Dies" also leaves us with a hint of danger and potential ruin in its final image, as if dreaming (or imagining) is risky in a world filled with ironclad facts such as trains speeding toward stalled cars. This element of grim danger is an early variation on the bleakness that en-tangles itself with the beauty in McDonald's beautiful-wasteland poetry. "Night Skiing on Lake Buchanan" contains a similar element of danger. As the poem makes clear, skiing at night is dangerous but also exhilarating. There is also a mysteriously beautiful quality in the poem's imagery: the moon is shining in "rhythm" on the water, and as the two skiers begin their simultaneous rise "to the roar of a motor / rumored to be before us," they feel as if they are "skiing on nothing / but shimmers." As in "When the Wind Dies," the couple experiences together this mysterious beauty, and "Night Skiing" again uses "lean" to suggest an imaginative act: "Spray in our faces / we *lean* to each other, / boards almost touching" (emphasis added). "Night Skiing" repeats the powerful act of communal imagining as its couple leans together "believing there is / nothing better / than what [they] are risking" (25).

Since imagination is an integral aspect of the skiing couple's ex-perience of the mysterious, and since "Night Skiing" makes such extended use of self-referential language (McDonald repeats "rhythm" four times and "feet" twice), it's hard not to see the poem as a comment about the act of creating poetry. This, in fact, turns out to be true not only of "Night Skiing" but also of "Midnight at Dillon." Like the acts of skiing, fishing, or merely struggling to make a life together, poetry occasionally offers a glance at the wasteland's mysterious beauty, but that glance demands a willingness to take risks and to engage the imagination communally. Part of the risk lies in facing up to the bleak realities that often mask beauty in the postmodern world. By taking those risks and asking the reader to take those risks as well, McDonald demonstrates how beauty resides in the midst of starkness and bleakness as well as how easily it can be overlooked in a harshly fact-ridden world so apparently hostile to mystery and the imagination.

"Midnight at Dillon" continues to explore how communing imaginations discover beauty camouflaged in rather bleak surroundings. "Midnight" pretends to be a poem about fishing, and it is that, but one soon realizes that the experience described is no ordinary excursion. There is something bleak and ruined about the poem's setting. As we discover, the lake itself has been fashioned out of hardship—homes have been flooded to make room for it—and the fishing companions are a rather hard lot who "bless the barbs" of their hooks by spitting tobacco juice on them and drink bourbon to keep warm. Paradoxically, these stark realities are the very elements that help bring about their experience of the mysteriously beautiful. As with "When the Wind Dies" and "Night Skiing," there is a note of danger in "Midnight at Dillon" from the very beginning, and the poem's terrain is bleak, the night cold, the fog "thick as walls around us, / cut off from shores and slumber" (64).

"Midnight at Dillon" reveals not only an experience of mysterious beauty, but a communal desire for that experience, an urge to search it out, as if that is all that can rescue one from "the sleep of this world." Here, then, are companions seeking beauty to counter the mundanity and bleakness of their surroundings. As we move toward the climax of the poem, McDonald again applies highly self-referential language (choosing words such as "line," "music," "foot," and "rhythm") to remind us that this is a poem about the mysterious experience shared not only by companions fishing but also by reader and poet in the act of creating poetry. The trembling exhilaration one feels at "the first hard whip of the line" applies equally well to fishing companions and to the poet and reader. The fog provides the most powerful element of mystery in the poem; it's as if we are separated from all that is solid and actual. "Fish of all sizes" swim in the unknown waters beneath, "all of us floating in darkness above them, / needing whatever lies hidden." The jarring moment of contact with mysterious beauty—"the first hard whip of the line"—

(whether we are speaking of creating poetry or fishing) relies upon
the imaginative communion of companions:

> Only the fleece of our coats can keep us warm,
> and bourbon, sipped from the bottle and passed
> back and forth in the boat like communion,
> the fellowship of the spirit of fishing.

There is some inscrutable element that draws us in, something "like
music."

> Getting a grip on the rhythm,
> we cup our rods and test the reels for tension,
> feed out another foot of line
> and go on breathing, ready to feel
>
> the first hard whip of the line
> from under, to hold in our hands
> the wonder, the assurance
> of things not seen. (64)

That moment (whether fishing or reading a poem) when we feel
stunned, even mystified, by "the first hard whip of the line" is what
matters most. It is wonder, our sense of awe in the face of unexpected
sublimity, that rescues us from the numbness of the barren or "the
sleep of the world" as the poem puts it, even though such awe-
inspiring beauty cannot be disentangled from the bleak elements
surrounding it.

These poems that blend the postmodern wasteland with its mysterious beauty continue to appear sprinkled throughout McDonald's
work since *Witching on Hardscrabble,* and they often offer interesting
variations on the theme. In *The Flying Dutchman,* for example, Mc-
Donald gives us another fishing poem that evokes, in this case comically, beauty in the midst of the mundane. "Seining for Carp" locates
the mysteriously beautiful in one of the most ordinary of all fishes,
the carp, and then goes on playfully to examine the defeat that the
speaker and his companions suffer while trying to seine the carp out
of their playa lake. As in the above poems, a communal experience
takes place during the course of the poem. The speaker and his companions consider the carp worthless,

> nothing
> worth eating, ugly, scaly leeched-out heirs
> of five-and-dime goldfish my daughters
> freed one summer (64)

and are thus intent on ridding the lake of these trash fish. But they are thwarted in their effort, which at times takes on a hint of danger similar (though playfully treated) to the risky experiences of beauty in *Witching on Hardscrabble.*

As in the other fish poems, the efforts at fishing here gradually become mystical, though it is comically mystical, evoked out of pure exasperation. When nobody can catch anything but carp (evidently the carp are easy to snag when they are unwanted), the fishermen trade their poles for scuba gear:

> Putting aside our rods
> and lures, we scuba dive ten feet down,
> searching the bottom of this hardpan
> playa lake, the water clear as a lagoon
> and barely cool.

But now that the fishermen truly desire to catch them, there are no signs of the carp, turned suddenly inscrutable: "Where they hide must be in fissures of stone / or shadows of our heels as we swim by." The hint of danger appears here in the form of comic exaggeration. After searching in vain for even a single carp, the divers begin to resurface:

> The first one up kicks off the flippers,
> digs in and pulls us in like climbers
> dangling down the sheer face of a cliff
> we have struggled up for days. (65)

Obviously the physical risks here are negligible; instead, the real risk lies in the companions' failing to understand that beauty is inextricably entangled with bleakness in the postmodern world. And in fact, after a good deal of scuba-diving exertion, the fishermen come up empty-handed as well as empty-headed.

The delightful irony of the poem is that the carp turn out to be both undesirable and desirable; they take on a kind of symbolic significance. Though representative critters of an arid terrain with a few playa lakes scattered about and occasionally filled with water, the carp also signify an ineffable quality entangled with that aridity: they are a part of that postmodern landscape that I refer to as the beautiful wasteland where beauty is always bound to the bleak. While the carp are spurned and disdained at the poem's beginning, they become, by the end, "the secret carp" swimming in a gorgeous lagoon instead of an ordinary playa lake. Interestingly, the fishermen's failure, as comic as it is, brings the group closer together in their suffering, but it is as if they themselves are a catch, trapped in the net of their desperately ordinary lives and being hauled to their inevitable end. After rinsing the net clean, they "close together, fold-ing, / feeling the plain week ahead close over [them]" as they wish "for someone to come walking over the waters / of [their] lives" and guide them, tell them

> to let down there, down
> there, where the water is clearest, where the secret
> carp wait in the open, catchable, all the carp
> in our lives easy to seine and toss to the cats.

McDonald seems to be offering us a cautionary note about our desire to evade what is bleak and harsh: we must be careful not to overlook the beauty in our apparently stark lives. The plains themselves seem flat, the hardscrabble barren, but the hardpan bottom of the most or-dinary playa lake contains the clearest water and "the secret carp" (65). Beauty is there before us if we only have the courage to look.

Beauty and bleakness are merged powerfully in "With My Father in Winter," a poem from *The Digs in Escondido Canyon,* which por-trays a son's recollection of fishing with his father. During the course of the poem, we come to realize that the son's memory occurs during the father's funeral; the harsh reality of death entangles itself with the beauty of the memory. The poem begins with the son's telling about a fly-fishing excursion with his father:

> We hiked through woods to pools
> I believed no one but he
> could find. He knew all trees
> by faith, never glanced back,
> his fly line flipping fast
> under aspens, the fly
> flicking upstream to pools
> no wider than his rod.
> His eyes searched eddies
> and stones for cutthroats
> shimmering deep in currents
> sapphire cold. (48)

The father has a certain mysterious, near-magical intuition for finding fish and is greatly skilled at flicking the line (note the self-referential moment) into the most inaccessible backwater to snag a cutthroat. "Shimmering," "sapphire," "eddies," and "deep currents" develop the moment's tranquil beauty, and yet "cutthroats" casts a hint of vi-olence and brutality into the midst of this imagery of tranquility. Even the loveliness of "sapphire" is qualified by its immediate as-sociation with "cold," which reminds us of the winter in the title and anticipates the funeral setting soon to be revealed in the poem. Artifact-like in its description, itself a kind of polished stone, the poem slowly discloses the idea of a beautiful wasteland and the speaker's mysterious experience of such a terrain.

The second stanza gradually reveals to us that, in fact, the first stanza is the son's recollection of fly-fishing, a recollection which takes place at the moment of his father's burial:

> Now, geese overhead
> aim north, and somewhere
> a hooked trout flounces.
> Even here among these stones,
> in snow, I hear it splash.
> On a stiff green carpet,
> I stand bundled like a boy
> under a flapping canopy
> and stare at black mud
> frozen in chunks
> while someone's words
> flick out across a hole. (48)

The piece follows an elegiac pattern that many of McDonald's poems adopt after his first few books; he begins with a moment in the past and suddenly shifts us to the immediate present, usually by the signal word "now," as in this poem. The powerfully jarring effect here lies in McDonald's ability to overwhelm us gradually with the realization that the speaker's father has died and we're at his funeral. Subtle phrases clue us about the setting; "among these stones," "stiff green carpet," and "a flapping canopy" ease us into the funeral scene and set up the final lines of the poem which resonate powerfully back through the piece, enigmatically weaving together the beauty of fly-fishing with the wasteland imagery of the funeral. The phrase "someone's words" takes on multifaceted meaning when we realize that we're at a funeral; the someone refers not only to the minister conducting the service but also to the now silent father who speaks from the past. But even beyond these two, the words uttered by "someone" belong to the poet as well, who flicks them across the chasm of the poem's risked language. Along with the speaker, the reader experiences the mystifying combination of joyful beauty and mournful grimness. McDonald helps us experience the awestruck terror that a son feels at his father's funeral, but combines this paradoxically with the beauty not only of fly-fishing but of the poem itself. The minister (as well as the poet) risks misunderstanding as words seem to become merely an artificial fly flicked across a black hole. But the art of that flick overcomes misunderstanding, ironically because its beauty allows us to comprehend the devastating bleakness with which it is so oddly bound.

McDonald continues to explore the idea of the beautiful waste-land in *Where Skies Are Not Cloudy*. For example, "No Matter Where We've Been" starts with the confession, "I swore I'd never come back / to the plains, eight flat acres / and stars so bright they buzzed" (5). The speaker here attempts to explain his return to a place that even he considers desolate and unappealing. McDonald felt this way about the plains when he was a young man: "I had a lot more loath-ing for this part of the country than I did love. I thought I would never come back to Texas. I wanted to go to Cornell University to study when I was an undergraduate. The Finger Lakes district sounded beautiful to me" (Baughman 272). Of course, the speaker of the poem does return (as did McDonald), and "No Matter Where We've Been" tries to explain why anybody would choose to live on such a wastelike terrain. Partly the answer lies in what Uncle Bubba says to the speaker about the plains: "no matter where we've been, / it's home" (5). But given McDonald's hardscrabble irony (and Uncle Bubba's rather grotesque characterization in other McDonald po-ems), Bubba's words sound more like a curse than a maxim to live by. With typical sarcasm the speaker continues to sing the praises of the plains:

> Our boys make a fortune
> dragging home rattlers in towsacks.
> The prairie crawls with tarantulas,
> hawks in all weather.

What more could one ask of a place than to have rattlers, tarantulas, and hawks always about? Still, the poem shifts to a more earnest tone as we move toward its end and the real virtue of living on hardscrabble unfolds:

> There's little we could lose, here,
> little we could hide.
>
> We've almost stopped pretending
> clouds are mountains.
> If we can't accept these fields,
>
> our own souls with all their wind
> and cactus, we ought to leave.
> Even at night, our shadows sprawl:
>
> this moon is up for hours. On fields
> this flat, someone's easy to find
> and always calls us friend. (5)

Living on hardscrabble, a person cannot hide from himself, nor can he believe, so easily, in illusions or self-deceptions. The harsh reality is that we either "accept these fields" and "our own souls" no matter how flawed they may be, or we "leave" by whatever means possible. The apposition of fields with our own souls emphasizes McDonald's insistent identification of mind and place, inner and outer terrain. They merge in flitting images of mysterious beauty, a region where "our shadows sprawl" and "this moon is up for hours." The moon, here, is simultaneously beautiful and terrifying in its luminous, omnipresent glow, suggesting the full measure of the beautiful wasteland's impact on its inhabitants' psyches. But perhaps most important about "fields this flat" (which begins to suggest not only inner and outer terrain but also the terrain of the poem itself) is that companionship is always possible, and as McDonald implies repeatedly, such communal understanding (friend and friend, husband and wife, reader and poet) is an essential element in facing the inevitable fusion of bleakness and beauty in the postmodern world.

The wasteland imagery almost overwhelms all sense of beauty with which McDonald binds it in some of his most recent work. In "The Summer Before the War" and "Black Granite Burns Like Ice" from *Where Skies Are Not Cloudy*, the psychic terrains portrayed recall the isolated, alienated voices of McDonald's early poetry. In "Before the War," the speaker thinks back on Vietnam as TV advertisements for '60s music open memories like old wounds. Actually, the speaker first recalls riding bulls with his friend Billy Ray "before Saigon," but afterward, "Nights come back like taps to haunt us / privately, not boldly like a rodeo where all could watch" (28). As in "With My Father in Winter," the poem is elegiac in tone, opening with a memory and then returning us jarringly to the bleaker moment of the speaker's present situation. The music, the rugged aesthetics of bull riding, and "waltzing with blondes" merge their beauty with the harsh reality of the speaker's present-day loneliness and tormented private suffering, part of which derives from his perceived beauty of the past (28). The ruin of the speaker's present life is so overwhelming that any contrasting beauty (even out of the past) exacerbates his pain. For this speaker, at least, hints of beauty in a predominantly wasted terrain produce anguish and isolation.

McDonald often uses references to art (as in his self-referential poems) to explore the enigmatic experience of the beautiful wasteland. The black granite in "Black Granite Burns Like Ice," from *Where Skies Are Not Cloudy*, refers to the Vietnam War Memorial (the wall), an image that appears often in McDonald's next book, *Counting Survivors*, the cover of which displays a reproduction of the wall. "Black

Granite" recounts the difficulty of surviving one's friends who died in the war:

> Watching the world from above,
> all fallen friends applaud
> in blisters on our backs.
> Wherever I go, there's fire.

For the speaker, and perhaps for all Americans, the war continues to haunt. The speaker has "been to the wall" and experienced the work of art by placing his "fingers on [his friends'] names." His reaction to the wall captures powerfully the beautiful wasteland motif in McDonald's poetry: "Black granite burns like ice / no lips can taste." For the speaker, the starkly sculptured beauty of the wall evokes both the unspeakable suffering of the war (killing, physical suffering, deprivation) and the private beauty of that experience (the friendship to which he refers, if nothing else). The poem (indeed, much of McDonald's poetry, in general) functions in a fashion similar to that of the wall; it is flat and reflective, stark in its appearance, dark, and the reader winces at the touch of its imagery:

> After the madness of Saigon
> I flew back through San Francisco
>
> to the plains, flat fields with cactus
> and the ghosts of rattlers.
> I feed the hawks field mice and rabbits.
> I'm no Saint Francis
>
> but even the buzzards circle,
> hoping whatever I own keeps dying.

The echo of "The Love Song of J. Alfred Prufrock" conjures up the imagery of psychic and physical ruin so omnipresent in Eliot's work, but there are hints in "Black Granite" of a companionship, a communal understanding of beauty in the midst of harsh reality that distinguishes McDonald's speaker from Prufrock. Images of beauty in "Black Granite" are scarce, but his "wife's green eyes" (58) pull us toward the lines that suggest the importance of the speaker's spiritual communion with his wife. The most tranquil moment of beauty in the poem comes at the end of the day when the speaker and his wife are together—"After dark / we rock on the porch / and watch the stars"—but lest we forget the bleakness of the poem's earlier terrain, McDonald's last stanza shows us what the two meditate on as they watch the heavens. They sit

wondering how many owls dive
at night per acre, how many snakes
per grandchild, how many wars
before all dreams are fire. (59)

The final use of fire, with its powerful ambiguity, emphasizes the entanglement of beauty and bleakness in the poem. The fire imagery
suggests both profane destruction and a kind of sacred (even if apocalyptic) intensity of understanding that the speaker is slowly coming to possess and that we come to possess along with him: while the
postmodern world stands in utter ruins, there is a beauty that abides
even in the midst of that devastation, a beauty which we come to
perceive through a communally imaginative act that often involves
the taking of a risk to achieve that understanding. McDonald implies that we must approach this harsh, postmodern beauty
through companionship. Otherwise the bleakness overwhelms the
beauty completely.

The mind on fire, then, suggests both ecstasy and torment, an ex-
cruciating awareness of beauty in the midst of the barren. The title
poem of McDonald's 1995 book, *Counting Survivors*, returns to the
suffering occasioned by such awareness. As in "With My Father in
Winter," "Counting Survivors" jars us as we gradually come to realize its setting, in church on Easter Sunday. The poem leaves us in the
same mysteriously stunned condition that we find the speaker in at
the poem's beginning. Images of the sacredness, beauty, and spirituality of the worship service are bizarrely entangled with reminders
of war: "The padded church bench / shudders like a medevac on
takeoff. / Saigon falls often in my dreams" (34). The poem ironically
echoes Eliot's *The Waste Land* where Eliot's speaker comments on the
living dead passing over London Bridge as they move toward their
daily jobs: "I had not thought death had undone so many" (31, line
63). In "Counting Survivors," the speaker comments on his own surprise at seeing "so many" returned home—"I'm stunned to see so
many of us home" (34)—and this echo of *The Waste Land* becomes
more ironic as we realize, by the poem's end, that the survivors are
(as in Eliot's poem) a part of the contingent of living dead, something
which the speaker implies in the middle stanza: "Most friends I
knew / are back in body. I miss good friends / who earned this service." The souls of the returned survivors are missing, and while the
"good friends" of the next sentence could be those who did not return
either in body or soul, the implication is that no friends have returned.
In a sense, nobody survives the war, since everyone who participates
is so radically affected by the experience. Still, the poem's setting and
occasion suggest a communal spirituality of sorts, a mysterious survival (or revival) that abides for those gathered at church. Both of the

final questions refer to those who are "back in body," the survivors that seem akin to the living dead. Thus, the parallelism of the two questions hints at the moment's mystery: "how do survivors live? / How do the dead arise?" (34).

Partly the answer to these questions lies in one's ability to reconcile the apparently hostile incongruities that exist between beauty and ruin. In the poems of *Counting Survivors*, McDonald chronicles varying degrees of success in this effort, moving from personas who live in despair at the beginning of the book (abjectly unable to reconcile the incongruities surrounding them) to those who seem to have finally achieved a reconciliation, even an affirmative understanding of the beautiful wasteland, as in "Mesas I Never Took the Time to Climb," the final poem of *Counting Survivors* and one of McDonald's finest pieces. However, we are far from such affirmation in the opening poem of *Counting Survivors*. "After the Fall of Saigon" portrays a tormented character who finds brief intervals of consolation in "good booze." But not even this can "burn the fungus out, / down where it doesn't show, / the mind's own groin." Haunted by what he has seen in Vietnam, he joins the contingent of living dead as the ironic reference to the wall makes clear: "Years after Saigon, he's like a wall: / lets no one know him, but his name" (3). Here, the wall is less a work of art than a barrier that isolates one. The speaker's bleak existence hides any of the sculpture's potential beauty, especially from the speaker himself.

McDonald refers to the wall again in "Out of the Stone They Come," where he fashions a portrait of a vet less isolated but as distressingly tormented as the alcoholic vet in "After the Fall." McDonald sets "Out of the Stone" in a time after the war in the Persian Gulf, where the speaker's son has fought. As if fashioning his own memorial, the son has "hung a framed painting / on his wall," which depicts a soldier his father's age standing before the wall. In the painting the ghosts of fallen soldiers, whose names are listed on the wall, reach out to touch the survivor:

> A soldier
> holds out a ghostly hand to touch him.
>
> Others beyond the wall look out,
> young as my son in their helmets.
> Out of the stone they've come
> with incredibly young arms
>
> because he's here, head bowed,
> surviving.

The father's viewing of the painting's harsh beauty occasions a more intimate, but also a more painful, relationship with his son. The son is no longer merely his father's boy; instead, the father now recognizes him as a companion soldier, a recognition that he fully awakens to after their trip together to see the actual Vietnam War Memorial. While gazing at and touching the wall, which is "cold as a mirror," the father sees his "son's own image in the stone" (16). The vision is simultaneously beautiful (reflective of the new spiritual communion with his son) and terrifically painful (the son's image in the stone associates him with those who have forever been altered by the experience of war). Experiencing both the painting of the wall and the wall itself brings the father and son closer together, which seems to enhance at least the father's ability to see beauty in the midst of the wasteland, though the vision is devastating, as the father's tears suggest at the poem's end.

In "Grace and the Blood of Goats," McDonald speaks through a voice less wounded than those above. He continues to convey a sharp twinge of bleak despair but assuages this by allowing his persona to persevere in the search for a recognizable beauty in his life. The speaker and his wife are vacationing in the mountains, staying in a cabin, trying to recover (or resurrect) a sense of their companionship: "We need what prairie eyes don't hope for, / what isn't ours to feed." If only for a while, the two need to feel unexposed, untroubled by the "hours of overtime" on the hardscrabble that interfere with their companionship. The speaker is hopeful and affirmative, but McDonald tempers this tone by combining images of beauty and romance with references to the stark landscape and carnivorous wildlife of West Texas. As the couple stands together at a window gazing at the moon, "silver beaten thin," they can't ignore the presence of owls that remind them of prairie hawks back home. And the moon itself, while silvery and awe-inspiring, takes on a frighteningly barren quality: "Tonight, / even if we call to it, peace, be still, the moon / keeps bleaching before our eyes." The couple remains slightly lost as they search for a way to connect:

> We wait for grace
> in a world deserted, where the blood of goats
> can't save us. The babies we raised were worth it,
> but now we're alone, lost in a snow field at night
> in mountains. (63)

McDonald returns ever so slightly to the isolation and displacement that trouble the voices in his early books; however, he keeps his speaker intent on negotiating his way over the confusing terrain of the beautiful wasteland, on reconciling the incongruities inherent in such a landscape through a renewed companionship with his wife. The couple pledges more careful attention to each other, physically and verbally: "Tonight, we swear we'll worship flesh / and tongues with more patient ears" (63–4). But McDonald doesn't resolve the poem in an easy affirmation; instead, both husband and wife understand that "we won't change much, but anyway we swear" (64). Still, McDonald suggests that perseverance is one way to face the postmodern world's beautiful wasteland.

McDonald creates several characters who successfully reconcile the incongruities of the beautiful wasteland at the end of *Counting Survivors* in poems such as "When the Children Have Gone," and "Mesas I Never Took the Time to Climb." In the former, he quietly depicts the consoling companionship between husband and wife, paying special attention to simple acts such as sitting together outside during sunset. McDonald himself takes pleasure in these simple acts. As he reveals in a recent interview, he and his wife Carol are fond of watching sunsets in the evening: "We like to sit outside and rock in darkness, even though it means we are out there where it happens. Often, it is quiet, here in West Texas. Sometimes we listen to the splash and battle of bass in the lake, the squeal of a mouse when an owl grabs it and flaps away." As this comment reveals, even when enjoying the placid tranquility of rocking in darkness, one is inevitably "out there where it happens." The beauty of a South Plains evening is inexorably bound with the bleak realities of life-and-death struggles. In "When the Children Have Gone," after the couple arrives back on the plains from a visit to the grandchildren, they settle into a sort of blissful yet simple end of day:

> Back home, we listen to coyotes howling
> the song we've sung for years. We live on beans
> and *fajitas* braised over mesquite roots,
> red peppers that scald our tongues. At dusk,
> we carry chairs outside and watch the sundown.
>
> My wife believes in the peace of dark,
> the burning stars. I watch light shimmer
> on her face, her flashing eyes. Now it begins,
> the golds and purple on the plains. Blink
> and miss it, like flecks of silver in her hair. (77)

In these final two stanzas, beauty predominates. "Her flashing eyes" echoes one of the few images of beauty—the wife's "green eyes"—in "Black Granite Burns Like Ice," but the wife's eyes, here, along with the "flecks of silver" in her hair connect her beauty with the cosmic beauty of the sunset. However, as in all of McDonald's poetry, beauty does not exist in a vacuum. The trip home, before we reach

the "peace of dark," is punctuated by images of roadkill and buzzards clacking their beaks, "black wings flapping a tight / possessive spiral back to bones." The "tight possessive spiral" reminds us
of the hold that harsh reality has in McDonald's postmodern world.
Beauty and the mystery inherent in its "golds and purple" abide but
cannot be unraveled from the spiral of "black wings flapping." The
line that captures the beauty of the sunset—"the golds and purple on
the plains"—speaks perfectly to this paradox if we catch the pun on
"plains" (77). Breathtaking beauty is superimposed on the flat, stark
barrenness of that which is plain—the "plainness of plain things" as
Wallace Stevens would have it (467)—in McDonald's postmodern
wasteland. Such an incongruity is difficult to reconcile; "Blink /and
miss it" as McDonald says. But the speaker and his wife seem, if only
briefly, to have understood, and McDonald leaves us to contemplate
this paradox and its relationship to their companionship at the end
of the poem.

I have tried to demonstrate, here, that beauty is not a transcendent
category in McDonald's poetry. Instead, it is inextricably earthbound, made relative (and relevant) to, rather than rising above, the
harsh circumstances of plain existence. The final poem that I want to
examine—"Mesas I Never Took the Time to Climb"—comes as close
as any McDonald piece to the mystery of transcendence. But in the
end, while the mystery abides, the poem insists on remaining tied to
its everyday prairie life with all the harsh characteristics that we've
grown used to associating with that life. The poem continues to celebrate companionship between husband and wife, but significantly it
moves beyond even that communal form of beauty to an examination of solitude near the end of the speaker's life. As in "When the
Children Have Gone," McDonald sets the poem in the evening, suggesting that his speaker, riding back home after a day's work, is in
the evening of his life. The light of companionship with his wife
draws him back home as has happened innumerable times in the
past: "My wife must know I'm coming, / lights bright in the kitchen."
The kitchen lights suggest the beauty of companionship that the
speaker knows, and he associates these earthly lights with the stars'
cosmic beauty; in fact, he seems to disdain any easy figuration of the
stars (as well as the rattlesnakes) as something other than they are:
"Our crops are rattlers and starry skies / we pretend are diamonds."
As in "When the Wind Dies," the tone here suggests that pretending
is a type of evasion, a swerving away from the recognition that the
stars' beauty is entangled with that which is plain, stark, and harsh,
not rare and transcendent. Crops, rattlers, and starry skies fit together into an equitable series for this speaker, though the series
may jar the reader who expects something euphemistically heavenly
from a mention of the stars. The speaker refuses to flinch from the

hardscrabble harshness; we learn that on this particular workday he has encountered a buzzard dying in the fields: "Today I found a buzzard in the field, / too weak to flap away. Panting, it hobbled / as if on stilts." The grim sight reminds him of his own impending mortality, and as he nears the lighted house, he speculates about his approaching final moments:

> Someday soon, I'll cut the fences down and let the bulls
> run wild. I'll ride my gelding straight toward a mesa
>
> I never took the time to climb. I'll dismount
> and slap the sorrel to send him back to the corral.
> I'll look at these flat fields from far above,
> the same parched sand and cactus after sundown,
> night shining not with diamonds, but real stars. (79)

In his projected moment of death, the speaker imagines an earthbound ascension similar to what one finds in Frost's "Birches," a "transcendence" that doesn't abandon the hardscrabble. He imagines himself "far above" the "parched sand" here, but he hasn't risen above the rugged landscape; on the contrary, he embraces that landscape in all of its harsh beauty and uses this understanding to approach his *real*izing of the stars. He, perhaps more fully than any other character in a McDonald poem, is able to reconcile the incongruities associated with the beautiful wasteland as he moves beyond pretending about the stars in the poem's final line: "night shining not with diamonds, but real stars." The speaker ascends after death not by rising above his West Texas existence, but by embracing its full reality, its harshness and its beauty, forever woven together.

To a great extent, then, McDonald's poetry is concerned with the mysterious nature of beauty in the postmodern world, and largely that mystery lies in beauty's inextricable entanglement with what is harsh, stark, barren, and often violent. Perhaps the greatest mystery is that beauty abides in such a world, but it is a beauty—in a place shimmering with the "purples and gold" of a sunset accompanied by the background shriek of a mouse snagged in the claws of a swooping owl—that is often maddening. But that is, after all, the beautiful wasteland that McDonald's poetry both reveals and ultimately celebrates.

Unignored Plunder: The Texas Poems of Walt McDonald

Dave Oliphant

In 1978, Bin Ramke, a native of Port Neches, Texas, won the Yale Series of Younger Poets Award for his first collection of poems, *The Difference Between Night and Day*. In the Foreword to Ramke's book, Richard Hugo refers to a poem entitled "The Feast of the Body of Christ in Texas" and suggests that, to illuminate "both the work and the poet's life," a critic "would probably take more than casual note" of this piece. In it Hugo finds evidence that by age twelve Ramke was developing "personal escape routes," since he realized that "the chances of heavenly redemption" seemed "remote," that there were "cities to go to, Chicago, Los Angeles. . . . Already the poet has begun . . . to create a world of other possibilities he can escape to." More recently, Mary Karr, who was born in Groves, Texas (a few miles from Port Neches), writes in "Coleman," the first poem of her 1993 collection, *The Devil's Tower*:

> When I finally caught a Greyhound north,
> I wanted only to escape
>
> the brutal limits of that town,
> its square chained yards, [oil] pumps
> that bowed so mindlessly to earth,
> the raging pistons of that falling
> dynasty. (1–2)

Bin Ramke and Mary Karr share a number of similar themes and attitudes which may or may not have grown out of a desire to escape the mindlessness and prejudice of Southeast Texas. Both poets were apparently educated in Catholic schools, and much of their writing is in the so-called confessional mode. In "Nuns in Sunshine" from Ramke's 1981 collection, *White Monkeys,* the poet recalls Sister Francesca in her

> full habitual splendor
> striding through classrooms
> winged and wafting the sharp-
> edged smell of starch,
> black and white as the answers
> in the Baltimore Catechism. (77)

In "Hard Knocks" from Karr's 1987 collection, *Abacus,* this poet remembers Sister Angelica, who

> banged
> her ruler, and we printed the same confession
> a hundred times, her shadow crossing
> our spiral notebooks,
> her eyes like old
> spiders. (11)

In "Nuns in Sunshine," Ramke also observes that

> It is hard to remember surviving
> childhood in Texas, the heat: it's hell
> they said gleefully, on women and horses.
> But think of the nuns! (79)

Karr's black friend Coleman—with whom she "straddled the [oil] pump as it bucked / a slow-motion rodeo" and watched "dawn breaking / in chemical-pink sky, refinery towers looming / like giants from a fairy tale"—"made the papers as a hunting accident" but was clearly the victim of "vigilantes" who had spotted him playing chess with a white girl (1–2). Despite the critical tone in most of these poems on their Texas experience, both Ramke and Karr yet return in memory to their native state, as in Karr's "Diogenes Tries to Forget," where she wants "a slice of pecan pie, some life / sweeter than this, like my childhood in Texas" (11). In "The Legion" Karr even acknowledges of her father's comrades, "[t]hat they should never leave / the Lone Star State had been / the fondest wish of each" (*The Devil's Tower* 29). Nevertheless, for those like Karr, who was "preoccupied with books," and Ramke, who "would not eat for days / because I liked / the strange dark feeling," Texas was essentially a place to quit for "other possibilities" (*The Difference Between Night and Day* 16).

Bin Ramke and Mary Karr left what is known as the Golden Triangle area of Beaumont, Orange, and Port Arthur in order to achieve considerable success as poets—Karr even publishing a best-selling memoir, *The Liar's Club*. On the other hand, after earning his doctorate at the University of Iowa, serving in Vietnam, and teaching at the Air Force Academy, Walter McDonald of Lubbock returned to his hometown to stake out his claim as the most prolific and profound poet in Texas history. His first book, *Caliban in Blue,* was almost entirely devoted to his war experiences, but one poem in that collection, "On Planting My First Tree Since Vietnam," forecast what would come to be a ceaseless outpouring of poems focusing on McDonald's native landscape, its flora and fauna (or lack thereof), its hardscrabble existence, and its people, like the singer of a country-western song who vocalizes in the title poem of McDonald's *Where Skies Are Not Cloudy* "as if these plains are all she needs" (52). Even though West Texans may need more than the plains provide, just as Ramke and Karr required more than Southeast Texas seemed to offer, the impression created by the sixteen collections of poems published by McDonald since *Caliban in Blue* is that his Llano Estacado (Staked Plains) area of West Texas has proved more than sufficient to inspire a wide-ranging and penetrating poetry of the highest artistry and insight.

McDonald's fourteenth collection, *Where Skies Are Not Cloudy,* contains what is but one of many key poems among the more than 1,900 he has published in an amazing variety of magazines both here and abroad. Entitled "The Barn on the Brazos," this piece recalls another prophetic poem in *Caliban in Blue,* "The Hammer," an earlier instance of the same retrospective power found in his later lines on a grandfather who

> pounded on mustangs,
> filing their hooves, fitting the cooled shoes
> and sinking the beveled nails, his hammer swung
> by a bicep hugely bulging. When I touched that arm
>
> my fingers couldn't reach. I rose on his arm
> toward heaven. (68)

The poem concludes with two stanzas that return to the theme of a missing past, or of not paying attention to what is always around us until it is too late:

> My knees and old boots creak as I bend
> to pick up nails. My wife doesn't laugh

at my cocked ear, tuned for the clang of steel,
the puff and sizzle of an iron shoe doused,
something to last until a work horse threw it,

lost forever in weeds, unless some boy
with a cane pole on his shoulder found
and cleaned the shoe with his hand, spat on it
for luck and tossed it over his head
behind him, not looking back. (69)

In the second stanza of this poem, McDonald, after finding that the grandfather's barn has been rifled, that "[e]ven the anvil's gone," remarks that he does not "blame anonymous neighbors for plunder / I've ignored" (68). To survey this poet's career, one would have to say that in fact McDonald has not at all ignored the valuables of his Texas life, that indeed he has mined them for all they're worth, and that following from his first collection where he planted his first tree after Vietnam ("scraping memory down through crust" 26), the poet has come, in such poems as "Setting Out Oaks in Winter" from *Rafting the Brazos*, to thrive in a place where "no trees stay green all summer . . . / heat-stressed, blighted, / full of drought," to learn and to teach the appreciation of where one is and what little one may have, to "swing [trees] overboard like treasure" and to soak them "over and over with water / pumped from our own deep wells" (120).

Unlike Ramke, Karr, and many other Texas writers, McDonald has not settled—at least not entirely—for the traditional view of Texas as hell or a fallen dynasty but has risen toward heaven on the arms of its people in whom he has discovered simple faith and strength of character. This West Texas poet also has forged a poetry of high seriousness from seemingly the most unlikely subjects. Taking the standard western movie scene of a lynching for stealing horses or rustling cattle, McDonald, in "Someday"—from his fifteenth book, *Counting Survivors*—sees a particular tree with "grooves in the bark like rope burns" and imagines "a thousand thieves / swinging the same ballet" and hears "the twist of ropes under tension" (75). Along with the notable diction of "ballet" and "tension," his alliterative sounds recreate the drama of such a Hollywood scene but go far beyond it in letting the reader mentally see and feel the full ironic and cruel effect of this dance of death. (Mary Karr's "The Lynched Man" also contains some fine moments, as when she writes, "He twirled like a tire swing / in the breeze that stirred the sugar cane" (*Abacus* 11). More moralistic, perhaps, is McDonald's "The Tap of Angry Reins," also from his 1995 collection, for here the poet refers to quarrels between friends which he likens to the bones of dinosaurs, to tongue-lashings that only bleach the tongue "like cow bones," and to little words that turn men into bulls gorging "all night in the mind's silo." The poem concludes with a call to "[b]ury the dead / and let good fences save us, if they can," an allusion perhaps to Robert Frost (39). More especially, McDonald's poems on his Texas experience summon up a passage in Book XI of John Milton's *Paradise Lost*, where the angel Michael reports that, after the post-lapsarian world has gone to "universal rack" and God brings on the Flood which only Noah's ark will survive,

> then shall this Mount
> Of Paradise by might of Waves be moved
> Out of his place, pushed by the horned flood,
> With all his verdure spoil'd, and Trees adrift
> Down the great River to the op'ning Gulf,
> And there take root an Island salt and bare,
> The haunt of Seales and Orcs, and Sea-mews clang.
> To teach thee that God attributes to place
> No sanctity, if none be thither brought
> By Men who there frequent, or therein dwell. (*PL* 11.829–38)

Since 1978 when McDonald published *One Thing Leads to Another*, he has continued to concern himself with his origins, how he came to be in West Texas and what it means to those who live there. In "Settling the Plains" from this second collection, he gives an account of a family arriving in a covered wagon, breaking down perhaps, wondering "What have we done" to come "ignoring all reports." Then, after the mother hugs her arms, the father shrugs and shakes his head, saying "hell . . . help me hitch up the plow" (26). Another poem entitled "Settling the Plains" appears in McDonald's *All That Matters*, and here the poet delineates the faith of those who "worked and sang" "[f]or here and for the afterlife," believing "whatever they put in the dirt / would live, if it was God's will / and the wind blew" (61). The very fact that McDonald has revisited many of the same themes (such as settling the plains) without depleting their possibilities for aesthetic expression and human insight is testimony to the inexhaustible fund of his region as a source for artistic inspiration. With his 1993 collection, the poet once again plumbs the depths of meaning in the lives of those who came to Lubbock's treeless prairies. In "Steeples and Deep Wells" from *Where Skies Are Not Cloudy*, the poet observes that on the Llano Estacado there are "no stones to hide behind," going on to comment that

> If any came blameless,
> here their faults were plain.
> No wonder they shoveled dug-outs first,
> somewhere to sleep out of sight.

His interpretation of the realities of a West Texas existence leads him to assert that "[n]o sense of guilt: that must be / what they sought," and for this they risked being

> stranded like crippled buffalo
> a thousand miles from Kentucky loam
> and lakes, pleasures of the flesh
> where sin came easy.

As part of his imaginative versions of the lives of his Texas forebears, McDonald offers a sense of their sacrifices, their hopes, their frustrations, but always he reveals how they faced the truth of their circumstances—"one crop away from being meat for buzzards"—and yet how they would neither leave nor renounce "a land so flat they dug deep wells / and raised plank steeples fast, / as lightning rods" (7).

Even though McDonald has clearly accepted the place he inherited from his ancestors, he has in no way denied that he is drawn to other landscapes and climates. In "After Years in the Mountains" from *Burning the Fence,* the poet remembers how

> In Colorado we had four seasons,
> real snow, always other rocks to see. . . .
>
> Always we found
> another trail or others like us
> packing in, climbing for Eden. (10)

In a piece from *Manoa* (fall 1990) entitled "After a Week in the Rockies," which it seems has not been collected in any of McDonald's published volumes (although he frequently changes the titles of his poems after they have first appeared in magazine form), the poet contrasts "a drizzle trickling gallons overnight" and "the odor of green pines" with "[h]ours of flat miles . . . the same dry sage and cactus," and wonders

> are we here by choice? Were our squatter fathers
> banished from regions where it rained?
> Our children have moved away, seeking their fortunes
>
> in cities. We'd do it a different way,
> if we made prairies. Rain like children would visit
> more often, buzzards like domestic dogs would lead us
> to calves before they starve, the summer sun
>
> would squint, not a hot, hypnotic stare
> enough to drop a bull. If we stand in one unshaded place
> too long, our boot soles burn. Lift up your
> faithful head and look around: it's home. (11)

This very fine variation on the typical infernal view of Texas—close in its depiction of burning boot soles to Milton's description in Book I of *Paradise Lost* of Satan's "painful steps o're the burnt soyle" of Hell—reveals McDonald's wish to recreate his fated place more in the image of a Golden Age or utopia. Yet in the end he sees it for what it is: a merciless habitation that can yet reward the faithful. And certainly this and countless other poems by McDonald have justified his belief and trust in his staked plains. Perhaps in a way this poet has adopted Satan's point of view that it is "[b]etter to reign in Hell, than serve in Heaven" (*PL* 1.562), at least to the extent that if Heaven only means mountains with plentiful rainfall and lush vegetation, Hell in some ways may inspire more imaginative, more thought-provoking poetry. Yet another example of McDonald's contrast between Texas and the appeal of adjacent areas like New Mexico and Colorado is his poem entitled "Colonel Mackenzie Maps the Llano Estacado," which seems to be another uncollected work, one only appearing in *The Texas Review* (spring/summer 1989). This piece presents once again the hell motif in a fine combining of historical and poetic dimensions. In addition, the poem creates with a sense of humor the desire for escape, incorporates an allusion to the nomadic Plains Indian who never settled in any one place, and builds through internal sounds and dramatic line breaks a formal design that carries with it the majestic McDonald ring and rightness of style and meaning:

> Chain by chain they dragged these plains, ten rods,
> ten rods, sometimes forgetting to count,
> not really caring how wide hell is,
> prairie flatter than desert good for nothing
> but native cunning enough not to settle.
>
> Soldiers rode for nothing but pay,
> knowing hell like enlistments can't last
> forever, ten rods, ten rods nearer the bars
> in Santa Fe, women and mountains,
> something to look at that wasn't flat. (55)

With his 1995 collection, *Counting Survivors*, the poet once more considers how and why he and his people ended up on the prairie. In "Rocking for Days in the Shade," McDonald asks,

>   are we here by choice?
> Great-grandfather left the cavalry
> for this? After renegade bullets and arrows
>
> he stayed in Texas where topsoil was sand
> and free. He said he needed sun to heal . . .

enough water to bathe in,
far enough from others
to build a shack with a back porch

and do whatever he wanted, rocking for days
in the shade, watching buzzards thirsty
for his blood, daring anything
to make him leave. (70–1)

In a poem from *One Thing Leads to Another*, entitled "To Derek, Still in West Texas," McDonald agrees that on the plains "there's lit- tle / to see . . . [i]t bores me, / too." Nonetheless, he goes on to ob- serve that "[o]nly the people count. Someday you'll / know how much that means" (24). Indeed, the poet has filled his poems with a sad but unforgettable gallery of figures: Uncle Edward who sur- vived World War I, a wife who left him, a son who went to prison, and his own gangrened diabetic legs; "Billy Bastard" who was given to cruelty to helpless creatures, slicing up a centipede till "all that lived were stumps" (4); and the owner of a corner grocery store who "marked each item up / however much he thought / would sell," cursing those around him for his disabilities suffered on the Bataan death march—all from *Burning the Fence* (18). Many of these same types of characters also appear in the poems of Charles Behlen, a na- tive of Slaton, a town near Lubbock which McDonald often men- tions, as in his sinister but amusing "The Girl in the Mackinaw and Panties" from *Anything Anything*. In the best Faulknerian tradition, both Behlen and McDonald describe vividly those who have man- aged to endure.

Not unexpectedly, then, McDonald entitled his 1995 collection *Counting Survivors*. In the title poem of this volume, he exclaims, de- spite the long list of names on the Vietnam wall touched by the poet's own fingers, "I'm stunned to see so many of us home" (34). In collection after collection, McDonald has recalled the survivors among his neighbors and kinsmen (all or many of the latter appar- ently invented), as in "Uncle Philip and the Endless Names," from this same volume, where the poet pays tribute to the man who "hated work, walked off a dozen jobs / before thirty," and won the war against the Kaiser

over and over, his doubled fists like tanks

the pension he never got
stuck in his craw, his quarrel with the war
all that saved him from steady work. (35)

From this figure, as from so many others in his various books, the poet has learned a form of survival, a type of trust and belief. And through his empathy with the numerous animals that populate his poems, McDonald unceasingly creates such exquisite lines as the ones about Uncle Earl's Saint Bernard, found in the poem entitled "Coyotes and Dogs," also from the 1995 collection:

> Cowboys taught him
> to howl sad tunes with the jukebox. Girls tossed him
> quarters, the only dog on the dance floor,
> waddling past couples locked in each other's arms.
> Lapping draft beer, he lay down by blondes
>
> and cowboys who tugged off leather gloves
> and let him lick stiff knuckles busted in rodeos.
> Fists that shot wild dogs and coyotes
> burrowed into folds of fur and made
> his massive paw keep time, thumping the floor.
>
> I remember how he howled and tugged outside
> after the sheriff left, the moon no jukebox,
> a dozen pickups but not one fist to pet him,
> sniffing packs of coyotes miles away,
> dragging the stiff chain tight. (55)

A related piece is entitled "The Last Saloon in Lubbock," from McDonald's 1999 collection, *Whatever the Wind Delivers: Celebrating West Texas and the Near Southwest* (with photographs selected by Janet M. Neugebauer). Here the poet envisions the life that went on inside the walls of a building which, as he passes by, he sees being torn down by a wrecking crew. Mainly he imagines what cowboys, "bulky in coats," who came to the saloon after breaking their backs herding cattle, needed in such a tavern, concluding that they went there "to get away / from skies more lonely than [themselves]." The poem focuses on "rouged women," "the swing of their crystal earrings," "girls in spotlights moaning the songs / I longed for." In the end, this bit of nostalgia achieves a kind of permanence for those who came before, "ghosts with throaty tunes / and the flash of starry earrings" (76). The poet too has needed what he calls here and elsewhere "the old songs," and he brings them back along with the vibrant imagery of a past that has given way to a "call for order on the plains." McDonald is concerned not to lose entirely that early life that shaped his own, but to capture its poetry that he glimpses in simple objects like a set of "starry earrings." This is true as well of "At the Stone Café," where the poet portrays a typical short-order waitress, "rouged, perfumed," and exposing "a flared / white cleavage" as she "waltzes off, // humming some country and western tune / that makes her human" (132). It is McDonald too who "makes her human," bringing to life such people of his region by revealing them vividly through characteristic touches, like the one in this poem where a cowboy "rises and whispers in her ear. She winks / / and flips his hat, leans back and sips her coffee" (32). As is so often the case with McDonald's work, the poet has rendered a rich complex of imagery and human interrelationships, uncovering them in an everyday Southwestern scene. At the same time, the writing is subtly poetic, the internal sounds (flips-sips, hat-back) adding wonderfully to the overall impact of this typical Southwestern vignette.

In addition to poems with a cast of colorful and moving West Texas figures and of the many farm and ranch animals of his region, as well as every imaginable creature from snakes and prairie dogs to deer, fish, hawks, buzzards, cicadas, and scorpions, McDonald has also written an impressive array of poignant pieces on flying, the airmen who died or disappeared in war, and those survivors who, like "The Food Pickers of Saigon" from *After the Noise of Saigon* and "The Children of Saigon" from *Night Landings,* scavenged at an airbase by climbing smoldering heaps of bulldozed food and discarded goods (another kind of unignored plunder): "the dump was like a coal mine fire burning / out of control, or Moses' holy bush / which was not consumed" (*After the Noise of Saigon* 5). But this Texas poet has never been limited to his own region or to his experiences as a wartime pilot. Even when he has written poems on the same subject, even giving them the same title, as in the case of "War in the Persian Gulf" in both *Where Skies Are Not Cloudy* and *Counting Survivors,* McDonald has resorted to little or no repetition, for each piece presents a new and engaging perspective.

Like Bin Ramke and Mary Karr, McDonald has also been a close observer of the world of human art. While his fellow Texans have written a number of poems that allude to classical music, McDonald has devoted lines to painters like Rembrandt and Picasso. In "Rembrandt and the Art of Mercy" from *Counting Survivors,* McDonald probes beneath the Dutch master's work to discover, contrary to the claim that the artist painted for money or for a lusting after painting itself, that it was flesh that Rembrandt "loved and pitied most," "flesh / / that's caught but never saved by canvas" (44). While this piece shares a biblical scene employed by Wallace Stevens in his "Peter Quince at the Clavier," it exhibits the Texas poet's own very distinctive style—direct, sure-handed, and full of sensual details that all contribute to the poem's clear and striking effect:

> Consider
> his florid elders astounded by Susanna bathing,
> his naked Danaë with her god of gold. Behold

the fragile, eggshell flesh of sad Bathsheba,
her toes and thighs scrubbed slowly

for a king. If only he could capture those
in ocher, rub her troubled eyes so they could see.
Notice the gold, pig-bristle swirls that touched
his dying Saskia's neck, her honey lobes,
the sweaty radiance of her breasts. (44)

This same theme had already been developed in McDonald's "Picasso and the Art of Angels" from *Where Skies Are Not Cloudy*, but
once again the poet does not in the later piece simply repeat himself.
In the earlier poem, Picasso is shown having felt the frustration of
not being able to paint what he envisioned the day he died: an angel

marvelously complex,

the skin tones perfect,
her flesh angelically erotic,
nothing at all like humans,
the skewed, cubistic angles
of the actual.

In the end, McDonald suggests that what the artist saw was "his
morning nurse, a local woman / working for pay" (36). This is a dra-
matically different point from the one made in the poet's poem on
Rembrandt and demonstrates once more the far-reaching, imaginative range of McDonald's writing.

Above all, this brief survey of the poetry of Walt McDonald pro-
poses that here is a writer who has in no way been hampered or con-
fined by the place in which he lives and from which he has drawn his
unfailing creative impulse. Although he more frequently reproduces
the insides of dance halls and the country-western tunes that whine
and twang their predictable sorrows, he also has given evidence in
poems like those on Rembrandt and Picasso that a Texas poet need
not be restricted to popular culture but can interpret as well the
work of the world's greatest artists whose themes were themselves
often drawn from literature. Time and again, McDonald has mani-
fested his ability to penetrate to the meaningful core of whatever ob-
ject or idea he happens to take for his subject. Most commonly he has
come to his wise and empathetic insights while contemplating his
immediate surroundings, as in a representative piece of West Texas
poetry entitled, delightfully, "Rig-Sitting" from *All That Matters*:
"On the derrick, I twist this wrench tight / as if the oil pipes of the
world depended / on it." Could this be McDonald's wry plains reply
to William Carlos Williams's "The Red Wheelbarrow"? Somehow,
like that New Jersey poet, the native of Lubbock determined early on

that his own writing should work with the tools he found lying about him, and like his familiar cactus, which "grows a quarter of an inch / each decade," to devote himself to the slow but conscious development of the local, elevating it to the universal. The remarkable result has been that, as McDonald says in "Rig-Sitting" and "Wildcatting" (echoing "The Snow Man" by Stevens), the "drill bit"(41) of his Texas poetry has managed with persistence to bite "miles through bedrock" in order to discover that "[n]othing is there until we find it" (40).

An Uneasy Truce: Wildness and Domesticity in the Poems of Walt McDonald

April Lindner

A regional poet to the core, Walt McDonald has recreated the plains of West Texas in vivid and thorough detail. The current Texas poet laureate and the recipient of four Western Heritage Awards from the Cowboy Hall of Fame, McDonald is primarily an academic, yet he writes of the ranching life with an authority few contemporary poets can muster. As Pattiann Rogers has written for the dust jacket of *Whatever the Wind Delivers*, "Walt McDonald knows the land of West Texas and the near southwest from the bone out. He breathes it. He lives within it. He is made of it. And he has produced a poetry that perfectly resonates with the sound and motion, the cadences and cares of the land, the life and the people that are his subjects." Rich with practical detail about raising livestock and trapping rattlesnakes, his poems derive much of their energy from the tension between the wild and the domestic. They explore the places where wilderness and domesticity coexist in an uneasy balance.

This tension plays itself out most vividly in his poems about animals. At one end of the spectrum we find "Stalls in All Weather" (*Counting Survivors*), which details the absolute dependence and passivity of cows:

> Deep inside silos,
> layers of spoilage ripen
> vinegar-sweet, stubble of sticky maize

fermenting wine for cows. They love
the bitter stalks, the half-digested
casserole of sap and fiber.

They loll those foot-long toothpicks
in their lips, grind them with grain
and swallow. Cows stare at snow fields
white as cream. If they remember calves,
the shudder of bulls at breeding,
they find relief in hunger.

They lower their heads like gourds
and scoop dark silage like manna,
full udders bulging,
grasped in the predawn cold,
the clang of gates and the tug of suction
all they need for now. (73)

Phrases like "dark silage like manna" and "they loll those foot-long toothpicks / in their lips" are gently comical. Simple and forgetful, with "heads like gourds," these cows are pacified by the ritual of daily life. The inability to focus on anything but their most immediate needs protects the cows from memories of trauma imposed by the humans who dictate when the cows will mate and when they will be parted from their calves. Absolutely dependent, these creatures are almost pathetic; like the pet goats in another McDonald poem, "The Goats of Summer," they are "easy to despise" (*The Digs in Escondido Canyon* 4). McDonald looks beyond the potential for humor in dumb livestock, however; "Stalls in All Weather" reveals the poet's fascination with the practical details of milking and feeding the cows and with the imaginative act of trying to peer into the unknowable mind of the domesticated beast. In doing so, the poet envisions domesticity as both a burden and a comfort.

We see a similar blend of comedy and near-pathos in "Old Pets" narrated by a father stuck with the abandoned pets of his grown children. The reader is told that "[o]ld bulls aren't worth the hay to save them, / but I don't throw away a glove because it's ugly," a statement both playful and rueful. Like the bulls, the father has been outgrown, and, in a sense, thrown away. Later, the speaker describes how he came to own the barn in which he stands: "A man with children built this barn / to last, but not one stayed to carry on his herd." Like the barn's original owner, the speaker has been left with no one to "carry on his herd." The poem's last line finds the speaker "dumping hay to old pets bawling at the barn" (*Blessings the Body Gave* 60). The word "bawling" in itself conveys both humor and pathos. Though not "bawling," the speaker, like the pets, is complaining. Pitiable for their dependence on humans, the domesticated beasts

resemble the father whose sense of self is dependent upon his relationship to his children. As in "Stalls in All Weather," a close attention to the process of farming shifts the poem's emphasis away from
emotion. The poem hints at the speaker's pain but is more interested
in the particulars of rural life.

While "Stalls in All Weather" and "Old Pets" concern themselves
with domesticated animals, the duty-bound speaker of these poems
is clearly identified with the beasts he tends. Here and elsewhere in
McDonald's oeuvre, the reader finds that domesticity is safe and
comfortable, but stifling for humans as well as for animals. A related
poem, "When the Children Have Gone" (*Counting Survivors*), describes a couple of empty-nesters whose land is repeatedly trampled
by herds of elk. The speaker and his wife watch helplessly as the
wild creatures pass through their property, leaving disorder behind.
Stand-ins for the couples' departed adult children, the elk eat their
fill and eventually leave. Despite its undercurrent of discontent, the
poem's tone is reverent toward the inconsiderate guests and toward the couple's grown children:

> We wouldn't want them pitiful
> and tame. We clean up gladly after elk each year,
> knowing they'll leave, never nod their racks as if thankful,
> slow and clumsy in our garden, graceful on the hills. (87)

The homebound parents must grudgingly admire the strength and
independence of their footloose progeny.

A similar dynamic exists in "A Cabin, Even a Cave" (*Blessings the
Body Gave*). Here, again, a long-married couple is decidedly rooted
in domesticity. Plains dwellers, this couple longs for a life in the
mountains, a landscape they idealize. The speaker's partner longs simultaneously for peace and excitement; she wants both "a meadow
without wild beasts" and eagles "wheeling in the sky," which would
"hook and tumble love-locked, / a mile-long whirl of white,
bald-headed sparks." Wild creatures provide both danger and vicar-
ious excitement. Addressing his spouse, the speaker claims, "you
want [the eagles] loving every dangerous second / and saved." The
spectacle would be thrilling precisely because it could end in disaster. Ultimately, however, the wife wants the eagles to be safe. It's significant that the wife's longings are for something quite
specific—wild creatures mating—because procreation and parenthood are the poem's real subject. Though the couple ostensibly longs
for a particular landscape, their sense of something missing stems
not from living on the plains but from living without the children
they have raised into adulthood. The mating of the eagles embodies
the excitement of procreation, an emotion the wife/mother has put

behind her. By poem's end, this wish for eagles becomes a longing for the couple's adult children who are transformed imagistically into eagles:

> We raised three babies on the plains, let go
> and watched them walk, then fly away. They call
> sometimes, like yodelers in mountains, seeing farther
> than we can see and waving, turning, and going on. (43)

Again, wildness is equated with independence, and again we see a tension between the wild and the domestic. The speaker must reconcile his pride in his children's independence with his longing to keep them safe at home.

Like the wife who longs for safety and danger at once, the speaker of "Riding Herd" (*Counting Survivors*) finds his own nature divided:

> Barbed wires on rusted nails can't hold
> lone bulls at home when they smell pasture.
> They thrust their bone skulls under barbs,
> tongues quivering for a taste of strange
>
> and shove until the post gives way. Days later,
> we find wires sagging, reset the post,
> and tighten bent wires like a fiddle
> and rope the worn-out bull,
>
> wishing there was only a fence
> between us and our hearts' desire.
> But something with spurs and a rope
> would find us, cursing and yelling on horseback,
>
> cutting us off from escape down arroyos,
> dragging us frothing and wild-eyed
> back to the sun-bleached yellow range,
> the same whirlpool of buzzards. (28)

Spoken in the plural first person, this poem at first seems to want the reader to believe that the poem's "we" consists of a speaker and a coworker or companion. By the poem's end, however, the "we" is clearly rhetorical; the tendency to long for greener pastures—for "a taste of strange"—is human nature as well as animal instinct. At the poem's start, its speaker identifies with the ranchers who restore order. By the poem's end, his sympathies are with the bull, a wild creature forced to live as a domesticated one. Both readings coexist in this poem; "we" are both the rancher and the bull. The "something with spurs and a rope" that invariably beats down our dreams is, by implication, within each of us, and not simply an external force. The wild, bullish self and the self that seeks to domesticate all wildness struggle for dominance within the speaker's psyche.

The human urge toward wildness is explored throughout Mc-Donald's work. In "Under Blue Skies" from *Counting Survivors*, the poet once again imagines himself into the viewpoint of wild animals, this time a calf and a rabbit that accept their deaths as a matter of course. In lines like "Whatever it was, it's over, / no more desire or fear forever," we hear an envy primarily of death itself, but secondarily of wildness. This secondary reading grows clearer at the poem's end, when the rabbit's death is depicted as "the safest death, simply to lie down / under blue skies and sleep, accepting / this as the way, not dreading anything" (65). Though acceptance of death's inevitability is possible for humans, it is perhaps less likely for us. Unburdened by questions like "why," and by the possibility of an afterlife, the animals in this poem know how to die with the proper resignation. Moreover, they get to do so under the blue sky instead of in a hospital bed.

At the other end of the spectrum from the passive cows of "Stalls in All Weather," we find the fierce and untameable bird in "Releasing the Hawk in August":

> Say something sober to a hawk
> and he'll rise flapping, curved talons
> ready to tear your heart out.
> He had that stare
> the scalding day we found him
>
> by a cactus, wing drooped,
> bruised by a hunter.
> After weeks of feeding him
> giblets and mice he snatched
> with curved beak and ripped,
>
> we knew we'd never be friends
> up close, too much alike,
> his wound the temporary warp
> of nature, the shape of genes,
> his way of saying save me. (*Where Skies Are Not Cloudy* 60)

The poem takes a surprising turn in its third stanza, when the speaker claims that the unbridgeable gap between man and bird is a result not of their differences but of their similarities. The words "up close" are key; from a respectful difference the hawk and the speaker might well coexist in peace. In close contact, however, man and beast must be mutually wary. Humans living close to the natural world cannot expect peace; they must content themselves at best with *rapprochement* and at worst with out-and-out warfare.

In the world of McDonald's poems, humans struggle to keep order in a natural world that tends to thwart that order. In "Mending the Fence," a Westerner's reply to Robert Frost's "Mending Wall," a speaker repairs the barbed wire fence meant to keep his cows in. We're told that "something shoves posts down / and makes good neighbors strangers." In a landscape where wilderness constantly threatens to encroach on domesticity, good fences really do make good neighbors. Here, however, the "something . . . that doesn't love a wall" isn't frost. Instead, it is any number of forces that would undo the order imposed by humans: whirlwinds, panicked cows, packs of feral dogs, and even "hunters mad at the moon / shooting at shadows"—in other words, human beings reverting to an animalistic state. Land that is cleared and fenced off may at any moment be reclaimed by the forces of entropy. The same principle is at work in animals as well, most notably in the feral dogs the poem describes as "stray pets becoming wolves." The struggle to maintain order in a landscape ruled by entropy even leads to wariness between humans:

> I wave to anyone on horseback
> or walking across my pasture
> under a sky of buzzards. If he's alone,
> if I haven't heard a shot for hours,
> I let him go, hoping I'll find
> no fence posts broken,
> no cow gut-shot and bleeding,
> her wild eyes staring at heaven. (10)

Any passing stranger is suspect; vigilance is key. The rancher must guard against the encroaching wilderness, a threat which takes both human and natural forms.

Uneasiness between humans and nature is evident in the ironically titled "Harvest" (*Counting Survivors*), in which helpless, abandoned pets stand in marked contrast to the feral dogs in "Mending the Fence." Domesticated and then rejected by humans, these dogs have small chance of surviving in the wild:

> No dogcatchers ride by, only cars
> with pets like rejected hearts. Our stock tank
> rescues dogs abandoned by cars with city tags.
>
> Dogs starve if they aren't born hungry for blood,
> part wolf, or cute as Disney dogs some farmer's daughter
> begs him to adopt. Stray cats survive on mice and birds,
>
> prowling somebody's barn. Stiff winds spread fires
> to fields where pheasants risk the rattlers.
> The sun leads cows to pasture, time for windmills

to spin their rapture, turning grass to milk.
Sometimes I squeeze a squirt to a row of cats
waiting with mouths wide with fangs. The farm

is harvest all year long. At night, rattlers
that survive the fires move rippling over rows,
and silent barn owls dive to pluck their staring eyes. (5)

Most of the "harvesting" in this poem is a matter of stronger animals
preying on weaker ones. But the strangest harvest of all is being
done by humans reaping a generous supply of something they don't
really want: someone else's cast-off pets. Though nature is depicted
here as red in tooth and claw, it is nonetheless more indifferent than
hostile. The city folk who drive to the country to drop off their house
pets are another story. Like the moon-mad hunters in "Mending the
Fence," these humans knowingly wreak havoc with the precarious
and hard-won balance between rancher and nature.

Maintaining this balance, holding ground against the forces that
undo domestication, is a daily battle for the protagonists of McDonald's poems. The poet himself fights a slightly different battle: the
struggle against the all-too-human desire to see symbolism where it
isn't. Nature's indifference, its very lack of meaning, is a hard sell;
most poets and readers of poetry hunger for meaning. Nevertheless,
McDonald exhorts his reader to resist the urge to personalize nature
or to see it as emblematic of anything but itself. In "The Signs of Prairie Rattlers," he quickly undercuts the title's portent: "Out here / the
eyes don't believe in signs." Rattlesnakes are rattlesnakes, nothing
more nor less. The poem satirizes the poetic tendency to find symbolic significance in wild animals by describing preachers who, in
their zealotry, resemble snakes.

Watch signs,
they warned with spitting tongues—coyotes
trying to mate with your dogs at noon,
a mirage that shimmers at dawn, lost owls
without a barn in daylight.

According to the preachers, these natural phenomena foretell "a
thousand years of peace," (33) a superstition that must seem ridicu-
lous to those who encounter owls and coyotes on a regular basis. A
related poem, "The Meaning of Flat Fields," makes a similar point,
denying the symbolic weight of landscape itself:

Landscape never tells us how to live
in the world. It never moves,

is moved, shifted in sandstorms,
silted by floods, thrust up as mountains

and cliffs millions of years ago.
Nothing that cold teaches us how to cope
with blood. We tell a landscape
what we hope it means, invent rich sounds

wise as well as ancient and give those
mournful names to landscapes—ocean,
horizon, stone. Nothing
that long ago knew what to do

but kill and flee from being eaten.
We've hurled the fear in ourselves
to the moon, our longing for peace
into sunsets. Hawks are no wiser

for watching the world from above,
no safer than rabbits balled up
in burrows, crouched with wide eyes,
not knowing when to run. (54)

Landscape—mountains, cliffs, and even the moon—serves as the blank screen onto which we project our hope and anxieties. We look to landscape for reassurance of peace, but any promise of safety we think we find there is false.

The urge to poeticize the landscape, to find meaning in it, is in a sense the urge to domesticate nature, to believe we can fully know it and therefore control it. Essentially, writing poetry about nature is an effort to make meaning from meaninglessness, to tame the wilderness. Of course, McDonald himself has been known to succumb to the human urge to assign meaning to animals and landscapes. As we've seen earlier, in poems like "Riding Herd" and "Old Pets," McDonald uses animals as emblems of human experience, thus giving in to the very urge he decries in "The Meaning of Flat Fields" and "The Signs of Prairie Rattlers." This tension—the poet's urge to turn nature to his own purposes pitted against the urge to accept nature on its own terms—is everywhere in the poems of Walt McDonald. Like the rancher who struggles to keep his fences in good repair despite the inevitable damage wreaked by weather and cattle, the poet himself struggles to make meaning in a universe he knows too well is essentially meaningless.

Walt McDonald, Poet of the Southwest

Nick Norwood

There can be no mistaking that Walt McDonald has already risen above the stature of the merely regional poet. Having published some eighteen books of poetry, won numerous national awards, and spawned a growing body of criticism about his work, including a recent special issue of the journal *Christianity and Literature* devoted to him, clearly McDonald has established a national reputation. The question is this: can we consider Walt McDonald a regionalist while still recognizing him as a major contemporary American poet?

The answer involves, among other things, the way we define "regionalist," and it involves our successfully identifying McDonald with a particular region. The first is an ongoing debate we would do best to avoid, but the latter seems to present less of a problem. McDonald is a native Southwesterner, and he turns to that region more often than any other in creating a setting for his work. Ironically, even the critical studies of McDonald's apologists include enough disclaimers about his regional status to indicate that it is a significant element of his reputation. In his essay for the *Christianity and Literature* issue, Darryl L. Tippens, for instance, acknowledges that McDonald "is sometimes called a war poet or a regionalist" and that since one must "write what one knows. . . . McDonald does this when he writes about Vietnam, Texas, and the Southwest" (191). Significantly, however, Tippens concludes that "[p]lace for McDonald is vehicle rather than tenor, and what he ultimately reveals through geography is timeless, universal, and spiritual" (191). Tippens's assertion is on the mark, I think, though he, like other McDonald supporters, undervalues the importance of region in McDonald's work and thus overlooks the important role it occupies in the inter-play between his geographical and military backgrounds. Though McDonald is no mere regionalist, he is a regional poet in the same way, I intend to show, that Frost was.

This may sound on the surface like another argument for or against regionalism (à la James Wright), but first of all it isn't, and second there is something special about the case of Walt McDonald, namely that he is a poet in the American Southwest and not the sexy, politically expedient Southwest of Tucson or Santa Fe, but Lubbock. This and the fact that he was recently elected Poet Laure-ate of Texas might lead some to more narrowly pigeonhole McDon-ald as a Texas poet, and there are still some people laughing at the notion that such a thing as Southwestern Literature actually exists, much less Texas Literature. I mean, it's really just cowboy books—right? Wrong, of course, but even those of us who have de-voted some region of our professional lives to the study of South-western Literature will have to admit that poetry has not been its strong suit—to put it mildly.[1] Though a number of the region's es-tablished prose writers have also published respectable po-etry—see, for instance, N. Scott Momaday's *In the Presence of the Sun*—and though some famous poets have spent a good deal of time in the Southwest and written verse about it—Witter Bynner is perhaps the best example —no great poet, no poet of unmistakable national or international prominence has been associated with the Southwest in the way that, say, Richard Hugo is associated with the Inter-mountain West.

The fact is that it's not too difficult to find major poets to identify with virtually every other region of the country *except* the South-west. New England is the benchmark in these matters, mostly be-cause of Frost, though we could also mention Edwin Arlington Robinson and others. Much has been written about Frost's regional-ism with most critics contending that he both *was* a regionalist poet and that he transcended the scope of the merely regional poet. The earliest reviews of his work—by Pound and Amy Lowell, for instance —identified him as a Yankee, or even Yankee-farmer, poet. Some have argued that Frost cannot be included among the highest rank of American poets precisely because of his regionalism, but those critics are in the minority.

In *Robert Frost and New England,* John C. Kemp distinguishes be-tween a sort of conventional or traditional regionalist and the kind of regionalist he considers Frost in his best work to be. The conven-tional regionalist, according to Kemp, is a spokesman for the region, a native, or "naturalized citizen," who offers an insider's view and whose work embodies the manners, customs, and especially the be-liefs or worldview of the region. He includes among this group most of the local-color writers of the late nineteenth century and says about them that they "settled for impressions that were all too monochromatic" and that their work is afflicted with "predictability and chauvinism" (103). Kemp specifically excludes Sarah Orne Jewett from this criticism, however, believing that, like Frost and Faulkner, she develops universal themes in her work and thus rises above her regionalist peers. In establishing a predecessor for Frost's second book, *North of Boston,* Kemp identifies Jewett's *The Country of the Pointed Firs* for the way it employs "observers who function as intermediaries between the reading audience and the rural world" (104).

It is among the group of regionalist writers Kemp associates with Frost, Faulkner, and Jewett that we should place Walt McDonald as a Southwestern poet: one who finds in his home region the materials he needs for developing universal themes, and one who has some claim to being an insider of the region but who is also enough of an outsider to view it objectively. Although the Southwest is the setting for many of McDonald's poems and though he often deals with the concerns of the region's inhabitants—drought, isolation, violent weather, animal husbandry, et cetera—he attempts in those poems not to express the Southwesterner's world view but to show how his own poetic worldview responds to the material the region offers. Again, the parallels with Frost's use of New England are unmistakable. Kemp asserts that, at his best, Frost controls "the tension between his sense of belonging to the region and his sense of being alien to it" and that he brings a "complex and heightened sensitivity to bear on the rural world." The poetry Frost thus produces "is not a platform for the regional spokesman and philosopher; rather it evokes an imagined world and a poet in that world." According to Kemp, Frost's successful New England poems represent "something altogether different from the regionalist's prosy lesson" (196).

In this same way, McDonald's Southwestern poetry offers more than regional perspective or artistic boosterism. His aim has never been to become Bard of the Southwest, and he acknowledges as much in a recent interview. "I've never thought of myself as a chronicler of a region or apologist for a way of life," McDonald says. "I'm open to the facts of my life and the regions I know, but I don't set out to record them or to argue for a creed" ("Evidence" 175). Rather than his using poetry as a way of representing the region, it is McDonald's successful and evocative use of the Southwest as the situation, the set of circumstances in which the poet finds himself, that allows us to call him a Southwestern poet. McDonald proves once again that a poet or fiction writer must employ a region's material to develop themes that go *beyond* its borders for the region to finally boast of producing a major writer. To use another writer and region as an example, no one has done more to establish the importance of

Southern literature than William Faulkner, and serving simply as a "chronicler" and "apologist" for the Southern way of life certainly would not have won him the Nobel Prize. McDonald's relationship with the Southwest proves beneficial to him and to the region's literature, even though it was never his conscious aim to promote that literature or to establish his reputation on the basis of a regional identity.

As a serious artist, McDonald seeks in the world around him those facets of life that may serve to better illuminate the whole of it. In her essay on "Forms of Incarnation," Helen F. Maxson argues that "McDonald finds in his native land metaphorical equivalents of human nature, experience, and culture" (227). Maxson is speaking of McDonald as an American, but her statement is equally true of McDonald as the poet whose "native land" is that part of America we call the Southwest. In its particulars he finds the objective correlatives to express his views on the human condition. The landscape of the Southwest itself provides both a source of stark images and a source of moral, aesthetic, and intellectual concerns for the poet to contemplate. The other regions McDonald knows are Vietnam and the mountains of Colorado, two places he often returns to in his poems. Generally speaking, the setting of his work moves among these two locales and West Texas. In that same interview mentioned above, McDonald hints, however, that West Texas is the geographical region for which he has the strongest affinity. He comments that upon the publication of his first book the poet Donald Justice asked him, "Where's Texas in your poems, Walt?" He says that Justice's question caused him to reconsider the possibility of finding the poetry of his own region, and he reports, "I began to feel the call of that wild, semi-arid West Texas that I knew better than I knew Iowa [where he received a Ph.D.] and Colorado, better than Vietnam" ("Evidence" 178). In the interview, McDonald also downplays the importance of region, saying that region is as much a state of mind as anything else, or conversely that a state of mind can itself constitute a region (177). These comments only further confirm that, as a poet, McDonald views the Southwest as the place where he happens to be.

The majority of McDonald's poems are set in West Texas, have Southwestern themes, or are in some way connected with the region, if only in atmosphere or nuance. Thus, he is more a Southwestern poet than a Vietnam poet or "war poet," as he has also been called. But certainly his experiences outside the Southwest are important to the poetic persona McDonald has created. We might say on the one hand that McDonald's Southwestern material is relieved by his poetry dealing with other regions and themes which are, if not exclusive of West Texas, at least not specific to it. And with regard to public perception, it may be that his Vietnam experiences, and the

subsequent poems that grew out of them, have kept McDonald from
appearing as merely a Texas or Southwestern poet. Ironically, then,
it is McDonald's experiences outside the region with which we have
come to identify him that make him a more reliable, interesting, and
insightful observer of it. His Vietnam experience and his military
and flight experience in general help him to see his home region with
perhaps a more objective, clearer perspective and thus also help to
establish his credibility. In McDonald the reader finds not a native
son making a case for the sanctity of his home turf, but rather a native of the region whose view of it has been tempered by worldly experience. Kemp shows that with Frost the opposite is true: the
identity that helped him finally establish his career as a poet was
based on his experience *in* the region with which he has come to be
identified, the eleven years he spent as a sort of pseudo- or part-time
farmer in Derry, New Hampshire. The myth of Frost the New England farmer helped establish his credibility as a unique poetic voice,
and the farmer-poet became a persona he exploited for the remainder of his career. "A contemporary orphic myth," Kemp asserts, "it
established a suitably bardic past and provided a sacred grove to
sanctify his singing" (41). As Kemp notes, however, it is when Frost
speaks as the outsider that he produces his best New England poems, especially those in the collection *North of Boston*. The difference
between those poems and the poems in the earlier collection *A Boy's
Will* is, according to Kemp, a matter of perspective. In the later volume, Frost positions his speaker as observer rather than "disguising
himself here, parading himself there" as an authentic New England
rustic (87). "This new perspective provided *North of Boston* with a
depth and vigor often missing in regional literature," Kemp asserts
(88).

For both poets, Frost and McDonald, the privileged status of being both insider and outsider benefits their poetry and helps them to
rise above mere regionalism. McDonald himself seems to agree that
his life outside of the Southwest helped produce in him a sense of being an outsider. He reports that before Justice had encouraged him
to look at Texas as a source of poetry, he had in a sense cut himself off
from the region. "For years," he says, "I had not considered this
world to be my home" ("Evidence" 178). A native of the region who
left it and later returned, McDonald knows Southwestern culture intimately, understands it, and can compare it to the culture of other
regions. In his overt Christianity and Protestantism, he shows that
he does in part at least share some of the region's mainstream beliefs,
just as the "real" Robert Frost probably contained a bit of the New
England rustic. But McDonald's outlook has been greatly expanded
by his experiences elsewhere—especially, it would seem, the life-
changing experiences of Vietnam.

A good example of a poem reflecting McDonald's position as both insider and outsider is "My Brother in Summer" from the early collection *Anything Anything*. In this piece, the speaker describes moments in the life of a West Texas cotton farmer, the "Brother" of the title. The sibling relationship between the speaker and the poem's title character establishes the speaker's insider status, but significantly the speaker describes his brother from an outsider's point of view. The speaker comes to us as an onlooker or observer contemplating the facts of another person's life, considering its problems and both its immediate and long-term concerns. The speaker seems to marvel at the persistence and ability to endure that his brother displays, and it is through this sensitive, penetrating reaction to that life that McDonald impresses on his readers the value of his perspective. Noting that his brother "wakes at five," the speaker relates how he "used to wonder, what is there to see / when even the sun rises after him." What the speaker's brother sees when the sun rises is "nothing but thousands of flat acres" and "each field / always the same as his" (12). In this way the poem evokes the monotony and anonymity of a farmer's life on the southern plains.

As with all of his poems set in the Southwest, in "My Brother in Summer" McDonald depicts vividly the sense of place in both its physical and cultural aspects by offering specific, concrete details:

> In the morning twilight
> he stoops and feels the dirt in nearest rows,
>
> sips his coffee and in the silence
> hears the cotton grow. . . . (12)

This level of description is necessary to make the poem real and convincing and to establish the nature of the speaker's perspective: he is a type of insider, a witness to his brother's experience. In also establishing his credibility as an outsider, the speaker convinces us that he is capable of becoming an objective and sensitive observer of that scene.

In addition to its privileged perspective and vivid imagery, what makes the poem exceptional is McDonald's ability to wring meaning from the situation and to imbue the farmer with a sense of dignity. It's a mark of McDonald's craftsmanship that he does this metaphorically through the plants the farmer grows for his livelihood: "a million / leaves at work, sighing oxygen / pushing itself toward its own white death" (12). But the poem's perspective alone may be the quality that provides the most power. The farmer of the poem remains real, which is to say he remains unselfconscious, not merely a farmer out of poetry but one bearing a resemblance to an actual farmer, a status it would have been more difficult to maintain had McDonald made him the speaker of the poem. The reader comes away with a good deal of respect, not only for the stoic farmer and his perceptive and sensitive brother, but also for the poet who created them.

Like Frost, McDonald has developed a persona whose presence is consistent throughout his work. Except for his occasional dramatic monologues in the voices of historical or biblical figures—"Goliath, Night Before Battle," for example—McDonald's poems all seem to come to us from the same speaker, one we associate, for better or worse, with McDonald himself. Reading the poems, we come to some conclusions about the poet-speaker's biography: that he grew up in the Southwest, later became a fighter pilot, served in Vietnam, and returned, eventually, to his native region. It's a voice we want to hear from, that demands a certain amount of respect, because it convinces us that the poet-speaker has lived an exceptional life and, more importantly, that he has perceived that life through the filter of a heightened sensibility.

A poem that well demonstrates the value of McDonald's mature perspective is the title piece from the book *The Flying Dutchman*. The speaker of the poem is a returned Vietnam veteran and former fighter pilot whose sense of isolation we feel from the opening lines when he reports that someone he "flew with / has gone to the moon and back" and that he, the speaker himself, hasn't "touched a rudder in ten years" (67). The speaker then explains matter-of-factly that his "only cockpit" now is "the family wagon," lines that effectively evoke the pathos of the situation: having escaped death, the speaker finds himself trapped in life. In this poem, McDonald helps us recognize the tragedy of each side of the dichotomy, one representing those who died in fiery crashes like the list of buddies whose deaths he briefly describes, the other representing those like the speaker himself who are forced to serve out the rest of their lives in a mundane world where the day's events too often do *not* involve questions of life and death. This is the primary source of tension in the poem, and for that reason we could rightly call it a "war poem" or even a "Vietnam poem." Curiously, however, this is also very much a West Texas poem, a point the speaker makes explicit in the last stanza where we see him "squirting a thin jet / to water Texas grass trying to survive / another drought" (68).

In this way McDonald incorporates the landscape of West Texas into the poem not just as concrete detail but also as a way of increasing the tension inherent in the situation. The words "survive" and "another drought" convey that landscape's harshness and sense of isolation, the demands it makes on its inhabitants by bringing the requirements of survival to the fore. The people there aren't likely to die of drought, but they will have to watch everything around them wither and die, and their own existence will often seem ugly (or perhaps, more accurately, lacking in beauty), stripped bare, laid open. The "cracked windshield" of the first stanza suddenly reflects a hot, glaring sunlight; we begin to see the landscape as desolate, forbidding, and pitiless. The poem becomes not only a statement about the situation of the returning Vietnam veteran but a characterization of the West Texas he returns to, a place where people's lives are consumed with work—survival—the jobs people find themselves driving to "at dawn." Its atmosphere is paradoxically sun-drenched and saturated with melancholy, a melancholy born of too much sun perhaps, and of the fact that its inhabitants include veterans returned from the war not to verdant, prolific lives but to merely surviving a kind of human drought. The West Texas landscape is characterized by the poem and helps to characterize the human situation of the poem: parched and blasted like the aftermath of war. In the last stanza we find the speaker holding the water hose and saying he can "feel flames" in his fingertips as he squeezes "to strafe begonias like a practice run." He then describes how, when he's "driving to work," his body still remembers his former life: "I keep feeling / a tingling in my hands / and the weight on my backbone in a turn" (68). The poem gives us West Texas, the American Southwest, as the setting for a trial of endurance, ordinary life in the face of extraordinary sadness, and perhaps only through the perspective of the poet who is himself a returning native, both insider and outsider, can a poem plumb these emotional depths.

Having established a persona as both insider and outsider, what remains is how McDonald will treat the region he views from this vantage point. To embrace it wholeheartedly would be to make the mistake Frost makes, according to Kemp, when he allows himself to become spokesman for New England by adopting the dour attitude of the New England rustic and viewing the rest of the world with a sort of clannish, xenophobic scowl. To take the opposite position and see only in the Southwest its often glaring faults—its provincialism, for instance, its lack of high culture, its crass commercialism, and bumper-sticker Christianity—would be even shallower, mere haughty contempt. McDonald allows himself claim as both a major American poet and as a Southwestern poet by dint of the unerring balance he achieves in his treatment of the region. Though he glories in the beauties of the Southwestern landscape, its people, wildlife, and cultures, he does not glorify them in the way that earlier Southwestern poets were apt to do. In its emphasis on the plain style and willingness to expose the region's faults—though always with a sort of gentle and forgiving irony—McDonald's poetry, fittingly,

embodies a famous line from Frost himself: "Anything more than
the truth would have seemed too weak" (*Complete Poems* 25).

The poem "Learning How in the Southwest" from the award-
winning collection *Blessings the Body Gave* demonstrates McDonald's
balanced approach. The poem describes an unidentified Southwestern town that, though it is not named, smacks of some place in West
Texas. "This town is like Montana," the speaker says,

> only worse—no trees, no mountain streams,
> no mountains. People here are loners and loud
> for hours in bars for greasy steaks and company.
> Hardhats from seven states drop by and brag
>
> how many gushers they've drilled since Christmas,
> baby's little booties encased in gold, not bronze. (61)

This is the tasteless, oil-bloated Southwest of West Texas, described
with candor, pulling no punches. Note especially the evocative nouns
and adjectives. Aside from McDonald's effective use of synecdoche,
it is significant that his oil field workers— the "hardhats"—though
they are "loud" and like to "brag," are "loners." The line is brilliant
in its economy considering the degree to which it goes beyond just
describing the men at the bar to speak volumes about the entire
region.

But as we should expect if we have become practiced readers of
McDonald's work, our oil field workers and the region they inhabit
are to be redeemed. Seeing beneath the Southwest's rough exterior,
McDonald finds something more valuable than oil:

> The five best women here know secrets
> no one wrestling derricks cares for
>
> except after hours, down in motels
> or trailers after the last bar closes,
> after the last dull darts have hit
> outside the target zone, the last fast women
>
> with bleached hair and freckles have staggered off
> with drunks who were their husbands after all.

What these "five best women" know, the speaker relates, are
"mother's tunes" that come "from more than the tongue, like honey
/ and homemade bread, learned when young, / commotion in the
heart older than cactus." The poet suggests that there is a foundation
under this culture, this region of thin soil and glaring light. It has a
soul, something beyond even the depth of "black shale." Beneath the
grimy skin and bravado of our oil field workers is a sensitivity and

appreciation of something finer, instilled in them through love, expressed metaphorically here as the "poetry in motion" given to them by their mothers "singing lullabies to babies / that cry and, cuddled, go back to sleep" (62). This strikes the reader as something other than regional chauvinism and empty sentiment or baseless mythologizing. The bar, the roughnecks, the "fast women," and the "five best women" remain quite real and convincing, and thus so do the mother's songs allowing for the redemption of the poem's primary figures.

The balance McDonald strikes here between the sentimental and the hard-boiled is a function of his measured view of the region. Strict insiders of the Southwest have been all too eager to assert the existence of its hominess. Anthologies of Texas and Southwestern poetry, especially those published before the 1980s, offer ample proof of this.[2] At the same time, strict outsiders, unable to see beneath the surface, have either overemphasized the mystical aspects of the region's dramatic landscapes and, to them, exotic cultures—think of the Southwest-inspired poetry of D. H. Lawrence[3]—or they have cringed in verse at what they see as the region's brutishness and impoverishment, as in William Carlos Williams's poems inspired by a trip to the Mexican border.[4] McDonald succeeds where strict insiders and outsiders fail because he knows intimately both the region's strengths and weaknesses and because he is neither overawed by nor over-enamored of them. He understands how each is tempered by the other.

But it takes more than perspective alone, balanced or not, to tie a poet to a particular region. It is the general atmosphere of the work, its tendency to evoke a specific region, that makes us associate a poet with that region. Atmosphere in this sense is created through the particular nuance of the language and through imagery. And it is in this respect that we may most think of Walt McDonald as a Southwestern poet. Southwestern imagery holds sway in McDonald's poetry, much more so than aircraft or war imagery. Notice, for instance, the number of times the following words appear in his work: *coyote, hardscrabble, calves, plains, snakes, cactus, wolves, wind, barbed wire, buzzards, hawks, rain.* Compare this list with a list of Robert Frost words—words like *birches, farm, hay, woods, mountain,* and, especially, *snow.* W. H. Auden comments that "nature in Frost's poetry is the nature of New England." By way of supporting that claim, he notes that in perusing the poet's *Collected Poems* he finds "twenty-one in which the season is winter as compared with five in which it is spring, and in two of these there is still snow on the ground" (346). We might make a similar remark about Walt McDonald's poetry, replacing "winter" with "summer" and noting that in most of the poems in which the season is winter there is still no snow on the ground.

When we think back on the poetry of Walt McDonald, not necessarily with a volume of the poems in hand but in a moment of contemplation, our memory of the work is suffused with harsh sunlight; the ground is flat, the grass dry and brown, the countryside sparsely populated, overhung by a wide metallic sky, strewn with bleached bones scattered among mesquite and cactus and old fence posts. We should see that our impression of Walt McDonald is bound to the American Southwest as surely as our impression of Frost is bound to New England. Far from being a limiting factor, it is part of the poet's strength.

Poetry to Trespass For

Dan Flores

I know almost nothing about W. H. Auden, the twentieth-century British writer-critic, except that once he wrote these lines: "I cannot see a plain without a shudder; 'Oh God, please, please don't ever make me live there!'" The exclamation point is his.

Auden offers up an opinion common in our time. Although the Great Plains at least once or twice in continental history has been a most-favored land, maybe in the form of a Clovisia the Beautiful, or a Comanche/Kiowa/Cheyenne Eden of the Animals all others lusted for, we live in an age of denigration for the Horizontal Yellow. Mountain ranges in piles across the horizon, the base reversal of plains, have formed our aesthetic ideal since the Romantic Age. And since it is our mountains that now preserve most of what is left of Indian America, and our plains are the most transformed landscapes in the modern West, those of us who hunger for *nature* flee to the mountains for new reasons.

Today I live in the mountains, where big earth forms give the encircling world a raggedly vertical, three-dimensional framing for life and motion. But I have lived on the plains, and the world there didn't give me Auden's sense of instinctive revulsion. In fact, I found my world there beautiful beyond belief, a place where if you live "out" and experience as much of an entire heaven and entire earth as is left on the plains these days, you'll find that the nature gods hold sway there if they do anywhere. The Llano Estacado, the great tableland of New Mexico and West Texas where I lived, taught me to be alive to the euphoria of simple existence in a way I'd never known before. At the same time, though, I also found the modern plains experience depressing and frustrating to distraction. In the end, I left. As I wrote in a recent book, *Horizontal Yellow: Nature and History in the Near Southwest,* "I was not able to stay . . . because of the dissonance in my head between the ecologically rich world I knew once existed here and the skinned and impoverished part of the Near Southwest I inhabited." The most privatized landscape in the entire American West—and I was in Texas, which magnifies the phenomenon—the Great Plains has not only been skinned by global market agriculture, it was almost all off limits. Here was this magnificent canyon country around the perimeter of the Llano Estacado, and getting at it was very nearly impossible. For the same reasons I couldn't live in Texas, I wouldn't be able to take Iowa or Kansas either.

My point is that even after twenty-two years of life on and in the creases of the Great Plains, I could not come to terms with it. So I ended up committing bioregional original sin: I left. But I continue to return, as a frequent visitor, to a country that resonates not merely as a homeland of my imagination but in the environmental future of the Great Plains and the American West. Modern society's hold on the Llano Estacado, which was once regarded as the major uninhabitable part of the Southwest, has been tenuous for a century now and grows more so as the global climate warms and the unseen Ogallala Aquifer dwindles to a few pockets of wet gravel beneath the ground. Like that of the Kiowas, or of the Clovis hunters before them, this is one of those mythic stories of inhabitation that ought to inspire and has inspired the human imagination to wonder about the limits and possibilities of life lived in a singular place.

One of the ways I and many others from this part of the world have tried to make sense of the Llano Estacado and experience its sense of place is through art—through the paintings of Frank Reaugh, Georgia O'Keeffe, Alexandre Hogue; the music of Buddy Holly, of Butch Hancock, Joe Ely, and Jimmie Dale Gilmore, or Terry Allen, or Andy Wilkinson; or, in literary terms, through the art of regional novels by writers like Elmer Kelton, Max Crawford, Larry McMurtry, or the creative nonfiction of Walter Prescott Webb, J. Evetts Haley, and more recently John Miller Morris's artful books of history and place. According to geographer Yi-Fu Tuan, art in every form that distills human experience of specific locales into a world instantly recognizable to the rest of us is one of the ways we humans order the flux of the world into the familiar of home. Space into place, he called it. Or, as Wallace Stegner would have it: this is how we create that much-coveted, shared "sense of place."

One of the paths home to the Llano Estacado for many of us has become a descent into the familiar through the simple act of sitting down in front of the fire to the landscape poetry of native son Walt McDonald. Although only a part, and a relatively small part, of his corpus of work, McDonald's pair of books with photographic archivist Janet Neugebauer about life in West Texas—*All That Matters: The Texas Plains in Photographs and Poems* (1992) and *Whatever the Wind Delivers: Celebrating West Texas and the Near Southwest* (1999)—stand in my mind as backpack-stuffers for anyone who tries to understand this seemingly simple but complex place.

When *All That Matters* was first published, I had just moved from the Llano Estacado, where I'd lived full-time for fourteen years, and most of that not in town but on a wonderful little piece of ground in Yellow House Canyon outside Lubbock, where the full power of the Southern Great Plains on the senses was irresistible. Now I was in the Rocky Mountains of Montana, where even the blue, green, and white coloring of the surrounding world disoriented me. Sitting in my apartment in Missoula, living in a town for the first time in a decade, I missed my canyon and my plains, and *All That Matters* was like a heartthrob of longing. Here's the way I wrote my impressions then in a review of the book:

> "It's wind, not rain, dry cattle need."
> This opening line in Walt McDonald's splendid new collection of High Plains poetry packs a potent and telling message. In just seven crunched words (six of them monosyllabic), McDonald portends the theme of this book. Here is Texas Plains. It is a spare, minimal place. The wind blows. The rain does not fall. Except for the odd coyote, a few pronghorns (poignantly, the subject of a poem titled "Things About to Disappear"), a pocket of captive prairie dogs in Lubbock, and that ubiquitous holdout, the coontail diamondback, little remains here of the magnificent wilderness of the last century. Instead, domestic stock animals from Europe and Asia trustingly eye the technology that keeps them alive in a transformed land where the water comes out of the ground rather than out of the sky.
> The Texas Plains is a country few outsiders seem to know or (seemingly) care to know. From afar it is perceived as topographically uninteresting, environmentally harsh, its people stiflingly conservative. Once, signing books in a Santa Fe bookstore, I found myself consoled by New Mexicans for being sentenced to live in "such a ghastly place." Had they done anything other than to drive across the plains, I inquired? Few had. Did they know the centuries-long symbiosis between the plains and the Sangre de Cristo Mountains? Other than the tiresome stream of tourists, they did not. Their parting question was easy to anticipate. "I live there," I said, "because it is absurd the way I love that country." Those who know plains history will know I was quoting Georgia O'Keeffe, writing from Canyon in 1916. But if I had read *All That Matters* then I could have quoted Walt McDonald, too: "I love this cactus land" (125).

"Now it begins," McDonald writes, "the endless golds / and blues, no forests, / no mountains anywhere. / Sunshine sixteen hours a day," in a country where there's "wind like a god," with "whirlpools of buzzards" in the skies and a scent on the air after a thunderstorm like "fresh honey in the hive." Cattle and horses, children and wives, Billy Rays and Joe Bubbas populate this world, where it takes "a million years to cut a canyon through the plains" but only "forty to pump it dry," where you can backpack for forty miles without finding "a stream so deep I couldn't step across on stones."

The feel of the minimal and of life lived close to the bone permeates nearly every work in this book. On "the earth we're beginning to call home," McDonald writes, there is the elemental reality of "only brown earth and sky, / and in between all that matters" (135). And there's this line, as close to the unfolding essence of life on the Llano Estacado as a worm in the core of an apple: "[i]f we didn't know the world is dying, / the Ogallala water table dropping / three feet every year, we'd swear this water / would gush forever" (81).

Love, sensual immersion, and unease in one package; in the universal sense, this is what a book of contemporary landscape poetry ought to be all about.

As the Texas Plains has come to know itself, to develop after little more than a century of inhabitation an emerging sense of place, it has depended on its native—and naturalized—sons and daughters to snatch from the fabric of plains life real and true insights about the place. I and plenty of others think that Walt McDonald's all-seeing eye and rhythmic voice are among the most gifted senses the Texas Plains have spawned. In the emerging corpus of Southern High Plains bioregional books, *All That Matters* is going to be a touchstone for indigenes. Here in the knot of the Northern Rockies, 1,500 miles from those blues and golds, it has certainly re-glued my feet to the caliche.

After reading it several more times, I haven't changed my mind about that book.

Although I continued to be a part-time resident of the plains after moving to Montana, 1999 was to be the last time I lived a good part of the year on the Llano Estacado. It was also the year McDonald and Neugebauer published *Whatever the Wind Delivers* (with a foreword by Laura Bush, who averred that she knew some of this country, which I believed), so I'd been spending some time with the new book and missing the deep canyons. One clear, frosty day I woke as soon as the mesas and cliffs of Yellow House Canyon became visible in black silhouette, made coffee as Turkey Mesa lightened to pearly-blue, and got off in time to make the ninety miles to Caprock Canyons State Park by 8 A.M. But the park was closed to allow hunters to have a try at eradicating the red African sand goats (a.k.a. aoudads) that in duller-witted times got introduced into these cliffs. So as I slowly drove the dirt lane around the north end of the park, I had to hatch out an alternative plan. It was a cold morning but brilliantly

sunny, one of those marvels—a still day on the plains—that sometimes occur for a day (usually no more) following a spreading high-
pressure cell.

And so I remembered Mexican Creek Canyon, the least known of
the three deep canyons the state park land here draped across, because in Mexican Creek's case the park lands are discontiguous from
the rest (they're sliced out in fact by a state highway) and preserve
only a section of the canyon. There are no trails into this canyon, and
no parking area. So there was nothing to do but park on the shoulder
of the road, an admittedly dim behavioral response to wanting to
walk across Texas that evolution's evidently not had the time to se-
lect out of us. In Texas, if you think you're going to end up trespassing, the smart move is to have somebody drop you off; parking your
car on the shoulder is almost as surefire a way to get yourself arrested as clipping into the local sheriff's bandwidth and announcing
on the air that among other sinful acts you're about to climb through
a barbed-wire fence. Even if it's with no more intent than to step on
the ground and look at the rocks, they arrest you for this in Texas.

However, having been so arrested nearby once already, I knew
the fine, and having done it once thought I could endure all the out-
raged indignation. As a taxpayer in the state, I figured that at least
part of Mexican Creek Canyon belonged to me anyway; if necessary
I was willing to fork over the $350 (hell, the goat hunters were proba-
bly paying more than that) and accept my criminality, provided I got
a chance to examine this canyon. From where I'd parked alongside
the road, I was looking out over it from just below its south rim, at
about midway of its total length, and damn but it looked deep, rugged, and beautiful. And like most of these Llano Estacado canyons,
this one preserved an interesting name from its past. Actually, I'd
crossed Mexican Creek Canyon—this morning I was recalling two
times in the 1980s—on other great trespassing jaunts northward,
through what's probably the very wildest and best of the Caprock
country here on the eastern side of the tableland. But I'd never explored the length of this canyon, and that serpentine couple of miles
as they uncoiled below the road overlook were extending an invita-
tion this bright morning.

I felt too sensuous to resist. So leaving an old car with out-of-state
plates (piling on the causes for suspicion) on the side of the road, I
slipped through the fence and angled down through the oak
shinnery towards the part of the canyon the map showed to be state
park land.

I had my brand-new *Whatever the Wind Delivers* in my pack. If an
arresting officer demanded to know why I'd so blatantly and wan-
tonly violated the sacred barbed-wire, I planned to whip it out in a
wild hope that the cop read poetry. If not, I thought at the very least I

could get Walt McDonald and Janet Neugebauer arrested along with me, in proxy, and maybe even pile up some chits against Laura Bush that (no offense intended to her) might help keep her husband out of the White House. (The more I thought about this the more it seemed that this line of reasoning might even get any charges against me *dismissed* in West Texas.)

Crime does pay. That day in Mexican Creek Canyon was a sweet, sweet day in paradise. I slid down sandy slopes and later climbed back up them. I sat and stared, tasted falling water, felt the rough clutch of sandstone walls, inhaled acrid sand-sagebrush on dry slopes and ferny mosses in dripping amphitheaters. I marveled at red rock, candy-cane gypsum striping, the blueness of the sky through the spidery white lattice of cottonwood limbs. I listened to little brown birds rustle the leaves in the canyon and ravens croaking their bored observations on the timelessness of all they saw below them. Whenever I was tired of walking or climbing, or I just felt like it, I opened up *Whatever the Wind Delivers,* and I read poetry and looked at old photographs of the Llano Estacado, with the real thing, the corporeal in the existential moment, surrounding me on every side.

Thus I read "Neighbors Miles Away," with its riff about "starving Comancheros" who "never dreamed" of pumping this "purest water three hundred feet to grain" (124) and did so in a canyon whose name is derived from their very real presence on the ground. And a few hundred yards farther on, I read "Starting a Pasture," a rumination (it's a century-long topic here) on exactly what this country might be good for now that "the Ogallala water table drops / three feet every year." Maybe "gazelles and impala / imported from other deserts, two of each kind / of animals in a dying world" (100), McDonald asks himself, as the accompanying photo lets you linger over the nineteenth century's resolution: Herefords as far as the eye can see. "Estacado," whose title I knew was taken from a pioneer town settled by Quaker farmers, extended the lesson to the twentieth century: "This wide prairie // with waving buffalo grass / reminded them of bread without yeast" (26). And on a day whose stillness was all too rare, I read "High Plains Drifter," with its Dorothy Scarborough–like conversion of the plains wind into a demon lover who won't leave white farmer women from Virginia (and other points east) alone. Ever:

> Meanwhile, his wife has a daily affair
> with the wind, southwest and lean,
> the silent type, a whistler
> who taps on the glass,

> slips in and strokes her hair
> and sweaty neck. . . . (74–5)

Half-the-day later, sitting silently and motionlessly beside the miniature waterfalls in upper Mexican Creek Canyon, surrounded by flitting, chirping, crawling, slithering life, I read pieces like "After the Monsoon," "Where Seldom Is Heard," and "The First Hard Thunder of Another Dawn," where McDonald traces out the fate of the wild in this country. In the first, "The wolves are gone, the buffalo, and the last game warden bored / with nothing to patrol" (18). And in the next two he deals with what's left—the world around me in my own time—like tarantulas "haunting the cactus," "squeals of mice and typanum of claws" (70), "mule deer and skunks, a trotting coyote and a prairie hawk" (52).

This led to a bit of independent-thinking mischief, my particular burden to bear. I put together photo #135, identified in the credits as "Hilary B. Bedford with some of the animals and birds he trapped and mounted" (and Janet Neugebauer ought to be congratulated for finding such an horrific shot of a loony pioneer gunman with his stuffed menagerie of half the endangered species from the region) and McDonald's poem "Rattler," just to absorb them side-by-side. What emerged were the visual and the lyrical manifestations of all that West Texas venom for the wild nature of the Southern High Plains, coiled together in one crazy photograph and five verses and sentences. In McDonald's poem, the diamondback rattler, a marvel of evolution and adaptation, is a monumental pain in the ass, a divine mistake:

> crazy and hostile, without a lawyer
>
> . . . nursing a grudge
>
> . . . nothing but a mouth
> with fangs and knotty large intestine,
> devouring all it can swallow, all it can kill.

The poem ends:

> We watched the old pretender
> coil and sway like a magic rope and squirm away,
> head weaving from side to side, as if nodding
> from cactus to cactus, *Mine, mine.* (38)

With downright lawyerly feelings, I say "amen" at the end of this last line and know full well now why I so rarely encounter other West Texans hiking in these canyons.

There's much in *Whatever the Wind Delivers* that would resonate for someone else—Texas two-stepping, buddies missing in action, children and grandchildren, flying a plane, and "The Last Saloon in Lubbock," which would resonate for me fine except that the poem's subject was banned from the city long before I ever arrived thirsty— but doesn't necessarily speak so closely to me. But what I do love, a sense of life lived close in to what I'd call (but McDonald never would) the Llano Estacado Bioregion, is there again and again. Different senses, same sensibility.

I ended the day in Mexican Creek Canyon spending nearly an hour in a place I yet dream about. Scrambling back up the south slope of the canyon to the car, I came to the topmost layer of the Dockum Group, the thick bed of Martian-red, Triassic Age sandstones that creates the vertical walls and brick-hued splendor of the canyons of the Little Red River. But I'd never seen an expression of the Dockum quite like this. I thus record for posterity that in Mexican Creek Canyon, on the south slope of the lower canyon, there is a spot, of a few thousand square feet merely, where red sandstone has eroded into the most sinuous mounds of fossilized red dunes. It was a marvelous place just to sit and look, or to read poetry, and sitting here I realized in late afternoon of that day of hiking and reading what I admired most about Walt McDonald's "landscape" poetry.

It's what anyone who loves literature almost always loves most, and it's no doubt the quality that makes McDonald's poetry so widely admired. Walt McDonald is honest. This is poetry like a historical document; you can infer truth of experience from it. Here's how I know. There is a historical arc on the Llano Estacado over the past 125 years, the outlines of which I've gone to some personal effort to trace out, that has made the natural world—grasses, canyons, native species of animals whose evolution here stretches back beyond imagination—flippant casualties of modern plains life, and scarcely anyone who's native to here ever bothers to wonder at the process. But McDonald's poetry isn't just aware of it; it treats this reality as one of his Big Truths of Which We Dare Speak. So this is a poet who doesn't gloss over, in a piece like "Nights at the Hi-D-Ho," that these beautiful canyons were offhandedly targeted as public dumps by the local populace. Or that, as I read in "Turning Thin Shimmer into Wells," to farmer/rancher culture here, "Prairies were never Eden even when it rained" (48), and that, in starkest terms, this is a country where "Home is grass / and thorns, as far from snow as Xanadu" (49).

Or—and this is the line, from a third-generation plainsman, that must have been so very, very hard to write (it's from "Learning to Live with Sandstorms")—"My father cursed the plains" (68). Shades of W. H. Auden! We made our hardscrabble livings here, McDonald implies, but we more or less hated the place the whole time.

It was getting on towards late afternoon, the High Plains light beginning to go that saffron-yellow I will remember in my last breaths, when I made the road a couple hundred yards up-canyon from my old Jeep. And there, sure enough, cleverly parked beyond the far bend in the road so my Jeep was just visible to him but perhaps I wouldn't spot him and run off into the rugged country where they'd have to hunt me down with dogs or helicopters, was the local deputy. Of course I had no intention of running off. In fact, as I strolled down the hill towards the car, I was instead rehearsing in my head how I was going to break it to this Texas lawman that a book had made me trespass.

I reached the car, opened the driver's side door and tossed in my pack, stood there saturating myself in the golden canyon light for a moment, and stretched. The deputy's car did not move. The lights did not go on. Unable to resist the magnificent glow across the cliffs and juniper-speckled slopes where I'd spent the day, places I now felt some intimacy with, I walked around the Jeep to the lip of the plunge and snapped a couple of photos while the abyss of Mexican Creek Canyon yawned at me. All was silence. No sound of an engine cranking down around the next bend.

With a last look at the canyon and a new appreciation of its mysteries, I climbed into the Jeep, inserted the key, and fired the engine. Through the rearview mirror I saw the deputy's car sitting motionless, making no move to roar to life and perform a Starsky-and-Hutch apprehension of the suspect. Curious. So I got out the binoculars and focused them on the windshield glinting in the afternoon sun . . . through which I could see the deputy, head lolled against the seat and mouth open, enjoying a late afternoon siesta.

For a long moment I sat there, toying with the idea of scribbling a note—"Thanks so very much for your concern; canyon's just fine; buy and read *Whatever the Wind Delivers*"—and tacking it to the curve railing. Then good sense prevailed, and I let out the clutch and drove off.

Why, after all, use up a perfectly good excuse for trespassing? Who, besides the rattler, knows how many more books Walt McDonald has in him?

IV. Aesthetic Strategies

Walt McDonald's Poetry: Images of Man's Acceptance of His Place in Time

LaVerne Popelka

Walt McDonald's poetry reveals a cyclic conception of time. Set against a backdrop of Vietnam, Colorado, and West Texas, his poetry contains images of recurring cycles and patterns in nature and in human life. His most prominent images involve the various stages of people's lives, but always a particular moment in their lives. Admittedly, time holds few bonds on people early in life, but its influence on them increases and changes as they mature. With simplicity of language and image, McDonald often captures this epiphany, that moment when people realize their niche in the cycle of life.

As he explores these epiphanies, McDonald's images of childhood demonstrate the development of people's attitudes toward death. Adults are aware of the danger that the future holds, but children are not, as seen in "The Party" (*Caliban in Blue* 50), "Faraway Places" (7), and "With Steve at Lake Raven" (*Burning the Fence* 54). In "The Party," a father relates his simple observations at his six-year-old's birthday party. His descriptions of his son's naïve attitude contrast with his own. By describing his son's nonchalant attitude, he is actually noting that adults are aware of the passage of time, the loss of innocence, and the eventual nearness of death. Singing all the way, the young boy has gone to the bathroom. Obviously, the innocent has no concern for closing the bathroom door to ensure privacy because he has not yet learned to be embarrassed. Furthermore, he comes back to the party with his pants unzipped and has a marvelous time, totally oblivious to his situation. The father explains that his son is borne away "raging in joy / toward seven" (50). The poem celebrates the passage of time for the innocent against the background of the father's maturity. It is the father who notices that the bathroom door is open and that the pants are unzipped. The son has not learned to fear time and its passage; the father realizes that his son has not yet lost that innocence but knows in time life will take it away.

The same contrast of perception appears in "Faraway Places" (*Caliban in Blue* 7). McDonald has remarked in a discussion of this poem that a man understands a "goodbye" and all it entails, but the child does not (Big Country Writing Workshop). In this poem, a father who has orders for the East, probably Vietnam, stands beside his young daughter near a placid duck pond, comparing her world to his. He must cross the Pacific Ocean to Vietnam (to face death), but in her world so small and naïve, her only childish understanding of any separation is the pond and the ducks on the other side. With the word "gold" and its connotative meaning of value, the father expresses his feelings. His daughter's hair

> . . . blows
> golden in the wind. Strange prospect
> to leave such gold, he thinks.
> There is no gold for him
> in Asia.

Cognizant of the forthcoming pain of separation, the father values their time together. He touches her again, but in her innocent stage and in her own microcosm, she "does not feel his claim / upon her gold" (*Caliban in Blue* 7) and ironically is only aware of the present and the ducks before her, not the future with its sense of loss which fills her father's present thoughts. By juxtaposing these individuals' thoughts, the poem emphasizes that an adult is more aware of time and its consequences than a child is.

A final example of this contrast is in "With Steve at Lake Raven," a poem in which a father takes a brief moment to enjoy life with his son and lets time slip by without confrontation. The setting is a lake, and the father, already in the water, beckons his six-year-old son to follow. The water, a universal symbol of life, both threatens and supports a swimmer, and treading water symbolizes the chanciness and the striving of a person's life on earth. Hence, the "trembling" of the boy can represent a momentary fear of mortality as well as deep water. Soon, the father and son race to the buoy. Under the ever-watchful eye of the father, the son goes first, making his way through the waves and reaches the buoy. The father then follows. The father and the son are at different stages of life, but for now they are together for a joyful moment beneath the swaying buoy, reminiscent of the pendulum of a clock. Time and life continue, and the father and son have their moment together. Summarizing his feelings, the father states, "I . . . laugh with my son / and think no matter, we are together now" (*Burning the Fence* 54). His phrase "and think no matter" conveys his sense of life's briefness, but he is content to live with what he has now. McDonald juxtaposes parents' and children's attitudes to show how one's understanding of time varies with one's stage of life.

In other poems, he varies this technique by letting a narrator recall his own childhood. The narrator's attitude is juxtaposed with that of the child he used to be. Four of these poems—"Billy Bastard and the Centipede," "First Blood," "Rafting the Brazos," and "Morning in Texas"—contain simplistic childhood experiences involving death. However, closer scrutiny reveals that they also emphasize stages of life. In each is a tension between the adult narrator and the child he once was. The adult is at one stage and is reflecting on another stage. As a child, the narrator had reacted one way to death; the adult now reacts another way, and more importantly, he realizes that his reaction has changed.

In "Billy Bastard and the Centipede," Billy Bastrop, called Billy Bastard by his friends, lives up to his name. He always finds mischief by cutting window screens, playing cruel tricks on cats, or playing with fire. One day Billy dissects a centipede with an audience of peers, one of whom is the child-speaker in the poem. One girl cries out in protest, but the others, almost spellbound, keep watching; Billy just grins. The speaker remembers that he stood there and did not protest the mutilation, but as an adult, he has a different perspective to that incident than he had as a child. With a clarity that only time can give, he recalls that the part of the centipede that still lived, the head with its eyes, "took each of us in," expressing the narrator's sense of guilt and inability to dismiss the incident from his memory (*Burning the Fence* 4).

Some children encounter death first through the deaths of animals, but eventually they face the death of a human being. Often, this encounter is rather impersonal. The adult narrator in "First Blood" recalls that he and a friend were on the way to school one morning when they saw a plane flying a pattern of circles; in the midst of this pattern, it hit some wires and crashed. They and the neighbors ran to investigate the crash site, but they heard no sound and saw no movement. The crowd chattered about how the young pilot had been buzzing the house of a girl named Shirley, who was not at home. Ironically, he was not on some great military mission; he was just having some fun. The narrator now realizes that he and Nolan were so engrossed in their excitement that they were tardy for school, but more tragically, they never sensed the sadness of the pilot's death or even its senselessness. In their typical childhood mentality, they each took a souvenir from the wreckage, and the narrator recalls succinctly that his piece "had some blood on it" (*Burning the Fence* 7). As a ten-year-old boy, this first encounter with death had little impact on him, but the adult recalling the incident realizes how much his reaction to death has changed.

The third poem in this group to contrast the child of the past with the adult of the present is "Rafting the Brazos." In this poem, death comes closer to the child when a young friend dies. With a simplistic style reminiscent of Ernest Hemingway's prose, the adult speaker in this poem recalls the summer that he and the other boys were rafting the Brazos:

> Someone always cheated. At fourteen
> games are serious as sex. Everything
> has rules and everybody breaks them;
> And so the day Durwood Stanley slumped over
>
> on his tube and dropped his paddle
> we passed him and jeered at whatever stunt
> he was pulling.

The narrator remembers how they were lulled into a false sense of security in their journey down the Brazos (whose original Spanish name *Brazos de Dios* is ironically "Arms of God"). The river kept "flowing as if it hadn't happened." For the first time, the boys learn that death can come to one their own age, can come amidst joy and childhood games, and cannot be reversed, no matter "how long" they pumped their friend's body and "how long" they blew into his lungs (*Witching on Hardscrabble* 50). Because Durwood did not drown, the fathers help the boys realize that they could not have done anything to save him. As an adult, the narrator comes to another realization: death could have taken him as well as his friend, and no one could have prevented it then and no one could prevent it now. As Lawrence Durrell explains, "Man, says the philosopher, as soon as he noticed the irreversibility of process in the natural world, became afraid" (5).

Death becomes more evident to children as they grow older. Sooner or later, the death of someone causes them to question their own time on earth. "Morning in Texas" (*Burning the Fence*) does exactly that. The narrator recalls an afternoon in April; he was in school when a grain elevator exploded and its "boom [was] like a bomb" (3). Unexplainably, a classmate, Juan Hernandez, jumps up exclaiming that his father was dead. Later in the evening, the narrator's mother, probably in response to her son's questioning, states that it was a "coincidence." The boy has reached a crucial moment in

life when he realizes his mortality and begins to anticipate his ultimate future—death. At bedtime, when his mother covers him with a
sheet, he announces, "Mother, I'm going to die." The use of the simple word "sheet" keeps the image of death around the boy. He lies in
bed, waiting for his spirit to leave his body. He never expects to see
the sun rise, but "Dawn came. Comes" (3). The past and the present
are juxtaposed; morning came, and many continued to come. That
last phase of life of the narrator is approaching with each passing
dawn. The narrator remembers the moment of his realization of mortality, his initiation into adulthood; it is a lesson he has not forgotten.

Besides contrasting childhood and adulthood, McDonald writes
of the transition between them. Three poems concern initiation rites,
rites of passage through which a youth formally becomes an adult
and is officially one step closer to death. It is ironic that civilized cultures place so much importance on time yet have so few rites of passage. In fact, among such cultures only weak examples can be found,
the best being the Jewish *bar mitzvah* held for boys at the age of thirteen and confirmation in Christian churches. Nonetheless, certain
other events come close to marking that major milestone, and Mc-
Donald often raises rather mundane or obscure moments to that
level. In "On Teaching David to Shoot," McDonald describes that
special father-son occasion when a father passes on the skill of shooting to his man-child, a skill whose roots lie in the basic responsibility
of providing food and protection for a man's family and thus ensur-
ing survival. The poem touches on the rite of passage into manhood:

> Clipped in place, the target
> waits like a child.
> Together we crunch back
> to our positions, and reload.
> I tell him ready, aim,
> And he takes aim. And fires.

The parallel is obvious. The target "waits likes a child," symbolizing
the childhood that is about to become the past. Carefully, the young
boy "takes aim" and "fires." With these words separated by a pause,
the child is gone, and the man emerges. The word *reload* is especially
appropriate to target shooting, but it also implies metaphorically
that life is just like a rifle. When one bullet or generation is spent, another must be ready to take its place. The son's attitude is positive; he
tries to please his father. Proceeding with no reluctance, he "takes
aim. And fires." The incident is a major one in the life of the child as
well as the father because the father has come to a realization of his
own. This whole incident does not pass without some remorse from
the father as he comments that "[c]ockleburs yellowed by the sun, /
stab my legs like old regrets" (*Anything Anything* 3). The past seems

to haunt him, and he admits that he would rather raise his son in another country, perhaps a country at peace, where there are only flights of bees. The poem provides additional insight into this rite of passage. When a father acknowledges that his son is now a man with the skills of a man, then the father must also acknowledge that his own mortality is closer. The pronouns in the passages before and during the firing of the gun are "I" and "he," indicating the separate stages of the man and the child. When they check the target, the pronoun changes to "we"; the boy is considered a man, appropriately inducted into the secret society of manhood, the ultimate fraternity, and the last stanza with its closure of "And fires" eliminates any traces of childhood.

Many of the rudimentary rites of passage recognized today resemble the ones observed by primitive people. Traditional examples include the teaching of self-defense, the separation of parents and child, and the hunt. "Scout Arapaho" (*Burning the Fence* 8) contains a more modern rite of initiation in the form of earning a Boy Scout badge. In character with the primitive initiation procedures, the boy is camping in the mountains alone to face the dangers of the elements and to prove his manhood. McDonald selects metaphors recognizable in every level of society and attaches meaning to them that at times seems almost metaphysical. The scout spends the night in a sleeping bag and emerges in three days, ready to prove his ability to function in this new world, actions that parallel caterpillars as they spin their cocoon and move into darkness, only to emerge in the final stage of adulthood. Our young scout emerges and shows no fear; instead, he seems to relish his new environment: he plays, he skates, he demonstrates bravery by enduring snow and freezing weather. Instead of killing a large animal, he stalks his prey with a camera. As he returns to civilization to receive his badge, he will be a different person.

Admittedly, McDonald's poems involving the rites of passage are frequently male-oriented, but in "Bloodlines" a girl experiences a rite of passage. In this poem, a sensitive moment between parents and daughter occurs, a common moment when parents and child have a conversation about where babies come from. The age of the daughter is not given, but since she is old enough to have seen a film at school about human reproduction, she must be ten or twelve. She comes home from school and places her hand upon the abdomen of her mother and comments that "I came from there." When parents remind her that they adopted her at two weeks of age, the little girl is confused; she has heard but has not completely understood. As she tries to grasp the concept, she questions where she came from, where babies grow, and who is her real mother. When the parents respond that they do not know, she asks, "Then how / can you be sure?" This questioning of parents is a major step in growing independence. Later, the parents check on her while she sleeps and find her wrapped up "cocooned inside the sheet" (*Anything Anything* 7). The animal image implies a metamorphosis, and the girl's new knowledge of the past will transform her.

Although many of McDonald's poems compare adult and child perceptions of death and describe childhood experiences including rites of passage, many focus on the adult reaction to death. Characters in McDonald's poetry try to rationalize death, escape it, or endure it passively, thankful when death does not knock on their door. In "The Jungles of Da Lat," the tiger symbolizes an unknown danger, perhaps death. The epigram beneath the poem's title comes from a newspaper article from Saigon about a tiger that has reportedly mauled a Marine and has become a man-eater feasting on battlefield carrion. This poem has an uncanny, frightening tone carrying an underlying primeval fear of being devoured. The tiger "sways" and "sniffs, eats, is satisfied." The word "death" is never used in these lines; it is not needed. These few, well-chosen words imply it. Like Hemingway, McDonald omits the adverbs and allows the reader his own interpretation. The newsmen, the "modern sorcerers," try to rationalize this incident:

> We sleep, protected by our own
> credulity.
> Our newsmen, modern sorcerers,
> explain away each horror,
> provide each jungle puzzle with
> a civil cause.
> See, it sways off
> through the cease-fire
> expecting its next feast. (*Caliban in Blue* 12)

The poem concludes with a haunting and ironic foreboding.

Some adults rationalize death; others literally run from it. The girl in the poem "The Girl in the Mackinaw and Panties" is trying to escape death. McDonald builds suspense by moving swiftly into the action and giving little background, allowing the image of coat and panties to speak for themselves. The driver picks up a hitchhiker, acts nonchalant, and makes little jokes about her attire: "Lose something / in a poker game?" He admits that he has to force himself to keep his eyes on the road. The suspense tightens, for "She keeps / looking back. Faster, she says" (*Anything Anything* 19). Something behind her is haunting or chasing her, and she knows it. Neither the driver nor the reader really knows from what she is running, but it does not matter. What matters is the fear itself.

In many of McDonald's poems, the characters endure the presence of death passively without trying to rationalize or escape it. They realize it is there, and they are grateful that it has not yet affected them, as are the parents in the poem "Ten O'Clock." The poem begins with the age-old crier's call, "Ten o'clock and all's well." The parents are relieved that their daughter has returned from a date by her curfew, and the scene is innocent enough. "[H]er dress still pressed, / unstained," and "The news is petty, / nothing disturbs." Even the fire has burned down, but the "red coals wink on, / off like tigers' eyes," indicating that the danger of death is still present. In the distance, through the snowy, cold night, set against this scene of tranquillity, a wreck occurs, ironically, "so soft" and yet "final." The parents "watch / each other's eyes," glad that their daughter is home and safe for now (*Anything Anything* 13). Death has not touched them yet.

More passive endurance is evident in "Llano Estacado." The driver of the car describes crossing the plains in present-day terms— "trails of asphalt," "cotton fields flat as our lawn"—after he recalls that the Indians once traveled across these plains following the buffalo. Civilization with its tractors and road equipment and neat lawns has changed the scenery of the plains, but something about this place has not changed and never will. "Buzzards in level circles" are in the sky in search of prey today just as they were when the Comanches crossed here. These circling shadows of death followed the Indians, and now they follow the driver, reminding him that death is omnipresent. He seems to acknowledge that it is present and that he cannot fight it. Like the animals in the Caprock who can only wait with "rapidly beating hearts," he knows death is there (*Burning the Fence* 12).

The narrator in "Giving Time" is a typical father who is aware that time is precious, but he is involved in his mundane tasks. His wife has asked him to spend some time with the children, and he replies, "Okay." After responding to one minor domestic crisis after another, he finally asks, "Now where are the kids?" (*Working Against Time* 5). Realizing the children could not wait any longer and have gone to bed, the father sees the faucet dripping and tackles one more chore. Although aware of the dripping of the faucet, an image implying the passage of time, he does not change his passive attitude.

In more modern technological terms, "Going Home" reiterates that people often encounter reminders of their mortality and react passively. In the first several stanzas, passengers in a commercial plane at high altitude describe the earth in contradictory terms. From their perspective, the earth seems to be "a dead planet" where an ancient people once lived. Lakes first seem "like amoebas" but become "like glaciers." The world below appears to be clean and peaceful, yet "clouds / hover like gunfire." The world is covered with clouds, and the speaker and the passengers are removed from this planet death, but just for a moment. Suddenly, the plane hits an air pocket and drops; the "hostesses hold on, balancing their trays / with our precarious lives." The plane resumes its climb; the hostesses with white knuckles assist passengers in the cleanup as a child and a mother cry somewhere near the front. They all realize that the earth is their home, and one way or another they must return to it:

> The earth, we confess throughout our
> shaken bodies, is still our home,
> a globe of graveyards and crashed planes.
> When we descend, the clouds thin out
> and there it sprawls,
> the rocks on which we live
> and where we all return. (*Burning the Fence* 46)

"Lake Solon" shows an adult's passivity toward death better than any other McDonald poem. Death rains down on a summer day as a swimmer's sunny moments are interrupted by a plane above reflecting the "[s]unlight like shook foil" as it drops ashes "like snow, / like flakes of coal" upon the lake. Apparently, someone's last request is being honored, and ashes are scattered over the lake. From the water, the universal symbol of life, the swimmer sees the plane fly out "like a stork," a symbol of life giving. Twice the speaker dives into the lake to purge himself of this reminder of death. No one else seems aware of this "fallout," adding to his loneliness and fear of the situation. His skin begins "to rust," reminding us that the swimmer is mortal and that death and decay are inevitable. Indeed, the swimmer can close his eyes and "float," but death will not vanish (*Anything Anything* 25). After all, this experience is only a reminder of death.

As these poems show, sometimes all an adult can do is accept the passage of time and the changes it brings, a thread that also runs through the title poem of McDonald's chapbook *Working Against Time*. The poem becomes a parable of humanity's struggle with time, showing an adult's resignation to it. The speaker, driving down the road, has encountered an unnamed obstacle. He backs up, then rams it, denting his fender. Again he tries, this time with greater determination—"I shake my fist." Now his face is bloody, and his windshield is cracked, resembling a "spider web." Believing that the obstacle is a monster smiling at him, he rams it again. On his last charge, he realizes that

> . . . it's not even trying to run,
> a grin wide enough to swallow me,

eyes big as tomorrow
seconds before we collide. (14)

The driver's rage is useless against a force he cannot defeat—time. The cycle of attack and defeat culminates in his realization that time is not to be overpowered like an ordinary foe, for he, like the spider's prey, is caught in the web of time and cannot escape.

In comparison, "Living on Open Plains" is a more realistic vignette about surrendering to time. The narrator speaks of a couple whose hearts are "circadian clocks" and who acknowledge the effects of time; their parents are dead, and their children have created lives of their own in various cities. The poem concludes with several rhetorical questions: "How does the sun set there?" "Where are the coyotes, now?" "Where is the sand running to?" At first, the sand appears to be the sand of West Texas; however, the sand is in an hourglass. The speaker's question "[w]here is the time going?" is a trite response to an inevitable phenomenon—the passage of time and the approach of death (*Night Landings* 37).

As illustrated by these poems, people react to death by rationalizing it, trying to escape it, or enduring it passively. However, people often challenge death. Some will tempt it; some will try to soften its blow by perpetuating life; others gallantly defy it when met face to face. "Caliban on Spinning" focuses on a pilot's temptation of death. The speaker states that spinning "an airplane right / is like a little death." Then the poem proceeds as process and instructs the reader, who is now projected into the pilot's seat, how to spin a plane. The narrator explains the process in imperatives—"Raise the stick back together . . . work the plane / rigid" (*Caliban in Blue* 3). The language implies movement and action, using words like *spinning, raise, kick, shudders, thrust, falling, surging, oscillations,* and *leveling*. These words are paradoxical; the poem states that the spin will be like death, yet all those action verbs imply life. The time cycle here in the plane is expressed in the terms of "spinning" and "oscillations." After the spin, the plane comes back to a steady flight, and the poem ends with enjoyment and a sense of calm and accomplishment. The pilot has challenged the forces of nature, has mastered the controls, has tempted death and now lives in control again and enjoys it. The plane itself seems to be alive, some force in nature; the pilot masters it, and each spin becomes better. If the plane represents time and its varying cycles, then man's ability to face it will ensure that the next cycle or stage will be better simply because he has endured.

Another way that people challenge death is to perpetuate life. In "Fathers and Sons," McDonald studies the way a man and his son must eventually exchange roles in a rite of passage touching both generations. In the poem, the father says that his son is not afraid of

any height, having climbed several major mountains and even having been severely injured in attempting a climb. The son is taking a
direct route to the top and hammers steel pitons into the rock when
the handholds are too far apart. The father climbs below, slowing the
climb and entrusting his fate to his son as

> [h]and over hand
> I give myself to the sheer face
> of his will, trusting each piton
> as it comes. I snap a karabiner through
> and loop the rope, insert each heavy foot
> and step out into space on nothing but his
> piton holding me, and his rope
> I climb toward fist by fist. (*Witching on Hardscrabble* 70)

Here the father and the son have reversed roles; the father must now
trust the son and follow his lead, and having taught the next generation to lead and trusting that lead, the father helps perpetuate the
continuity of life.

In "Finding My Father's Hands in Mid-life," as in "Progeny" and
"Fathers and Sons," hands suggest a relationship between generations. The narrator's hand is now his father's hand, and even the
blood in the veins is his father's. "So this is the fist / of my father."
When the narrator makes a fist, it represents the family with the father as dominant figure, a figure that provided security and love. "I
see his / half-moon thumb fold over four / tight fingers, a picture of
family" (*Night Landings* 67). This fist associated with family and
closeness also represents hope and determination, for through its
progeny a family line lives on and defeats death.

McDonald's characters are often at their best when they have a final face-to-face confrontation with death as in "The Hammer," a
tribute to the speaker's grandfather, for years a blacksmith, who is
dying. The heart's stopping and going is compared to the forging of
steel:

> Sixteen, the doctor said,
> each like the clang of steel on steel,
> the stiff slow bellows blowing sparks,
> stoking time. . . .

His heart/life, like the hammer and bellows, will not quit until the
job is done, but this time the blacksmith is preparing a shoe for the
"horse of death" (*Caliban in Blue* 31). Perhaps this blacksmith, whose
defiant heart has restarted several times, is like the burning fence
post in "Burning the Fence." As the old fence post "brittle as old

bones" resists the consuming fire and is "unwilling to stop being fence," he resists death (*Burning the Fence* 57).

An adult's resistance to death can also be unusual, especially when death comes unexpectedly. In "The Lifeguard," not only is the response unexpected, so is the perspective. In this poem, McDonald uses a perspective of a young man dying by drowning, and this victim's response to the immediacy of death is in sensual terms. First, he feels the hands of the female lifeguard upon his chest. As she is bending over him, he imagines that "her bikini top / sags open and you can see everything." Then, as she begins mouth-to-mouth resuscitation, he envisions it as a kiss. The victim is literally "dying with pleasure." The pattern continues, but just as the victim wants her to continue, she stops, and he begins "to freeze." Ironically, the moment preceding death is envisioned as a moment of passion: her legs are warm, he is cold, and at the moment when "you want her to go on forever," she stops (*Burning the Fence* 39).

Like "The Lifeguard," "The Neighbor" describes an adult's defiance of death. The narrator's neighbor, a farmer, has suffered a heart attack but, with the aid of medical assistance, lives. At night, in pain and alone, he dreams of doing his mundane daily chores like "letting the cat out," "plowing the last rows," and "gathering strawberries." He also dreams of

> . . . snapping the long beans
> the cat purring on his lap,
> children of all the neighbors
> sitting down before him,
> begging a story, a blessing,
> anything. (*Witching on Hardscrabble* 41)

The farmer relies on past experiences as he draws near his death, and memories are weapons against death that give him just a little more time. The closure "anything" implies that the children are wanting him to continue, providing him a reason to live.

In every stage of the life cycle of McDonald's characters, time has some effect. To children, time holds no threat, and they respond with joy and hope. As the children mature, they realize that time does hold some bond on them. The closer McDonald's characters come to death, the more they react to it. Whether they acknowledge that death is there and proceed as usual, appreciate life more and perpetuate it, or finally confront death, the strongest of them sing with a defiance that matches Dylan Thomas's in "Do Not Go Gentle into That Good Night."

Angel and Mirage: Concerns of Imagination in Walt McDonald and Wallace Stevens

William Wenthe

I. "Flat is a state of mind"

And, nothing himself, beholds
Nothing that is not there and the nothing that is.
                    Wallace Stevens, "The Snow Man"

It is difficult to imagine a figure more out of place in the Texas Panhandle—that semi-arid, naturally treeless, flat plateau of the Llano Estacado and its attendant red-walled canyons fretted with mesquite, scrub-juniper, and cactus—than Wallace Stevens's Snow Man. Not simply because he'd melt to nothing in the heat (in eight years here I've seen but two snowfalls sufficient to actually make a snowman), but more so because of the impercipience of the snowman, who beholds nothing, whether imagined or actual, and is consequently "nothing himself" (8). We tend to associate Walt McDonald with other poets who have detailed the landscape and work life of particular regions—Frost, Williams, Hugo, Wagoner. But I see also a deep affinity between McDonald's work and the imaginative project of Wallace Stevens, which is, contrary to the Snow Man, to behold what is not there, along with that which is. McDonald's poems are populated with goat-farmers, dryland cotton farmers, cattle ranchers: the descendants of pioneers who—given the grim fact of the elimination of the native Southern Cheyenne and the buffalo that fed them—came to this area to eke a living almost as unnatural to the landscape as the buffalo were natural. These personages, arrayed among a vast family of grandparents, uncles, brothers, cousins, and children—and, too, a bestiary of livestock, dogs, coyotes, rabbits, hawks, snakes, and others—form the retinue of a vast imaginative vision encompassing McDonald's particular part of the planet. "A mythology reflects its region," claims Stevens, and McDonald's poetry amounts to a mythology of the Llano Estacado (476). Like myth, his poetry performs the necessary work of imagination, leading to an understanding of the human position in the land, an understanding vital to Stevens and McDonald both. For Stevens, the imagination is self-fulfilling; for Walt McDonald it points to a larger, divine imagination; but for both poets it is a fulfillment of the human place in the world, a further, fuller habitation.

If flat is the dominant aspect of the Llano Estacado, then flat is also, to the poet who lives there, "a state of mind":

> Flat words for flat land,
> wide as a state. Flat is a state
> of mind. Imagine driving for hours
>
> without one hill, the cruise control
> asleep on sixty. Nothing but yucca,
> red cactus blossoms, pale green mesquite
>
> balanced on single trunks, pretending to be
> flamingoes. (*Rafting the Brazos* 79)

Wait a minute—flamingoes? As if to convince us we're not hallucinating, the poem that precedes this one in *Rafting the Brazos* explores the image in more detail:

> Often in my fields I see mesquite trees
>   balanced on one trunk, pretending to be
> green flamingoes. Wind in the west
>
> does that, shaking their leaves
>   like feathers.

In this poem, "The Witness of Dry Plains," the speaker confronts, as is often the case in McDonald's poems, the harshness of "dry, bone-scattered plains" (to a rancher, the notoriously thirsty mesquite trees are not a welcome sight "in my fields"). But there is more: there is the pressure upon the mind to find imaginative, spiritual sustenance, a "Witness" in all its religious implications. In this tropical trope of mesquite trees as flamingoes, the Texas plains intersect with the fulsome Floridian mindscape to which Stevens often turns. There is something in the imagination that desires to see this, for "I'd do it / a different way, if I made pastures." If flat is a state of mind, then the plains, "flat as a pelt on a highway / dozens of pickups pound flatter / daily," can be inhabited, can be dwelt upon, in mind and body. As opposed to the "last appetite" that led that hapless pelt to the highway, the speaker of "The Witness of Dry Plains" has an equal appetite of the mind. He observes—he needs to observe—a hawk riding thermals, at home in the air, and stooping from "high in the heavens" to a rabbit in the fields. Watching the hawk leads to a discovery, a vision in which the mind's desire is at peace with the actuality of the plains: "All is as it will be, in a desert. / Even the trees are balanced" (78).

"The relation between the imagination and reality," writes Stevens, "is a question, more or less, of precise equilibrium" (647). In McDonald's poem, the imagined flamingoes and the utterly real roadkill converge in the hawk and the concomitant discovery of balance. Again, Stevens describes "the nature of poetry" as "an interdependence of the imagination and reality as equals" (659). While these comments are basic to an understanding of Stevens, they can apply equally well in reading the poetry of Walt McDonald. In its own way, the landscape of the Llano Estacado is as extreme as the tropics to which Stevens turns for metaphors of imagination, and so it is—in its own way—an equally fertile ground for the imagination. Perhaps more so: presented with land flat as paper, as stretched canvas, the mind needs to fill that space. So it was for a tribe who, coming upon "a plain in the land of Shinar," were compelled to build the tower of Babel (Genesis 11:2). There is a similar urge toward verticality in Walt McDonald's poems: "On land so flat, they dug deep wells / and raised plank steeples fast, / like lightning rods" (*Where Skies Are Not Cloudy* 7). Windmills, hawks, and of course aircraft draw the mind skyward, and beyond the sky, to stars. Witching for water, digging for artifacts of ancient nomads—these draw the mind downward. Between the two—"caught between the earth / and angels," as the former pilot says—is where the human imagination dwells (6).

In the poem, "Living on Buried Water" (*After the Noise of Saigon*), the skyward and earthward vectors meet, again in the image of a hawk diving for a rabbit:

> Each time a hawk
> plummets and scoops a rabbit like a ladle,
> someone takes a stick and goes there,
> witching. Sometimes a twig drags down to water
> and we risk digging. We haven't found it,
> but we believe it's here. (7)

The pragmatic folly of witching for water is secondary to an imaginative need: to practice the belief that water might be found there, a belief betokened by the hope that a hawk's need might speak to a human need. It is the mind that seeks sustenance, more so than the body. Stevens echoes this process when he writes of the imagination as a necessary response to the harshness of existence. The mind, he writes,

> is a violence from within that protects us from a violence without. It is the imagination pressing back against the pressure of reality. It seems, in the last analysis, to have something to do with our self-preservation and that, no doubt, is why the expression of it, the sound of its words, helps us to live our lives. (665)

At the time he wrote this, the major pressure of reality facing Stevens and his audience was World War II. Indeed, the pressure of war, the burden of surviving it, are written of extensively in Walt McDonald's poems. He has even suggested that his beginnings as a poet may stem from his war experience:

> I came to poetry late . . . as a middle-aged Air Force pilot. After some of my friends went off to Vietnam, and one was shot down, then another, I felt a need to say something to them, or about them. . . . Flying and a war I went to briefly are two of about five regions that I keep prowling; they're my background, part of what I am. ("Evidence" 173)

One of the poems that refers to the aftermath of this war, "After the Flight Home from Saigon" (*All That Matters*), alludes notably to the phrase, "Oh! Blessed rage for order," which is Stevens's epithet for the imaginative desire in one of his most famous poems, "The Idea of Order at Key West" (106). But McDonald revises the idea: "This is the rage for order on the plains, / barbed wires from post to post" (8). At first these lines seem a rejection of Stevens, but the poem's focus on the solid routines of ranch work implicitly contrasts, by way of the framing title, with what the speaker has left behind, namely, the war in Vietnam. McDonald's poem situates this barbed wire—balances it even—in an emotional space somewhere between the rage of war and the image of a woman singing to the placid seas off Key West in Stevens's poem. At the conclusion of "Notes Toward a Supreme Fiction," Stevens addresses himself to the reality of World War II, suggesting that "[t]he soldier is poor without the poet's lines" (352). His point, I take it, is that of all human activity, none is more useless than war, without the compensating gift of imagination to hold out the prospect of something better, to place oneself in the context of "a war between the mind / And sky, between thought and day and night." At war or at home, then, the imagination is a function of the broadest concerns of "our self-preservation" (351).

II. Weather makes nothing happen

The building of the tower at Babel was wrongheaded, and led to a confusion of language. The witching for water where a hawk has dived is also wrongheaded—except for the element of play. Knowing that this witching will (almost?) certainly yield no water, the speaker places emphasis on possibility. The witching for water is a kind of ritual, a rehearsal of belief: the last line, "but we believe it's here," echoes—always in McDonald's poetry—with a larger, spiritual belief which, in his case, merges with Christian faith. But the imagination that underlies this exercise can also, if not brought into what Stevens calls "a precise equilibrium" with reality, hold perils. Thus, in "Crashes Real and Imagined" (*After the Noise of Saigon*), the speaker distinguishes between the aircraft crashes on television and the real crash of a fellow pilot. The sensational, fictive television crashes happen off-camera, "behind cliffs / or convenient forests," the pilot having avoided the terror by biting a—painless, we presume—poison capsule. Similarly, the speaker tries desperately to believe his friend was unconscious as he crashed, but the imagined hope only worsens the reality:

> For weeks
> we waked from our private dreams,
> feeling our own too solid flesh
> impacting in the common ground. (49)

The allusion to Hamlet's escapist wish for annihilation—"O that this too too solid flesh would melt"—underscores the tragic potential of imagination not grounded in reality. Likewise, the common ground of the Llano Estacado must also be accepted, and merely fanciful imaginings avoided:

> We've almost stopped pretending
> clouds are mountains.
> If we can't accept these fields,
>
> our own souls with all their wind
> and cactus, we ought to leave. (*Where Skies Are Not Cloudy* 5)

Or, as Stephens wrote in his notebooks, "The world is the only fit thing to think about" (906); and again, to underscore that reality must be recognized if the imagination is to build upon it: "The real is only the base. But it is the base" (917).

Imagination that fails to recognize reality is useless, but equally useless is a world without the work of imagination: "What if the sun / was never a god, a burning bush, / a chariot?" McDonald asks in "Macho" (*Where Skies Are Not Cloudy* 39). The answer might be a world as seen in "The Weatherman Reports the Weather," whose speaker can report data and facts about the weather, but not the human meaning behind them. He can map the jet stream, "the highs and lows / of regions under siege," the "barometer falling"; but his map does not include the grief for two boys killed in a car wreck on the wet roads—"My map won't show the crosses on that road" (60). The redundancy of the poem's title reflects a position in which facts are only facts, and the poem bespeaks the helplessness of that position: "Weather's a science: it makes nothing happen." That, of course, is an allusion to Auden's "poetry makes nothing happen" in his "In Memory of W. B. Yeats" (Auden 197). But Auden's poem, which is as much about the use of poetry as about Yeats, goes further: there, poetry is "a way of happening, a mouth." The weatherman cannot give voice to reality: "I let the news and brokers talk of death by drowning." Again, an echo of a major modernist poem: "Death by Water," which is the title of the fourth section of T. S. Eliot's *The Waste Land*. And here, too, the weatherman does not see the redemptive possibility offered in the following section of Eliot's poem, "What the Thunder Said," where water is associated with the thunder's utterance of the Sanskrit word for "sympathize." But sympathy is not in the weatherman's job description; he cannot forecast "children's fate, / not anyone's children, not yours, not mine" (61).

These allusions, together with the weatherman's private tendency to anthropomorphize the "manic-depressive weather," reach beyond the weatherman's literal climate and point towards the value of poetry's imaginative force. In Auden's poem, water is a metaphor for "the healing fountain" of poetry; in Eliot's poem, water promises redemption. To the weatherman, water is simply water, and too much of it, at that. Reality without imagination is a world of animal, but not human, life: the arguing uncles in "Bull" for whom "[f]acts like barbed wire / fenced them in, old bulls snorting / at each other" (*After the Noise of Saigon* 29); uncomprehending goats shocked by an electric fence in "The Sting of the Visible" (*Rafting the Brazos* 29); the doomed buck with an arrow in his flank, "wondering what to do, / what to do." (*After the Noise of Saigon* 21). The contrast between animal and human underlies the remarkable poem, "Wishing for More than Thunder" in *Counting Survivors* (another allusion to *The Waste Land*). Here, the ignorance of grazing steers is bliss, for whom "the grass is manna" and "alfalfa paradise"; who "never wonder / if God's in his heaven." The speaker, however, sees "[m]irages hover like angels fanning the fields," and steers "hook their horns in invisible robes, / / shaking their heads to graze." Unlike Stevens's Snow Man, who sees nothing, to imagine angels in mirages is to see what is not there, together with the nothing that is. More importantly, it is to see the difference. The act of imagining these angels is necessary to human survival, or survival of the human, like the witching for water where a hawk has dived. But equally necessary is to hold that imagination in equilibrium with reality; hence the drawing back at the end of the poem, the balancing of these "angels" against the practical, physical need:

> Watching steers graze

> in a lake of shimmering light, seeing angels
> fanning themselves, we wonder if even they
> could make it rain, how many spin on a windmill,
> how many squeezed would make a decent cloud. (4)

III. "We must know something"

Before I venture one step further in my comparison of Walt Mc-Donald and Wallace Stevens, I must point out a crucial difference. McDonald partakes of a tradition of religious poetry in which the poetry directs itself toward, or is upheld by, a religious belief; Stevens belongs to an aesthetic tradition in which poetry is a kind of substitute for religious belief. As Stevens bluntly puts it, "Religion is dependent on faith. But aesthetics is independent of faith" (906). Yet Stevens does not see religion and aesthetics as opposed, or polarized, in their intentions: each has in common the need to claim an intrinsic value in human existence, a "vital self-assertion" (748). His position arises from a question common in Modernist thought and art: if one does not have a religious faith, to what, then, does one turn to satisfy that need for intrinsic value? For Stevens, it is art, imagination:

> The paramount relation between . . . modern man and modern art is simply this: that in an age in which disbelief is so profoundly prevalent or, if not disbelief, indifference to questions of belief, poetry and painting, and the arts in general, are, in their measure, a compensation for what has been lost. Men feel that the imagination is the next greatest power to faith: the reigning prince. (748)

To Stevens, then, imagination is an end: the "Supreme Fiction." It is self-fulfilling, ". . . since nothing is more certain than that the imagination is agreeable to the imagination," and by that self-fulfillment, it is the means "by which we project the idea of God into the idea of man" (736). To McDonald, imagination is necessary to explore, experience, the possibility of what is beyond imagination, namely, the Divine. If the end of imagination differs for these two poets, the process of imagination is nonetheless necessary to both, and the comparison can lead to a fuller appreciation of the place of poetry in our lives.

But, in Walt McDonald's work, as in the best of the religious poets, this imaginative quest for faith does not come easy. His poem "Nearing the End of the Century" (*After the Noise of Saigon*) situates the speaker in the same question of where to turn to satisfy that need for intrinsic value. Tellingly, it begins with an epigraph from Stevens's "Evening Without Angels":

Nearing the End of a Century

Let this be clear that we are men of sun
And men of day and never of pointed night
WALLACE STEVENS

Night of the comet, space without angels,
only our eyes to find whatever light
is there. The stars are rose-ember

over coals already gray. Orion
rises angry in the east.
Night after night he prowls the same

black forest of stars, tracking
the spoor of nothing he remembers.
In zipped twin sleeping bags

before Saigon, we claimed billions of stars
to wish on, perfectly foreign,
the absolute absence of meaning. (22)

The speaker looks at stars, but not heaven—there is no faith to provide any "light" other than the physical. The recognizable Orion is an empty myth; identifying the constellation is mere force of habit, and thus it appears angry and amnesiac. This view gives way to the memory of an even more "foreign" view of stars, viewed from the fields of Vietnam. The opening asserts the world of mere fact presented in Stevens's poem: "Air is air. / Its vacancy glitters round us everywhere" (111). Stevens then presents the response to this vacancy, the human urge to project the self upon it, and inhabit it with religious belief:

> Its sounds are not angelic syllables
> But our unfashioned spirits realized
> More sharply in more furious selves.
>
> . . . .
> Sad men made angels of the sun, and of
> The moon they made their own attendant ghosts,
> Which led them back to angels, after death. (111)

Similarly, McDonald's poem turns to this same urge to project the self into reality, that reality may, in turn, reflect back a religious meaning:

> We counted myths made up by others
> like us, needing to believe in something,
> projecting filaments like spiders
>
> spinning tales to turn stark fear
> to faith. Somehow we survived that war
> and raised our share of children.
>
> Nights, you turn for me to hold you,
> although I have no answers. (*After the Noise of Saigon* 22–3)

As yet, there is no faith. Stevens, too, in the lines which became the epigraph to McDonald's poem, asserts that we are bound to the world of fact, the pressure of reality. But not irredeemably so. For the imaginative projection, if released from the quest for absolute faith and turned to its own self-assertion—nothing, after all, being more agreeable to the imagination than the imagination—can shape reality to the human need for validation: *"Yet,"* he writes (my emphasis), "the wind / Encircling us, speaks always with our speech." Stevens's poem concludes with praise of night as the time when, the harsh light of day being muted, the imagination is most responsive:

> Bare night is best. . . .
> . . . .
> Where the voice that is in us makes a true response,
> Where the voice that is great within us rises up,
> As we stand gazing at the rounded moon. (112)

In the final movement of McDonald's poem, the speaker does not find this "true response"; rather, having "no answers," he is left with a further questioning:

> Our best minds query a comet we'll
>
> never see again for clues. Rockets probe

the one unanswered question, millions
of light years back toward the beginning,

before myth. We say whatever is,
we'll accept. But we must know,
we must know something. (23)

Corollary to the unanswered question—How did the universe
begin?—is the question of how we fit into this universe. Myth has attempted answers and failed; now, the most advanced science, "our
best minds," takes its turn. Despite the unlikelihood of a satisfactory
answer, the speaker insists, "we must know something." That "must"
can be read two ways: that we need to know something, or that we
already know something. The former reading affirms the need for
imaginative participation in the world that both Stevens and
McDonald share; the latter reading, however, marks a difference between them. For in Stevens's view, what we know of human validation is what we make, and the making must be constant; one of the
criteria of the Supreme Fiction is that "It Must Change" (336). To Mc-
Donald, it would imply something already known, pre-existing,
"before myth": the ground of religious belief.

IV. "I can hear stars burning"

To the longing for knowledge in "Nearing the End of a Century," I
would contrast another poem, "Nights in the San Juan" from *Rafting
the Brazos,* in which knowledge is surprisingly commensurate with
desire:

Bed and chairs, table and stove,
home for a week in the mountains.
Because the logs are stacked

we love them, two rooms
that would be a shanty
on the plains. Cold water faucet

that drips all night.
Bare ceiling, two beams split.
A board floor easy to sweep clean

through the cracks.
Curtains too short, too thin
to block out the moon.

Nothing is level, flush.
You sleep against me
on the uphill side,

the wood fire cold by midnight.
The forest so still, so dark
I can hear stars burning. (13)

As in the last movement of "Nearing the End of a Century," the husband and wife are together at night. Conditions are hardly luxurious,
and the details of it are presented with a spareness and precision worthy of a T'ang poet. The sense of acceptance, indeed embrace, of the
Spartan conditions, together with the love between the husband and
wife, builds a contentment which overflows ordinary, sensory apprehension—a fullness which bursts into a felt connection to the stars.

In "Nearing the End of a Century," stars are "the absolute absence
of meaning"; but here, the stars sidestep the very question of meaning altogether and emerge in full presence: he hears, not his own
voice as in Stevens's "Evening Without Angels," but the stars. The
connection to stars in the cabin in the San Juan mountains is neither
a pathetic fallacy nor the Modernist irony of Stevens, ever self-
conscious of his invention of a human bearing to reality. Stevens,
too, admits of such moments, "times of inherent excellence," which
are "not balances / That we achieve but balances that happen"—
moments he calls, in another section of "Notes Toward a Supreme
Fiction," "accessible bliss" (334, 341–2). Still, these moments are in-
terludes in Stevens's larger quest toward that supreme fiction—"the
fiction that results from feeling," which is, ultimately, "a place dependent on ourselves" (351, 346). McDonald's "I can hear stars burning" opens up the possibility of a vital connection between the
human mind and the world in which it moves. In short, the connection stems from without, not within.

This connection, or the need for it, underlies the emotional closure
of the later, dazzling poem, "For God in My Sorrows": "This, this is
what I need, without lights or cities / man-made and dying, somehow to know I'm known" (*Blessings the Body Gave* 78). This poem—
another meditation on lights, from tracer bullets to stars—revises
the statement "We must know something" that concludes "Nearing
the End of a Century." The desire is for an apprehension that, like the
imagination, is freed from the confines of physical reality; but unlike
the imagination, is something more than the product of the human
mind—indeed something beyond both reality and imagination. The
poem "Grace and the Blood of Goats" states this desire—"We need
what prairie eyes don't hope for, / that isn't ours to feed": that is,
something that satisfies a hope beyond the speaker's own conception of hope, a nourishment that, unlike the food he gives to goats at
home, is not in the realm of the human to give. The poem then names
the answer to that need as "grace": "We wait for grace // in a world

deserted, where the blood of goats can't save us" (*Counting Survivors* 63). This "blood of goats" refers not only to his own goats, but hints at the Dionysian rituals involving the sacrifice of a goat, out of which Greek tragedy ("goat-song") is conjectured to have begun. Beyond human enterprise (here represented as goat-farming), beyond myth, beyond art, grace is a kind of divine imagination: a sense imparted from outside ourselves that things are more and better than the physical reality.

The last line of "Nights in the San Juan" suggests a moment of such grace, and points the way to certain poems where—increasingly it seems in McDonald's later books—the realm of imagination and reality are, in Stevens's phrase, "in precise equilibrium" (67). There are, as the title poem of one book says, "Blessings the Body Gave." The perfection includes contingency: "Blessings the Body Gave" is a recapitulation of "Nights in the San Juan" with the husband and wife spending time in a mountain cabin, where the car gets stuck in the mud, where the stay is bounded by time—"our last hours alone in the mountains" (98). And yet they are figures of Adam and Eve, where forest sounds are "like two of everything approaching to be named," as if the physical world itself were acknowledging, and presenting itself to, the imagination.

V. "What marvels she could sing about"

These moments of grace depend nonetheless upon the imagination's readiness to receive and apprehend them. It is an alertness and openness of mind akin to the quality of sympathy, which opens us to the feelings of other persons; accordingly, the fulfillment of imaginative possibility means opening up to others as well as to one's own mind. In McDonald's recent book, *All Occasions,* we are given an extraordinary example of such fulfillment:

Diamonds in the Carnegie Museum

Our guide was blind and kind, chatting about diamonds
we half circled like a wagon train in a box canyon,
no way out but united for the night,
bound for Montana. She was thirty-five or forty,
without a ring. Her dazzling eyes rolled back

and blinked. She was singing, prattling
about diamond mines and dreams, but singing,
her voice charming us to look. She loved those halls
she never saw, loved all of us she had touched
in the lobby, touched each one only once

but knew us, or made us believe she did.
I wondered what marvels she could sing about
or show. She turned and tapped her way
with a penlight-thin retractable pole,
turned to the bulletproof transparent glass

and sighed. She was a bride among diamonds
and we mere cousins in from the cold, lucky to share
what she held at arm's length every day,
too precious to wear, crushed coal and fire
in the heart of earth too radiant to see. (61)

The museum guide is a figure for all of us: with the contingency of
blindness, she loves what she cannot see. Imagination allows her to
see things beyond the physical—her eyes, blind, are "dazzling"; she
holds "marvels." Her description of the diamonds and their history
merges into "singing," and like the poet, she charms us to look at the
world, and to see more than the world. The parable of this poem is
like an inversion of Plato's parable of the cave in Book VII of *The Re-
public*. There, the image of the soul brought to knowledge is that of
a prisoner dragged from a cave to the outer sunlight. Here, the
speaker is led by a "blind and kind" guide from the resplendent light
of showcased diamonds, to an underground place "in the heart of
earth" which, surprisingly, is not too dark, but "too radiant to see."
What does she have to carry forth this journey, but love and imagination? The splendor of imagination far exceeds the tenuousness of our
knowledge in the material world, that "penlight-thin retractable
pole" that leads her to "bulletproof transparent glass." But that
imagined splendor is also real, even as the unseen realm of the Ideal
was, for Plato, reality.

"What we see in the mind is as real to us as what we see by the
eye," claims Stevens, in a line from a notebook that could as well be
an epigraph to "Diamonds in the Carnegie Museum"—if the poem
needed one (903). For the point that Stevens wishes to arrive at is, ultimately, a blending of the two terms, reality and imagination. Or
put another way, that the imagination, as expressed in poetry, constitutes a part of reality:

> It comes to this, that poetry is a part of the structure of reality. If
> this has been demonstrated, it pretty much amounts to saying
> that the structure of poetry and the structure of reality are one
> or, in effect, that poetry and reality are one, or should be (692).

The basis of this claim is the notion that structural resemblances,
which abound in nature, are reiterated in the mind's capacity to perceive resemblances, and to create further resemblances not bound to
the stricture of physical reality—that is, metaphors. Simply defined,

imagination and reality can be seen as opposites; but the action of the mind upon reality, the reality of the mind's actions, inhabits a liminal space where imagination and reality blur, converge. This space is one into which rational, linear discourse falls and disappears, as if into a black hole; but one that poetry—indirect, "slant" as Dickinson would say, metaphorical, rhythmical—inhabits and enjoys. A space, then, where mesquite trees are flamingoes.

While Walt McDonald is best known for his poems of the West Texas landscape, the work of imagination performed in his poems extends to the broadest human concerns, expressed by Stevens's terms of imagination and reality, terms that Stevens would distinguish only in order to demonstrate how they merge. After defining the mind as "the imagination pressing back against the pressure of reality," Stevens claims that "the expression of it, the sound of its words, helps us to live our lives" (665). But how does poetry help us to live our lives? In a contemporary climate that includes belief and skepticism, there are limits to how much a poem can teach to its readers, in terms of what one might believe, what one might accept. Recent critical attacks on the notion of the "author" aside, there are few poets writing today who would consider themselves to be authorities, fewer still who would admit to it if they did. What poets present is a particular observation, a particular expression, and from that observation and expression we take what we will. Still, there is one thing that poems teach us—across the synchronic spectrum of contemporary styles and voices, across the diachronic chain of literary history—and that is responsiveness. The poem stages a poet's response to circumstance, and though interpretations may differ, the poem presents, to turn Auden's phrase, a way of responding; furthermore, the poem bears with it the notion that an acuity of responsiveness is itself meaningful. And whether written by the most ardent formalist or swashbuckling experimentalist, the poem teaches responsiveness to language, the medium in which, more than any other, we express both self and circumstance. For myself in the Llano Estacado, my experience tells me, and the guidebooks and Audubon Society checklists confirm, that there are no flamingoes here. As a reader, a writer, a person, my reading of Walt McDonald's poems show me ways that, nonetheless, I might look.

How to Spin Rightly: Walt McDonald's Vision of the Artist

Janice Whittington

Walt McDonald often peoples his poems with men who are struggling to survive in a dangerous world. Flying and war poems dominate *Caliban in Blue*, his first volume of poetry, but as his work progresses, other poems appear—poems about the land, whether the mountains of Colorado or the high plains of West Texas. Using landscape, its creatures, its people, McDonald creates a place where life is a challenge for both human and creature. Always there exists the element of risk in McDonald's poetry, risk involving difficulties faced in the world, whether on the land or in the air. Yet in his poems the struggle of snake, farmer, or pilot ultimately becomes the act that fills life with a stark joy. And as he writes about flyers, farmers, even artists, McDonald also explores a person's need to create—to learn a craft and master it—and by doing so, he ultimately writes about his own craft: writing.

"Caliban on Spinning," the first poem in McDonald's first collection, becomes a foundation for all of his work, opening various themes and motifs, and as a result becomes a poem that can be read as a metaphor for writing. The poem centers on Caliban as he explains how to spin a plane, but more significantly, the instructions involve how to spin "an airplane right." To spin wrongly would mean death, but ironically, danger is everywhere, for even to spin right "is like a little death." Caliban's instructions are precise, leaving out no part of the maneuver. In fact, like the numerous dials and gauges a pilot faces in the cockpit of a plane, the poem is packed with specific, physical actions, and the reader—who takes on the role of the novice pilot—must complete these actions. The physical body becomes drawn completely into an experience that involves all senses, immersing the reader in a sense of physicality, even sexuality, when the simile suggests the engine "shudders / like a lover bound," and

> Thrust with your right leg faster,
> ram home and hold the rudder there.
> Arch the curved stick hard as you must
> to keep it on the stops.

The images duplicate the energy of the flight maneuver, but the poem's focus is not merely on the physical experience (sex). Caliban's insistent voice focuses not simply on spinning but on spinning "right" and warns that "You will wonder, / will it come apart? Do not let go." This question, and the opening comparison where spinning "is like a little death," is an image charged with danger. The maneuver is not easy, nor is it carefree. But in this maneuver, danger is counterbalanced by Caliban's insistence on following instructions that work, and through that adherence to instruction, the pilot can keep a sense of balance. Caliban explains that

> you must master it to spin well.
> Forcing control, follow the oscillations
> down through the first swing,
> the vast earth spinning before you
> like a dream. (3–4)

Control becomes the salvation that keeps the pilot balanced in the swirling confusion of a maneuver that suspends him between heaven and earth. And preparation for the spin is necessary:

> If you entered well-timed at the top
> with long enough to fall,
> you can lead your plane
> deeper and ease out. . . .

Even with success, there is an underlying danger, and the pilot must stay alert: "Fine trim everything again / Check all gauges, notice the wings / smooth, spanning the horizon." The pilot recognizes that danger is inherent in the act of flying; however, control and knowledge, finesse and work, lead to that ultimate result which is a joy in "the feel of steady flight, / after the spin." As Caliban presents lessons on how to spin a plane, the flying maneuver becomes a metaphor for living one's life. The pilot must wield a power, an assurance developed from knowledge: "(you should know the plane is steady

—/ a few preliminary stalls would tell.)" (4). Instructions on flying broaden to instructions on how to live one's life, how to face any challenge.

Caliban's advice can extend to the craft of writing poetry as well. Flying involves danger, as does living, as does writing poetry. McDonald's poem prepares, instructs, and challenges, but not merely in the single context of a flying maneuver, nor in the extension to how to live one's life. This poem forms a primer for writing poetry as his patterns for style emerge in the language, line breaks, rhythms, and internal sounds.

In an interview in *Vistas,* McDonald speaks of the craft of writing poems and gives this advice to his students: "In poetry, when you write details, you're taking a risk. Poetry is implosive. The emotions are shared by language; make your language more muscular" (28). As Caliban instructs, step by step, McDonald blends content and form with strong verbs that give an immediacy and significance to the act: "raise," "shudders," "thrust," "ram," "arch," "ride." He chooses a technical language of rudders and ailerons, making the maneuver believable to the reader. Also, with the use of the second person, we the readers become the novice pilot listening to Caliban, and we are caught up in the experience. Caliban goes through the motions and instructions, and the imperative voice enriches with verbs of command, yet McDonald describes the maneuver with a minimum of adjectives. Instead, McDonald gives the poem specific nouns, minimal modifiers, and strong similes. The first simile starts the poem—"Spinning an airplane right / is like a little death"—while stanza two begins with another as the "engine shudders / like a lover bound." Stanza three begins, "The nose will drop off / like the earth falling beneath you into space," and a fourth simile occurs in lines 29–30 with "the vast earth spinning before you / like a dream." These last two similes connect the act of flying to earth, a human's natural element, and this connection meshes two major images recurring in McDonald's poetry—the land and flight.

In this poem, line breaks often take risks, echoing the danger in the content. In line 21, McDonald writes that "the plane will shudder," and with the line break, he holds the fearful sense of "shudder" just that extra instant before the next line continues in the word "desperately." Here also the use of sound shows in the subtleties of McDonald's verse. The haunting sounds of "shudder" echo in "desperately," as the consonance continues over the line break. Internal rhyme fills the poem in examples like "ram home and hold the rudder there" and "hold rigid, ready." At the end of the poem, sound also echoes sense as Caliban continues with his instructions:

> Check all gauges, notice the wings
> smooth, spanning the horizon.
> Enjoy the feel of steady flight
> after the spin. (4)

Just as the pilot completes the spin, the poet eases the language out of the emotional frenzy and powerful details of earlier images and into sibilant sounds in the last lines, simulating the smoothness of flight. With "Caliban on Spinning," McDonald begins his first collection with a poem that has multiple levels, both thematically and stylistically, and creates an early commentary on the art of writing.

"Mesas I Never Took the Time to Climb" from *Counting Survivors* (a collection published in 1995, almost twenty years after *Caliban in Blue*) is almost a companion poem to "Caliban on Spinning," though structurally they seem an incongruous pair. "Mesas," far shorter—almost half the length of "Caliban"—is arranged in uniform stanzas of five lines each instead of the varied, longer stanzas of "Caliban." "Mesas" is a poem grounded in the land; "Caliban" is about flying. Yet the mature persona of "Mesas" rides the saddle much like the pilot rides the cockpit of "Caliban." In "Mesas," although the poem is not about actual flight, the persona identifies with the dream of flying, wondering about the "buzzard in the field / too weak to fly away." He asks, "Will it miss / the soaring, the glide toward horizons?" as if a pilot reflects on his own cessation of flight. But flight exists everywhere around him—in the buzzards "above us / wheeling a slow blessing on flesh" and in the "[h]awks [that] see no farther / than I could see from a mesa." Now, he imagines that if he climbs the mesa, "I'll look at these flat fields from far above, / the same parched sand and cactus after sundown, / night shining not with diamonds, but with real stars" (79). With these images, an expanded sense of flight pervades the poem.

Again, flight can be a metaphor for the craft of writing. Stylistically, the language of this poem shows the evolution of McDonald's craft. Again the poet fills his lines with strong verbs like "I nudge this sweating gelding," "Old leather creaks," "Coyotes prowl at night," and "I shove old boots through stirrups," all of which show vitality, action, and muscularity even in the ordinary struggles of the persona as he lives his life on the land, not in the sky. As always, McDonald's vivid yet ordinary verbs enrich the experience. Additionally, the crisp images shine through specific yet simple nouns: "gelding," "leather," "mesquite," "rattler," "hawks." Creating sensory details of the poem, the poet brings the reader to the place, personalizing the intimacy, allowing the reader into the experience along with the persona. In "Mesas," McDonald's choice of figurative language differs from "Caliban." The metaphors in "Mesas" show the faith of the poet in his own images as they "live in a bowl of sand," and "crops are rattlers and starry skies / we pretend are diamonds" (79).

The frenzied insistence and the imperative language of "Caliban on Spinning" changes to a sense of ease in "Mesas I Never Took the Time To Climb," incorporating smooth language and rhythms to reflect experience, patience, acceptance. It eases into a language trimmed to the essential images. Internal rhymes build a tapestry of sounds, slowing the reader in lines like "Old leather creaks and I lean between mesquites / and cactus." Another example demonstrates how McDonald manipulates sounds as well as line breaks for his purposes as he describes the weakened buzzard:

> Panting, it hobbled
>
> as if on stilts, others above us
> wheeling a slow blessing on the flesh. Will it miss
> the soaring, the glide toward wide horizons? (79)

With "hobbled," McDonald emphasizes the awkwardness of the buzzard, and the stanza break sustains that awkwardness for an instant until "as if on stilts." Then the poem changes as sounds build and swirl and the long "I" sounds of that last line suggest the smoothness of gliding.

In the last lines of the poem, McDonald exemplifies mastery of his craft, incorporating assonance and alliteration to create internal rhymes:

> I'll dismount
> and slap the sorrel to send him back to the corral.
> I'll look at these flat fields from far above,
> the same parched sand and cactus after sundown,
> night shining not with diamonds but with real stars. (79)

The persona is accepting, even visionary, and the language reflects his contentment.

We can also see the persona as a spokesman for the poet who knows his craft, who leans between the thorny mesquite and cactus. With experience, his control is second nature, and he is "content in a saddle, that perfect slap of leather chaps." The new mesa he as poet will climb "is there / if I want it" (79). In this view, he recognizes and appreciates the "real stars" he has.

From these two poems, we can move to others that take craft or art as their topic. In "A Brief History of Glass" from *Anything Anything*, McDonald traces the history of glass making, and the first stanza begins with "Egyptians fired the first glass." Their talent is amazing, as is the demand for their works, and

> [f]or Cleopatra they could make mirrors
> smooth as the Nile, thread
> viscous spools of glass delicate
> as the hair of Isis, blow
> silica replicas of rams' horns
> and coil tiny asps with fangs of glass.

As he presents the glassmakers, McDonald emphasizes their talent and the work they do; working with a dangerous element, they "fire" the glass, the hot, risky substance that is powerful yet delicate. As the poem unfolds, McDonald emulates the artistry of the glass blowers in diction and line breaks. With words like "smooth" and "viscous spools," he creates the visual and tactile images as well as sibilant internal rhymes of the poem; again in "silica replicas of rams' horns," the sensuous sounds of the language reflect what the artist creates. McDonald's line breaks become as delicate as the glass they describe, teetering on the edge of fragility, making a finely crafted pause that allows the reader to catch a breath, as if saving glass from breaking: "glass / delicate as the hair of Isis." Several lines later, he creates an opposite effect, as Mary "bought, broke / one of these flasks for the feet of Jesus" (38). Here the line break falls on the heavy word "broke," echoing the action itself. With such, McDonald creates his own art while discussing art.

Glass is associated with danger and power throughout the poem, and McDonald's language changes, becoming less fragile in stanza two as he describes the punishment for the artists who gave "spun secrets of Venetian glass / death." The break stands between the delicacy of the glass and the brutality of the punishment, holding the reader briefly in the world between. The last stanza brings the reader to the present, and the allusions become more strident. Smooth glass swans reflects a loss with "their vacant eyes dimpled." The "Post-Dresden dolls" allude to World War II, and the dolls' "rose skin / seared with fire, line other shelves." Throughout the poem, the purity of art has been manipulated, and the result here and now is horror, and McDonald's diction mirrors that horror in the ironically quiet language of the poem. These dolls are like the dead: "bodies in a morgue," and the image continues this emphasis with "their glass eyes / open, almost like mirrors." McDonald has tied the beginning of the history of glass to the present, starting with scenes of beauty connected with destruction: the flask is broken to cleanse "the feet of Jesus," the future already set; the glass is smooth as a mirror for

Cleopatra, as are the small figures of "tiny asps with fangs of glass";
Venetian glassblowers are imprisoned for their talent; World War II
and Dresden connect with dolls and their glass eyes; finally, we read
of the "glass luster / on the shoes of serious young men / down deep
in the missile silos of Kansas" (38). Thus McDonald's poem steps beyond being only about glassmaking to reflecting McDonald's style
in all of his writing: strong, vivid images, powerful yet simple language, rhythms that reflect and create mood, and power in closure.

In "Picasso and the Art of Angels" from *Where Skies Are Not
Cloudy*, McDonald puts the speaker of the poem into the mind of Picasso. Again, McDonald's subject is art and the artist, yet as he steps
into the situation, he steps into the mind of not just Picasso but anyone who is creating. In stanza one, Picasso "dreamed he saw an angel" on the day he died. Instead of merely wondering at the vision,
Picasso "wept he could never paint her, / marvelously complex." Picasso forever reaches to a new work of art, forever seeks to paint perfection. True to his passion, the artist continues to be an artist, and
McDonald approaches this artist's mindset with vivid images:

> skin tones perfect,
> her flesh angelically erotic,
> nothing at all like humans,
> the skewed, cubistic angles
> of the actual.

In these lines McDonald juxtaposes the concept of perception and reality and yet does so in reverse. Picasso sees reality as "skewed,
cubistic" and his vision as "angelically erotic." The description contrasts what the readers know of Picasso's method—showing the actual in terms of the cubistic. Thus, McDonald reverses the actual
with the sensual. In the poem, Picasso's vision of the woman who
"was only / his morning nurse, a local woman / working for pay" is
beyond reality, as is his art, and even as he is dying, the artist
"reached for his brushes." The poem emphasizes the artist and his
passion to put his vision down on paper or canvas, regardless of
what others see as truth, and McDonald's images transpose what is
considered the interpretation of appearance versus reality. Similarly, the title of the poem both suggests the artist's capabilities and
plays a bit with language. This is the art beyond the ordinary; this is
the art of the extraordinary talent, the "art of angels," but in the language and the poem, it is also the art of angles (36).

"In the Rare Acquisitions Room" from *Rafting the Brazos* also celebrates art and the artist. The speaker sees the "fourteenth-century
oil-on-board" and relates it to what he knows, what he is familiar
with, from "bluebonnets" to "Texas mesquite." Overwhelmed, he

feels that "[t]he face of Mary is so real / if I could reach through the glass / I could shake the small medieval hand." The reader sees the connection between the poet—the artist of words—and the artist of the painting. The images the speaker appreciates in the picture show in the poet's language, and the "meticulous" hand of the artist becomes the careful image of the poet:

> the brow of Joseph behind her
> knotted over this puzzle
>
> of truth, his vestments
> more like a Venice merchant's
> than a carpenter's,
> the details of his frown
> preserved forever like a bone. (46)

The stanza break itself is meticulously wrought, allowing the reader a moment to wonder, to "puzzle," and learn what the puzzle is—the mystery of the Virgin birth—then to realize McDonald's poem takes the view from Joseph's perspective. The final simile closes the poem in a haunting image of color, of art's capturing a moment forever in time.

Art, like life, like poetry, is not always about beauty, for neither the images nor the language is always attractive. In "Mirror Image" from *Working Against Time*, McDonald's diction becomes harsh and crackling, echoing the struggles and perversity the artist has tried to capture in his work as this poem looks at "Michelangelo's / unfinished head / of a lost soul." The poem is startling because of its short, choppy lines that are almost unfinished feeling in themselves. The verbs incorporate and mirror the image they present, as

> the forehead bunches tight
> like bat wings,
> the nose jerks back
> into a snout,
> the eyeballs bulge.

McDonald is a poet painting with rhythms, sounds, and images, and in doing so, reflects the vision of Michelangelo, artist to artist. Finally, the recognition of the lost soul's being "all things we ignore"—"the astonished stare / of the hopeless, / the face of the damned"—shows an awareness by artist and by poet of the other side of the mirror, the dark side of humanity which sets itself up as a challenge to paint, to sculpt, to write about (13).

A different approach to art and the artist appears in "Rembrandt and the Art of Mercy" from *Counting Survivors*. Here, McDonald approaches the artist by taking first the assumptions of "they say" and "they claim." Then the poem shifts at the end of stanza two as the last line reverses, seeing the artist in a new way: "No, what he loved and pitied most was flesh // that's caught but never saved by canvas." The speaker acknowledges the artist's need to save something unsaveable, to face a challenge that cannot be overcome: "If only he could capture those / in ocher, rub her troubled eyes so they could see" (14). Is the artist, in fact, paralleling the poet? Is the poet also attempting with each poem to capture something on paper that is perhaps uncaptureable?

Through these poems, McDonald has written about the craft of famous artists, but many of his poems approach the concept of the artist in a closer, more intimate situation. Artists are not merely those ancients whose works hang in galleries, but artists are among us. In several poems, the speaker's wife is an artist. In "His Side of It" from *Rafting the Brazos,* the poem explores the artist's need to create and the danger involved in such a need. As the woman gathers items for her art, "she'd get out, / climb down another canyon, risking her neck / along the edge." McDonald actually uses the word "risk" as he puts the wife on the edge of a canyon, collecting. "Finally, she'd stagger back, / arms filled with lava, / petrified stumps, anything hard." The obvious sexual imagery shows in the impatient young husband, too tired of this stopping along the way and yet filled with love and desire for his wife. As he watches her return, he is "beer sorry and horny," but the attraction is more than sexual; there is an acknowledgment of more than bodies. He joins her as she goes for another load: "off we'd go down the canyon / for fossils or shells, arrowhead / whatever she couldn't get enough of alone." This woman is creating by gathering fossils or rocks, but she adds another kind of artistry because their togetherness is itself a creation:

> before the long climb out
> we'd meet on a bed of flint chips,
> ignoring snakes and indifferent trucks
> somewhere beyond a blur of thistles,
> her skin hammered with sand like gold leaf. (63)

Although danger surrounds them—flint chips, snakes, trucks, thistles—she has seen the beauty of the world around her, has drawn him into this world, and he has become one who sees that she herself is the work of art, with "her skin hammered with sand like gold leaf."

In "Witching on Canvas" from *Counting Survivors,* again the speaker's wife is the artist, the visionary who discovers—in the harsh realities of West Texas—a beauty that reveals itself as she "witches mesquite and cactus / from hardpan caliche white." The speaker recognizes that she puts her art aside for duty to family: "I've watched oil borders dry / while she draws babies' bath." (Here, word choice deliciously makes her one who "draws" in a different way.) The speaker even recognizes "she goes without sleep // without a brush in her hand for weeks." She is still an artist, he realizes, needing to paint and drawn to her canvas. In her art she brings life as she "draws windmills and streams / and makes them flow" (43), but her art takes on a wider scope. Beyond the limits of the canvas, she creates; beyond the duties of her home, she creates, facing whatever struggles and challenges arise.

In "Memento Mori" from *Witching on Hardscrabble,* again the artist is the speaker's wife, and the speaker notes, "I've seen her pose a skull / on a barrel cactus she has centered / in sand like caliche." Taking the elements which surround her, the artist nurtures growth in the middle of seeming death:

> She tilts the white bone, searching
> for shadows with eyes in the holes,
> the wide horns the only signs
> about the skull suggesting cow.

The artist is surrounded with images of danger, of death: bone, shadows, horns, skull; again the artist is using these elements, not backing away from the risks. Just as

> she brings out of canvas a desert
> driving down trails she invents
> thousands of cattle she raises
> from dust, hiding their dry, durable
> muscles under nothing but paint.

The artist becomes a bringer of life, and she creates from the same palette of colors and objects McDonald's own poetry covers, these elements from the West Texas land. On a "slab / of an oak tree" she has

> brushed out of nothing
> a thorn-barreled cactus
> wearing a skull, painted in clouds
> and ground we could stand on. (12)

She has made more than what was before, creating not only on the oak slab but also in her life, anchoring both her art and life in truth, this "ground we could stand on."

McDonald approaches again the motif of the artist as inventor in "Getting It Done" from *The Flying Dutchman*. The persona's wife is almost a magicmaker as the speaker

> watched amazed the same burnt sienna
> land we live on begin to glow
> under the brush, palette of ocher sand,
> glinting light she invents from nothing
>
> but tubes and bristles.

In this example, McDonald's line breaks become the focus; the brief extended "nothing" allows the reader to pause. The wife does more than paint. Extending her art, "she gathers and blesses / turquoise, obsidian, anything to bring color / to copper, making a garden of stone and cactus." Like the artist of the poem, McDonald breaks the line for emphasis. Once again, the persona sees her artistry as moving beyond the canvas or the garden: "Even me, she polishes nightly with roughest / of kisses, giving up on nothing / she's started." The line break creates a pause after "nothing," adding to the significance of the following line, and again the speaker emphasizes the craft, the skill, and the patience of the artist as she takes

> years and three children
> to paint over and over this scene in the desert
>
> where we live, only brown earth and sky
> and in between, all that matters. (69)

The artist makes beauty in what surrounds her; so does McDonald in his poetry, tracing the beauty of the skull, of the cactus. The title "Getting It Done" expands to mean more than the drudgery of work; it becomes the phrase that encompasses the approach to one's craft, and the poem reveals a delight in the process.

The persona also discusses the artwork of his wife in "The Waltz We Were Born For" from *Blessings the Body Gave*. In this poem, her craft appears in the form of making wind chimes from simple objects. She takes "bits of steel / from engines I tear down," and "ties copper / to turquoise from deserts." Out of the harsh land, the artist has found elements of creation, and her creations echo in her family: "She strings them all / like laces of babies' shoes." From these simple items, from these simple family connections, the wife's wind chimes become "hosannas dangling on strings." The poem is a celebration of the speaker's wife as artist and her ability to take the ordinary in her art and raise it close to heaven, a parallel artistry of "dazzling devotion" (109). McDonald celebrates the artist and his or her craft, whatever it may be, celebrating the elements, the difficulties, and the ultimate struggles that result in a life lived right.

In his latest collection *All Occasions,* McDonald follows the same pattern, presenting the artist in the shape of the speaker's wife in a poem entitled "In the Alchemist's Household." Craft of the wife takes on wider dimensions as McDonald plies his language into creation metaphors. The poem begins with the artist in her studio and her interaction with her children when she "waves our big-eyed children / back from the kiln." The separation between art and life is non-existent as is the separation between artist/mother. Again the persona recognizes the woman's skill in using elements of the land where she lives, having watched "her spin exquisite vases / from clay, jar of the same sienna sand / we live on." The ability to create goes further, and the earth metaphor takes on a larger significance:

> she turned
> mere kisses into screams
> and tiny fists, squinty infants
> who turned her breast milk
>
> into teeth and giggles, and fists
> that lifted puppies up and snuggled.

The artist creates from sand, but she goes beyond, becoming artist personified, creating life, which, in turn, creates more life. Everywhere around the persona, he sees transformation from the wife's hands; her art makes life and even eases death as "she turns long nights to dawn / by bedsides of the dying" (109).

Only one poem from McDonald's collections approaches straightforwardly, at least in its title, the act of writing. "Plains and the Art of Writing" from *All That Matters* prepares readers for an *ars poetica.* Instead, McDonald returns to both the land and flying for his poem, and the reader is left to make the connections:

> A prairie lays its mystery face up
> on the plains, nowhere to hide
> from black, spiraling mobiles
> in the sky, the sun a bully
> breeding hawks and buzzards,
> no shade worth claiming,
> at night the moon, all-seeing eye
> blessing barn owls floating
> soft feathered over the earth,
> without a sound.

McDonald creates a blend of land and flight, and danger is everywhere. The harshness of stanza one ends with "I love this cactus land," and in the second stanza, the language softens, calling "the moon a headstone," suggesting that beauty exists for one who looks for it. Like the rattlesnakes of the poem, the poet feels "long muscles flowing / over the old, familiar sand," language metaphorical enough to suggest his approach to writing. His landscape is like an artist's blank canvas; the tools of his art are words, and he returns to "old, familiar sand" to discover new images and ideas (125).

V. Religious Imagery, Thought, and Implications

"Dark Pearls": An Introduction to Walt McDonald's Poetic Journey of Faith

Darryl Tippens

> The kingdom of heaven is like unto a merchant man, seeking goodly pearls: Who, when he had found one pearl of great price, went and sold all that he had, and bought it.
> —Matthew 13:45–46

> 'Tis therefore happy that we have two Worlds to hold on. To enjoy true happiness we must travel into a very far Countrey, and even out of our selves; for the Pearl we seek for is not to be found in the *Indian,* but in the *Empyrean* Ocean.
> —Sir Thomas Browne, *Christian Morals*

> The one dove bleeding
> with eyes like a kitten,
> the throat rapidly beating,
> the dark pearls.
> —Walt McDonald, "On Taking a Grandson Hunting"
> (*Counting Survivors* 58)

As early as his first volume of verse, *Caliban in Blue,* published in 1976, Walt McDonald names the central dilemma and preoccupation of his life. On the one hand human beings are creatures of earth, bone, and ash. To say that we are "Caliban" is to say that we are "Adam" (Hebrew *adamah*), that is, clay, soil, matter:

> Pilots always knew
> man is matter,

felt the secret
ooze past our hips
each take off. (5)

Our muddy connection to Adam and Caliban is seldom absent from the poet's thinking. In *Burning the Fence,* published in 1981, the narrator recalls a troubled flight, when the commercial aircraft suddenly drops hundreds of feet, terrorizing the passengers. The poem concludes:

The earth, we confess throughout our
shaken bodies, is still our home,
a globe of graveyards and crashed planes.
When we descend, the clouds thin out
and there it sprawls,
the rock on which we live
and where we all return. ("Going Home" 47)

However, humans are anything but satisfied with "this muddy vesture of decay," as Shakespeare called it. Mortals feel the upward pull. McDonald, an Air Force fighter pilot from 1957 to 1971 and formerly an instructor at the U.S. Air Force Academy, knows the lure of the ethereal. With Gerard Manley Hopkins, McDonald also celebrates "Man's mounting spirit," as it tries the limits of mortality; though "scanted in a dull cage," McDonald's protagonists are destined to soar.[1] They are brutes with intimations of immortality. Though they may be Calibans, "things of darkness," they are Calibans "in blue." Such Calibans, with hearts of Icarus, transcend earthly limits:

No clear decision
makes us fly—(wings
do not sustain us,
Icarus our patron saint)— (*Caliban in Blue* 5)

In the more than 1900 poems produced by McDonald in the last twenty-five years, one finds a panorama of human suffering and joyous potentiality founded upon the fundamental conviction that we are citizens of two countries, one earthly and one empyrean. As he writes about the disciplined routines of life in West Texas, as he punctures the level plain of existence with sharp memories of Vietnam horrors and heroics that a man can scarcely express, he finds that our lives are rounded by a great Christian paradox: we are born of the soil but homesick for a heavenly country. It is crucially important, when reading McDonald, to recognize that the poet feels complete freedom to write *individual* poems that savor almost exclusively our earthly boundedness (with little hint of transcendence), while others make clear our celestial destination. Still others bring the two domains, the earthly and the eternal, into close conversation. When the poet observes this planet closely, in deep stillness, in "the peace of dark" (*Counting Survivors* 77), the sacramental dimensions of human beings interacting with sky and land become evident.

McDonald shares the faith of the great seventeenth-century physician, Sir Thomas Browne, who wrote that human beings are amphibians "whose nature is disposed to live not only like other creatures in divers elements, but in divided and distinguished worlds" (103). It seems fair to say that McDonald also views human beings dualistically—creatures of earth and sky, Adam and angel, Caliban and Icarus, body and soul—destined to travel between "divided and distinguished worlds." In George Steiner's terms, McDonald's characters "are monads haunted by communion" (140). Constantly defying the gravity of their mortality, they seek something higher. They succeed; they fail; but in flight, however brief, they discover that they are more than dust.

Yet McDonald is reluctant to jump quickly to themes of heavenly glory. One must savor the world in which we have been planted. The poet, therefore, expresses a deep love for the elemental beauty of *this* world, where we *now* live: "only brown earth and sky / and in between, all that matters" ("Getting It Done," *The Flying Dutchman* 69). The sacred realities often lie hidden. Hence, earthly themes of absence and suffering often predominate, as well as themes of family and communal life, the effects of a region on the hearts of its inhabitants (specifically, Vietnam and the American Southwest), the continuing desolations of war in the lives of combatants and their offspring, and the hardness and the beauty of nature. He often writes what seem like straightforward, minimalist descriptions of ordinary people in ordinary and extraordinary situations, using what Jack Myers calls "the strong, flat character of the contemporary International Style" (95). Because so much of McDonald's work reflects his Vietnam experience and the rugged life of Colorado and West Texas, he is sometimes called a war poet or a regionalist, but to so designate him is vastly to underestimate his reach.[2] One must write what one knows, of course, and McDonald does this when he writes about Vietnam, Texas, and the Southwest. "I discover poems from the regions I own—or that own me," he says. "If my regions happen to be on actual maps, that's coincidental" ("Evidence" 177). Place for McDonald is vehicle rather than tenor, and what he ultimately reveals through geography is timeless, universal, and spiritual. Indeed, anyone attempting to understand the source and goal of McDonald's art must pay close attention to the poet's profound and ever-present spiritual concerns.[3]

Without *seeming* to address sacred topics, McDonald contemplates his elemental subjects so acutely that the ordinary is transubstantiated into the numinous. Like T. S. Eliot, he sees "the boredom, and the horror, and the glory" as contiguous and inevitably linked ("Evidence" 178). In this respect he is also akin to George Herbert whose "hieroglyphic" method transmutes the ordinary into the holy:

> A man that looks on glass,
> On it may stay his eye;
> Or if he pleaseth, through it pass,
> And then the heav'n espy. ("The Elixir")

McDonald shows us through the prisms of Scriptural narrative and personal experience that the deepest truths are found in classic Christian paradoxes—that loss is gain, that the desert can bloom, that earthly bodies are kernels of the eternal, that silence yields wisdom, that solitude empowers presence, that suffering adumbrates glory, that death yields life, and finally, that darkness enables spiritual insight.[4]

Admittedly, Walt McDonald's vision is often oxymoronic, merging the bleak and the transcendent. His poems come to us as "dark pearls"—rich, lyrical treasures that may go unnoticed by those seeking sleek, bright, optimistic productions. His works may be equally undervalued by those who prefer to dwell on the horrors of existence. McDonald's position is neither pessimistic nor triumphalist.[5] His poems carry the news that there is a way out of the impasse called life. McDonald cites William Carlos Williams to explain his own reason for writing: "It is difficult to get the news from poems. Yet men die miserable every day for lack of what is found there" (qtd. in "Deliverance"). For McDonald, a great deal is at stake: the truths of human existence, the authentic news, whatever the cost. In his hands this sometimes tragic news turns miraculously into good news.

Happily, a growing number of scholars, critics, and readers are recognizing McDonald's poetic achievement. He is the recipient of numerous honors and prizes including the Ohio State University *Journal* Award for *Blessings the Body Gave* (1998), the Juniper Prize for *After the Noise of Saigon* (1988), the George Elliston Poetry Prize for *The Flying Dutchman* (1987), and the Texas Institute of Letters Voertman's Poetry Award. His poems have achieved a wide currency, having been anthologized in over sixty collections.[6] Even so, surprisingly little has been written about the *specifically Christian* dimensions to McDonald's body of work. To understand this poet well, one must read through the accidents of subject matter and location to encounter the lyrical essences, which are intense images of a life informed by the Christian faith.

"In a world deserted"

Walt McDonald is a poet for apocalyptic times. From the hardships of growing up on the "hardscrabble" plains to the personal catastrophe we know as Vietnam, McDonald meditates deeply upon "the eternal wound of existence," to borrow Nietzsche's phrase. Though some of his poems are serene and replete with the joys of beauty, family, and faith, most often they recognize that "shadow itself may resolve into beauty," that "the twin oceans of beauty and horror meet" (Dillard 69). Like Shakespeare, he remembers that "quick bright things come to confusion" and that beauty is soon swallowed by "the jaws of darkness." A deep sense of loss makes him a poet of dereliction and elegy. "Isn't loss everyone's story, after Eden?" he asks ("Evidence" 184). His poems are often tranquil meditations upon loneliness and absence: "I've seen / the world on fire, from bunkers, each man alone, hunkered down / at night to survive the sirens" ("For God in My Sorrows," *Blessings the Body Gave* 77), or "I'm old enough to value / loss, but I can't bring my brother back." In "Grace and the Blood of Goats" he writes:

> We wait for grace
>
> in a world deserted, where the blood of goats
> can't save us. The babies we raised were worth it,
> but now we're alone, lost in a snow field at night
> in mountains. (*Counting Survivors* 63)

The pain of alienation is often quietly understated: "I flew off to war / and came back home alone. These are the facts" ("After the Fires We Once Called Vietnam," *Blessings the Body Gave* 41). Much energy is expended in simply surviving the crisis, which requires enduring the loneliness, measuring the losses, and searching for meaning in the grief: "There's always something to be done / alone" (*Night Landings* 70).

Vietnam becomes a code word for loss writ large, the metonym for all losses. About his comrades he writes: "People I knew kept disappearing." In McDonald's world, the severing of vital links is commonplace: "Pitons and karabiners / like the tightest bonds / break loose" ("Reasons for Taking Risks," *After the Noise of Saigon* 84). One of McDonald's most memorable elegiac poems, "All That Aches and Blesses," laments the immense psychic chasm between father and son:

> More than the heart, we give ourselves away
> in skin, the blessing over all we are.

> We feel the deepest loss of fathers
> not in our bones, but skin they'll never touch.
> (*Night Landings* 74)

Here the poet not only acknowledges the sense of loss but a strenu-
ous protest against Gnostic tendencies; we are "hopelessly and
blessedly physical," as theologian C. Leonard Allen has expressed it.
We are not, Allen goes on to say, merely "incarcerated spirits or
Minds occupied with meditation upon Being," but bodies, real bodies, breathed upon by the breath of Life. "We know and are known in
gestures, embraces, smiles, laughter, caresses, eating, drinking.
With every limb we signal like semaphores the rich and distinctive
texture of our lives." Our sense of loss, then, is rooted in our bodies
as much as in our minds, and the ways in which we feel our losses in
our bodies and express these losses in words are clues to profound
spiritual longing.

Nature often confirms the poet's sense of abandonment. Beneath
the lofty vastness of the night sky, which the poet experiences both
as a lonely pilot and as a Texas rancher living far from the reach of
the city lights, the poet-narrator undergoes a Pascalian crisis. Pitched
beneath the infinite, desert spaces of the dark firmament, McDonald's lonely observer wonders about the possibility of meaning. He
is caught between the fear of nothingness ("the absolute absence of
meaning") and the absolute need to believe:

> Night after night he prowls the same
>
> black forest of stars, tracking
> the spoor of nothing he remembers.
> In zipped twin sleeping bags
>
> before Saigon, we claimed billions of stars
> to wish on, perfectly foreign,
> the absolute absence of meaning.
>
> We counted myths made up by others
> like us, needing to believe in something,
> projecting filaments like spiders
>
> spinning tales to turn stark fear
> to faith. (*After the Noise of Saigon* 22)

The narrator, speaking to his wife, tries to fathom how survival is
possible when so many questions remain unanswered: "Our best
minds query a comet we'll / never see again for clues." He concludes
with an assertion, pitched somewhere between despair and hope:
"We say whatever is, / we'll accept. But we must know, / we must

know something" (22–3). Loss and loneliness feed guilt, a deep and "endless guilt of surviving" (*Night Landings* 79) that cannot be erased by time: "Saigon falls often in my dreams" (*Counting Survivors* 34). McDonald's survivors are haunted sufferers who must be counted "casualties" equal to the war dead. In McDonald's poetry, Vietnam is not so much a discrete historical event as it is a recurring, mysterious, personal, Job-like pattern of experience, demanding some form of theodicy, some answer. In summary, one might say that suffering (of which the loss of human fellowship is the most painful form) is the primary construct through which McDonald views and reports the human story.

Manna in the "Fabulous Desert"

We find in McDonald's verse just what Frank O'Connor found in excellent short fiction: "an intense awareness of human loneliness" (87); however, loneliness is not the last word in McDonald's world. Rather, it is—at least potentially—one station on the road to spiritual purification and insight. It is true that at times McDonald drifts perilously close to the rocks of despair—the "desert experience" is his quite literally—yet his plains turn "suddenly fabulous." His desert blooms and his rocks yield living water; his Dark Nights yield luminous insights, and redemptive possibilities lurk below the crusts of the driest hardscrabble terrain.

If it is true, as McDonald says, that "[e]very poem is a metaphor of how it feels to someone to be alive at some time, at some place" ("Deliverance"), then one might say that McDonald's poems are metaphors of how one can awaken to new depths of spiritual life, despite life's calamities. Paradox frequently attends McDonald's poems: places of stark loneliness and drought become locales that yield rich nourishment. Regarding the poet's strategy, he writes, "when I let down my bucket in a plains region doomed to dry up, I found all sorts of images for poems, even if I could live to write for forty years in that suddenly fabulous desert" ("McDonald"). Like the Desert Fathers dwelling on the fringes of a fallen world, McDonald offers Christian hope as a way out of our dark situation. Mere stoic endurance, while necessary and admirable, is finally insufficient for the journey of life. And so, while McDonald admires the rigorous stoicism of James Dickey, he believes there is more to life than struggle: "Unless there's more than endurance," McDonald surmises, "then the atheists are right" ("Deliverance").[7]

To be sure, there are recurring periods of doubt, as when the poet narrator stands before the long, black wall of the Vietnam War Memorial. This episode, somberly portrayed in the title poem of *Counting Survivors*, rests upon two mysteries: how survivors manage to function in everyday society after a great trauma and how the dead are raised:

> Most friends I knew
> are back in body. I miss good friends
> who earned this service. I've faced the wall
>
> and placed my fingers on their names.
> I wish for Easter all year long.
> I watch parades from curbs
> and wonder how do survivors live?
> How do the dead arise? (34)

The concluding query simultaneously suggests faith and doubt, a dialectic with which the poet seems at home. Are the survivors set *in opposition to* the war dead; or are the survivors *appositional,* that is, striking *examples* of the war dead—the "living dead"? "How do the dead arise?" may constitute an assertion of despair ("It is *impossible* for the dead to be raised") or an affirmation of hope ("Though the dead *are raised,* we cannot explain the mystery").[8] Elsewhere in the McDonald canon there is greater confidence and reason to hope. Resurrection motifs are not uncommon. Though we are earth, as he tells us in countless ways, we also are "old bones mired in mud we've proved / can rise and walk again" (*Night Landings* 78). "[A]ll men are able to rise with the help / of clowns" (*After the Noise of Saigon* 87). Hope often emerges from descriptions of struggle in nature: "we kept on crawling through water / for a shore we believed was worth it" (*After the Noise of Saigon* 83). Natural beauty is eternity here below, and so the hardscrabble West Texas landscape becomes another Promised Land, "heaven's tableland." Though something has been lost and will be lost again, something always remains. There is manna in the desert:

> At last, for a brief while,
>
> all is well. Even the bulls
> graze head-down and silent
> as if they believe this hour
> goes on forever. These
>
> Are the days of plenty,
> a year without locusts,
> wind in the rigging of saplings
> staked out and thriving. ("Manna International," *Night Landings* 71–2)

In biblical narrative, after humans rebel against the divine will, first there is punishment, then an outpouring of mercy. This divine grace initiates a new beginning, often symbolized by the birth of a child. Babies bear the promise of a new and better future, sometimes a messianic future: "For unto us a child is born" (Isaiah 9:6). Similarly, children and mothers figure prominently in McDonald's poetry as agents of mercy. A mother is a "mystery of give and take / laid open to strangers and neighbors in need." Modeling a life of kenotic selflessness, the maternal figure is a Christ-like redemptress, pierced by briars and stickers, as she races barefoot to save a child nearly asphyxiated after swallowing a marble: "she ran to that baby on adrenaline / and faith." She embodies grace: "a comely woman, mother, nurse, / who believed herself simple, submissive, afraid, / not knowing how able she was, how recklessly brave" ("With Mercy for All," *Blessings the Body Gave* 29).

In "Learning How in the Southwest" an unseen mother sings a melody late at night in a shabby oil town. Her heartfelt lullabies counter the loud, lonely revelers, the "[h]ard hats from seven states," whose commotion is empty and cold:

> That's when some mother's tunes drift
> softly at midnight, alarming songs not taught
>
> In oil fields, an ache for words that come
> from more than the tongue, like honey
> and homemade bread, learned when young,
> commotion in the heart older than cactus
>
> and black shale, a spark before the gas is capped—
> music from school or church, poetry in motion
> only such women give singing lullabies to babies
> that cry and, cuddled, go back to sleep.
> (*Blessings the Body Gave* 61–2)

Two poems about adoption convey an immense sense of hope against a backdrop of loss. The children adopted by the narrator and his wife symbolize messianic promise: "Such hope / never happened again . . ." (21). A kind of Advent season brings these babies as gifts; the caseworkers are "half trauma nurses, half Santa Claus." Similarly, in "That Child Abandoned upon the Porch," the narrator connects the report of an abandoned child to his own adopted son, and ultimately to the Christ Child. These messianic infants are "swaddled babies" overseen by angels, shepherds, and guiding stars (51).

Though children and mothers often signify promise, even they cannot sustain the poet through every dark passage: "The babies we raised were worth it, / but now we're alone, lost in a snow field at night / in mountains" (*Counting Survivors* 63). McDonald's poetry takes an apophatic turn. Faith proves possible at last, not because of what we *can* see, but because of what we *cannot*. Bearing this out are McDonald's poems which envision a radiant, dazzling darkness in the tradition of Nicholas of Cusa, the advocates of the *via negativa*, and the apophatic spirituality of Christian Neoplatonism. This knowing in and through darkness is suggested in McDonald's stirring "For God in My Sorrows":[9]

> I try to ignore the stars, a billion witnesses
> that I give myself to black skies, not even gravity holding me
>   back,
> cast into outer darkness. Not stars always on fire, not fire,
>
> but beyond, whatever scattered them: *that* power.
>   (*Blessings the Body Gave* 77)

The poet is not seeking God through some empirical inquiry. Astronomical "proof," the "speech" of the heavenly luminaries (Psalm 19:1), that is, natural theology, is not particularly helpful. "Black night / has answers I don't want," the poet declares. He seeks something above and beyond—something *after* the stars dissolve:

> But after stars collapse,
> after all that mass snuffs out like a match, after whatever
>
> Peter meant by the known world melting with fervent heat,
> how much remains?
> . . . .
>   Do those black skies have answers after all,
>
> terror no less than daylight, night vision blinded by the star
> we'll never see at this distance? Is it blackness I seek,
> after all, total loss, like turning my back on the highway
> and shutting my eyes tight as if those billion fires were gone,
>
> leaving me free to pray without the crutch of fire,
> not even flashlights? What, beyond wars and weapons, beyond
>   stars,
> what could I find? The light that guided wise men?
> No, that's done and over, servant of the source I yearn for. (77)

Even the star that guided the Magi does not interest him now. Instead, the poet seeks a witness *beyond* material evidence, beyond sense:

> I believe
> as I know my hand is here before me in the dark, my eyes
> stretched wide—sun, moon and stars almost forgotten—
> I feel faith inches away from my face, thumb and split claws

cunningly made to hold a rope or grope along the wall at night
for a light switch. When I close my eyes, magically,
it's here. This, this is what I need, without lights or cities
man-made and dying, somehow to know I'm known. (77–8)

Needless to say, McDonald's quest for faith is not settled in a single poem. There's too much struggle, too many experiences, too much "negative capability" to settle the quest. But "For God in My Sorrows" does affirm his belief that God is there, that he knows us, and that we somehow can know him too, despite, or even because of the darkness.

"Evidence of hope / not seen"

In the recent volumes *Counting Survivors, Blessings the Body Gave,* and *All Occasions,* McDonald articulates his Christian convictions with increased clarity. For example, in "The Dust We Are Made Of," a poem concerning an archeological dig, the poet reveals his particular method for suggesting faith through the careful observation of concrete objects and in the common features of the desert Southwest. The poem begins matter-of-factly: "All summer under klieg lights / we stroked the dirt with trowels." The excavators slowly uncover mundane items: an arrowhead, a jawbone, a "bowl crushed to dust by a boot"—the commonplace relics of unexceptional lives, the bric-a-brac of prehistoric desert-dwellers soon to be catalogued and displayed in some "regional museum." But soon these "signs of modest toil" turn into "clues" and "signs" of something unexpected and rare. Line by line, layer by layer, as we "dig" the poem, we uncover a "deeper" reality beneath the pottery shards and bones of mammoth and bear:

> We found bronze kernels never baked,
> like golden ears hung up to dry
> on southwest porches. We had eaten tortillas
> of such crushed corn. Here, people like us
> lay down in darkness. We sifted dust
>
> we were made of. What did they fear?
> Near midnight on our knees
> we catalogued clues for regional museums,
> the signs of modest toil, evidence of hope
> not seen, the kernels not consumed.

Suddenly, the concatenation of things (corn, people, dust, darkness) is no longer random. The archeological dig turns cosmic. There is design here. These ancient people "lay down in darkness" and felt fear like we do, and they also left important clues about life's direction.

The poem ends with a surprising burst of good news. Though these primitives are now dust, as are their implements and artifacts (and as we shall soon be), still there is "evidence of hope / not seen, the kernels not consumed" (*Counting Survivors* 45).

The concluding passage, remarkably economical, sonorous, and strong, is itself a solid kernel of hope, declaring through subtle biblical allusions the redemption of the body and the promise of eternal life:

> Very truly, I tell you, unless a grain of wheat falls into the earth and dies, it remains just a single grain; but if it dies, it bears much fruit. (John 12:24 NRSV)

> But someone will ask, "How are the dead raised? With what kind of body do they come?" Fool! What you sow does not come to life unless it dies. And as for what you sow, you do not sow the body that is to be, but a bare seed, perhaps of wheat or of some other grain. But God gives it a body as he has chosen, and to each kind of seed its own body. (1 Corinthians 15:35–8 NRSV)

John's Gospel explains that our bodies are seeds of "corn" (John 12:24 AV); St. Paul adds that our bodies are "sown in corruption" and "weakness" but raised "in incorruption," raised in "power" and "glory." We are planted "terrestrial bodies" but raised "celestial" ones (I Corinthians 15:42–44 AV). In view of the New Testament, McDonald's title "The Dust We Are Made Of" is richly suggestive and heavily ironic. Though we are dust, Adam, *adamah*, our bodies are also blessed seeds destined to flourish in the eternal. Because the golden kernels have not decayed or atomized, because they have not been "crushed to dust" like the earthen artifacts that contained them, we have hope. These "bronze kernels never baked" are living seeds, in fact, promising eternal life. Echoing Hebrews 11:1 ("For faith is . . . the evidence of things not seen"), the poem affirms that we have "evidence of hope / not seen."

Thus, "The Dust We Are Made Of" illustrates how McDonald successfully avoids what novelist Mary Gordon calls the "twin dangers" of the religious life (which are also the twin dangers of the writer's life)—abstractionism and dualism. "Abstractionism," writes Gordon, "I define as the error that results from refusing to admit that one has a body and is an inhabitant of a physical world. Dualism, its first cousin, admits that there is a physical world but calls it evil and commands that it be shunned" (27). Just as Paul insisted on the blessed fact of an everlasting physical body, so McDonald never gives up on this world we call home, nor does he even for a moment lose interest in the power and the glory of creation. He continually gives us objective correlatives, luminous verbal images, which stand for and convey to readers the mysteries of an enchanted, God-created earth and sky. "The Dust We're Made Of" illustrates how the believing poet manages to stay very close to material things, to celebrate particulars, to notice and to love things intensely, yet not to love them for themselves, but for what they can reveal to us. McDonald offers us "dark pearls" (*Counting Survivors* 58), poetic seeds of faith which, once planted, grow and illuminate the hearts of searching readers.

According to McDonald, life is often hard, at times anguished, yet this world is also glorious, God-infused, and worth the trouble. Our vocation in this vale of soul-making is to search out Creation for these dark pearls and to cry out to our Maker until we put on our amazing armor in a new world called eternity. McDonald's experience in the skies over Vietnam may have initiated the quest, but that soul-searing experience also led him to look for the reality before and after the stars. Walt McDonald's poetry declares, finally, that we Calibans and Icaruses must rouse a confident readiness to enter the darkness of the future called faith—not settling for the blue, but for something well beyond it:

> What matters
> is timeless, dazzling devotion—not rain,
> not Eden gardenias, but cactus in drought,
> not just moons of deep sleep, not sunlight or stars,
> not the blue, but the darkness beyond.
> (*Blessings the Body Gave* 109)

Intimations of Higher Matters: Anagogical Closure in Walter Mcdonald's *Burning the Fence*

William Jolliff

In *Poetic Closure: A Study of How Poems End*, Barbara Herrnstein Smith writes:

> Whereas the weak closure of much modern poetry can be under-stood partly as the result of the prevalence of formal and the-matic structures that offer minimal resources for closure, the reverse is also likely: the prevalence of free verse, for example, probably reflects, in part, the impulse to anti-closure. (243)

Though published thirty years ago, Smith's claim seems as accurate today as it was then, and it applies equally well to more recent po-etry. One need not discount the vigor and productivity of the New Formalists to maintain that most poetry currently being published is of a kind that offers little structural support for creating satisfying closure. We are not surprised, then, to see Smith's assessment, or prophecy, manifesting itself on the pulpy landscape of several hun-dred journals. Far more surprising, given such a state of affairs, is the fact that one frequently reads contemporary free verse poems that *do* achieve satisfying closure of one kind or another—not simply the watchcase click of a too-obvious craft, but that satisfying sense of integrity and completeness, which, to echo Smith again, "makes sta-sis, or the absence of further continuation, the most probable suc-ceeding event" (34).

A likely question, then, is this: given the relative paucity of re-
sources that free verse offers to achieve closure, how do the poets do
it?[1] Needless to say, this question will not receive a full answer here.
I will attempt to make a modest beginning, though, by demonstrat-
ing one way in which one contemporary poet, Walt McDonald,
achieves closure in one of his collections, *Burning the Fence.*

The book opens with "Morning in Texas." Set initially in the narrator's grade-school classroom, this poem seems at first to center on
the reactions of his classmate, Juan Hernandez, who, hearing an explosion in the town,

> jumped straight up
> burst the desk top
> shouted My papa oh
> my papa's dead!

Juan's premonition proves to have been correct. And though, as the
speaker's mother assures him later, it was "[j]ust a coincidence /
Juan couldn't have known," the fear, and, we may imagine, the mysterious cause of that fear, persist with the narrator:

> All night I lay there
> starting to explode,
> feeling my spirit crouched,
> ready to burst (3)

until his long night ends with the reassuring final line, "Dawn
came." That is, the line is reassuring until we read the second half, a
one-word fragment, "Comes" (3). Apparently the second half of a
compound predicate, the second occurrence of the verb supplies an
emphatic pause—a technique common enough in the portrayal of
conversational syntax. Yet it is that single word that suggests the necessity of our second level of understanding the poem. Isolated, it
becomes a kind of "transformational line ending" (Myers 165–6),
though in this case the semantic change takes place not because of
the demands of an additional line, but because the isolation of the
term gives it emphasis and creates some ambiguity. With the tense
change taken seriously, and very conservatively, it may be expli-
cated to mean, "And dawn still comes," implying that "the fear is
still with me as an adult, even as I write this poem, and it is still alleviated only by the dawn." But to stop with that reading seems unnec-
essarily rigid. The absence of a clearly defined syntactic purpose
created by the isolation of the fragment "Comes" allows us liberty—
or makes us bold enough—to generalize the fear still further. When
we do so, the line seems to allow that, as a principle, dawn *continues
to relieve* our recurring fears, fears that are an incessant strain of our

existence, of the human condition. As I hope to demonstrate, Mc-
Donald repeatedly closes his poems in a manner that encourages this
kind of interpretation, and since the phenomenon occurs repeatedly,
it seems appropriate to give it a name.

A likely source for the needed term is Jack Myers and Michael
Simms's *Longman Dictionary of Poetic Terms*, the handbook that seems
most conversant with what goes on in poetry workshops today. In
their nomenclature, what McDonald is using would seem to be an
"Eastern ending"—that is, an ending in which the closure "continues to develop quietly and to complete itself after the actual printed
ending of the poem has been read" (92). Their usage, derived from
the fact that many Asian poems work this way, seems accurate to our
purposes as far as it goes. But, while it may be roughly correct, there
are certainly many different reasons that an ending might continue
"to develop and complete itself," and my thesis is that McDonald is
creating a particular kind of closural effect.

As it happens, the most thorough study of closure is still that of
Barbara Herrnstein Smith. She devotes a lengthy chapter to a discussion of what she calls "Special Terminal Features," much of which
pertains to our discussion here. In that section she details several
particular ways that closure is gained, techniques that may be used
alone or in combination to strengthen closure. But it is her prefatory
insight to this discussion that speaks most clearly to the phenomenon we see occurring in McDonald's poems:

> The devices of closure often achieve their characteristic effect by
> imparting to a poem's conclusion a certain quality that is experi-
> enced by the reader as striking *validity*, a quality that leaves him
> with the feeling that what has just been said has the "conclusive-
> ness," the settled finality, of apparently self-evident truth.
> (152)

Two pages later, she clarifies her focus:

> [T]hat particular experience of validity which, when it occurs as
> the conclusion of a poem, strengthens or secures the readers'
> sense of finality and stability. In general, it appears that the con-
> ditions which contribute to the sense of truth are also those
> which create closure. (154)

These statements describe accurately, though not fully, what is
going on in McDonald's "Morning in Texas": that dawn comes and
continues to come strikes us as valid—the affirmation is true. But
neither here nor in the forty pages that follow does Smith suggest a
more particular "terminal feature" that addresses what we have observed in McDonald's work. Nevertheless, based on her trajectory, I

suggest that the "special terminal feature" McDonald is using be called *anagogical closure*. I offer the phrase with some trepidation, realizing that I may be accused of one of the more frustrating postmodern sins: that of reintroducing a traditional rhetorical term only after having reconceptualized the meaning sufficiently to suit my strengths and confuse all comers. What I have tried to do, on the contrary, having experienced strongly in several of McDonald's poems the qualities that, according to Gabrielle Rico, "are the basis of aesthetic activity"—"consciousness of a unified whole and consciousness of intense pleasure" (54)—is to identify the prevalence and highlight the closural significance of anagogical suggestion, understood quite traditionally.

In "The Banquet," Dante suggests that a piece of writing

> ought to be expounded chiefly in four senses. The first is called literal, and this is the sense which does not go beyond the strict limits of the letter; the second is called allegorical, and this is disguised under the cloak of such stories, and is a truth hidden under a beautiful fiction. . . . The third sense is called moral; and this sense is that for which teachers ought as they go through writings intently to watch for their own profit and that of their hearers. . . . The fourth sense is called anagogical, that is, above the senses; and this occurs when a writing is spiritually expounded which even in the literal sense by the things signified likewise gives intimation of higher matters belonging to the eternal glory; as can be seen in that song of the prophet which says that, when the people of Israel went up out of Egypt, Judea was made holy and free. And although it be plain that this is true according to the letter, that which is spiritually understood is not less true, namely, that when the soul issues forth from sin she is made holy and free as mistress of herself. (121)

McDonald's "Morning in Texas" does just this. His anagogical closure carries us from an understanding of one little boy's bedtime apprehension to a fear that characterizes human existence. The poem's closure "gives intimation of higher matters."

Indeed, anagogical closure is common, if not dominant, throughout *Burning the Fence*. In "University Library," the first eight lines are a straightforward description of that building—any metaphorical richness must be imported by the reader. But the final six lines focusing on graduate males use language rich in sexual suggestion:

> Deep in the stacks in fourth floor
> carrels, graduate males massage
> slide rules backwards and forwards
> mastering bodies of knowledge

by degrees and dreaming beyond facts
of the inscrutable design of young wives. (6)

So clear is the comparison of the imagined wives to the graduate
work being done that one is tempted simply to say that the sestet has
a controlling metaphor. What forces our reading beyond the explica-
tion of metaphor is, once again, the last line, in particular the phrase,
"inscrutable design." For these young engineers' work, we assume—
if we drive the cars they design over the bridges they build—is not
"inscrutable." They are, after all, "mastering" their crafts. But they
are dreaming of what they cannot fully understand: the mysteries of
the closest human relationships. The passage works on us as metaphor until that final line leads us beyond metaphor, reminding us of
a truth higher than gross weights and stress factors. Human analysis
ends, and the mystery begins—right there in the library. McDonald's phrase, "inscrutable design," in Dante's words, "gives intimation of higher matters belonging to the eternal glory."

"Tornado Alley" similarly directs the readers to the anagogical
level. Like "University Library," this piece is divided into an octave
and sestet, but here no metaphor prepares the reader for anagogical
closure. In the first thirteen lines, the poet presents an apparently
matter-of-fact account of a family going down to the basement to review their storm preparations. The images are metaphorically rich,
but the figures seem to find completion in their most immediate significance: "spiders dark as funnel clouds swirl themselves down /
and swivel into cracks. Lawn chairs webbed with dust / lean on the
walls." It is only the final line—"We search the sky. There's time"—
that suggests a significance greater than the ordinary preparations
imply (13). The final emphatic sentence, "There's time," reassures
us, we assume, that there will be time to compete this task before the
first tornado comes. Clear enough. Yet some ambiguity settles in.
For in fact, the speaker is reassuring us concerning a fear that has
never, in the poem, been developed. So our first reader response, "I
am assured," is quickly followed by our second: "But wait a minute
—I don't recall being worried." There is, it would seem, no impending calamity, no storm warning, heightening the poem's tension. *So
just what is there time for?* Again, we must assume, given our strongly
felt sense of closure, our "consciousness of a unified whole and consciousness of intense pleasure," that this ending does fulfill some
other need that we readers have been feeling. Some other disaster
must be coming. But what? Since no additional particulars present in
the poem offer themselves, we turn to the fear that most typically
characterizes our human condition, the fear of death, which is certainly one of the "higher matters belonging to the eternal glory," if
we excuse a certain lack of blessed assurance or define "glory"

broadly enough. Having been invited to a higher level of meaning, the anagoge allows us not simply to reread the poem as enriched by a controlling metaphor, but instead to identify more closely throughout with the fear implied by the poem—in particular, the very human attempts to stave off the inevitable.

Once one begins to think anagogically, these endings in *Burning the Fence* become one of our reading expectations, and one that is frequently fulfilled. In "First Solo" a new pilot is being warned about some of the dangers of landing, dangers based not on weather or enemy fire but on mental or psychological struggles that could betray him. When the poem ends with "Give everything you have to the runway, / You will have all night to dream," we read the poem almost immediately as anagogical (21). Here it certainly does not hurt that McDonald is drawing upon the traditional metaphorical language of sleep and death, which in themselves enhance closure, yet the significance of the final line, since we have become accustomed to reading anagogically, fulfills our expectation by suggesting things eternal. The rhetoric of flight in "Going Home" plays similarly upon us. In this narrative, an aircraft hits such turbulence that even the flight attendants "smile grimly, their knuckles white / as they distribute the napkins." Crisis over, the poem ends:

> When we descend, the clouds thin out
> and there it sprawls,
> the rock on which we live
> and where we all return. (47)

One can of course read the final two lines simply as an allusion to traditional funeral rites or even more simply as double entendre. But since by this time we have begun to read McDonald for an anagogical meaning, that tends to be our preferred interpretive move: literally we return to earth with every landing, and anagogically we return, dust to dust, the way of all flesh.

In the poem that supplies the collection's title, the quasi-personified fence does its best to resist burning, or at least to resist showing its fire. The flames "waver within cracks"; the posts "hold in their flames." The fence, we learn, is "unwilling to stop being fence" (57). Read as anagogical closure, what is portrayed is the resistance of the temporal and material to accede to its limitations. The personification hinted throughout makes the application of the effect to the reader a short step indeed, and suddenly we are reflecting the "higher matter" of our own im/mortality, so difficult to admit, to let go. "Measuring Time" confronts a similar struggle. In this poem, the speaker is recounting a progression of deaths: family members, friends, comrades. That done, he states that "the hands go around, around" (29). Given the title, the image of the clock is clear; just as importantly, the repetition echoes and suggests a continuity similar to that we perceived in "Morning in Texas." The hands will keep on turning not only for friends, but for the speaker as well. "I" measure the time, and the time is coming around.

Anagogical expectation comes into play once again in "World War I Soldiers." The poem is the narrator's reflection on an old photograph of the town regiment of Louisville, Kentucky, going off to war, and he scrutinizes the photo for good reason: "I search the faces for father. / My eyes rake each platoon, return to one man / in the second rank." He assumes that this is his father, or at least ponders that idea, and asks:

> If he had died
> in Flanders, who would have seen
> this man I see,
> who would've cared? (24)

These lines would be enough of an ending for any good poet; they suggest to us the eternal smallness, the diminishing temporality, of what are perceived in the present as great and heroic acts. But the poem does not conclude there. Instead, McDonald goes on: "I stare at the others. / Each one marches alone," curious lines since, after all, the men are marching more or less together; the fact that we have been told previously that "[t]hey aren't even nearly / in step" foreshadows but does not prepare us for the grave significance of the final line (24). The emotional import of the poem has been the fact of our human aloneness, and that idea is beautifully iterated by the restatement of their unpracticed marching—a statement that we immediately perceive as an anagogical truth: they are not only alone in their marching pattern, but we are alone too—all humans are ultimately alone. Though hardly "glorious," this is an "intimation of a higher matter," a more spiritual idea, if you will, than human limitation and temporality.

The clearest instance of anagogical closure, however, may be in the uncharacteristically green "Evolution." In an image that recalls Theodore Roethke, "Wisteria tendrils / bounce about in the wind" as we consider "the speed of sunlight / lasering the leaves." We share the narrator's wonder until we are confronted with the "vegetable intelligence." The light knows "somehow where to go" (51). Having been invited and conditioned throughout the collection for at least some religious awareness, the intelligence of the light, like the work of the plant, takes on a heavenly significance: higher matters are intimated. Thus the poet celebrates the intelligence that sustains life and light.

As I evaluate my own readings of these texts, it seems even to me that my claims are suspect, that they may place more in the poem than is really there. And of course it is possible that I do see visions of death behind every dark night, that I assume a herd of elephants behind each mundane clap of thunder, or that, more seriously, I may be over-reading the poems in a way that devalues their more literal excellence. That is a potential problem with such readings, a problem to which centuries of allegorical, moral, and anagogical readings of the Bible may attest. But given the risk, what continues to push my own conservative reading tendencies in this direction is the fact that what I am calling McDonald's anagogical practice seems, in the context of this volume, readily distinguishable from the types of endings most easily mistaken for anagoges: those which depend upon double entendre, and those which I will call, for the sake of consistency, "literal" endings—those final lines of which the primary claim to closure and aesthetic gratification is essentially non-figurative.

A few brief examples may help clarify these distinctions. In "Claiming Kin," McDonald tells the story of Uncle Edward who, after a rough and rugged life, ends up sad in his old age, calls the speaker's mother on the telephone and "weeps for his boys," asking,

> How
> can I make it up?
> *There*
> *there,* she says,
> not knowing how. (23)

The beauty of this ending is that the mother's words, as well as the speaker's description of those words, support several complementary meanings. They may very literally mean that she simply doesn't know what to tell her brother to do; they may mean that she does not know what to do about Edward; or they may mean, since she is the speaker's mother and since Edward's is such a common complaint, that she doesn't "know how" with her own children either. A more subtle closing, yet still classifiable as a double entendre, is found in "First Blood." In that poem, the speaker recounts a childhood experience in which he and his friend watch a small plane crash. A lovelorn pilot was apparently buzzing a former girlfriend. The poem ends flatly: "Each of us / took a piece of the plane. / Mine had some blood on it" (17). What makes this ending work is the fact that the statement, flat and powerful, is no doubt literally true; but the doubling suggests that such boyhood fascinations as watching a plane crash are bought at a high price. That the ten-year-old didn't perceive this second aspect, while the narrator and the reader do, is what makes the double entendre a satisfying irony with which to close.

Successful literal endings also abound in *Burning the Fence*. "Plowing Through Ashes," for example, a lyric which recounts hunting through harvested sorghum fields, burning the stubble, preparing the field again, and planting, ends with these lines:

> and in May
> he [the speaker's father] rigged the tractor up,
> lowered four worn plows
> into the ground
> and planted grain. (5)

There are many good qualities about these lines. They affirm, reassuringly, the cyclic nature of agrarian practice, and the ashes image has sufficient resonance in archetype and in religious tradition to make it satisfyingly suggestive. But the closure does not, it seems to me, offer "intimation of higher matters belonging to the eternal glory." In another poem, "Cabin," McDonald portrays a couple pondering where to build. After recounting the many advantages of a particular high site, McDonald ends with their vision of the future: "and in spring we'll dust / shake blankets fresh outside, / and beat the rugs" (7). This closure works because it describes not only a literal fact about what will need to be done, but also because it resonates, literally still, with the healthy pleasure of cleaning and the more ironic pleasure of beating a rug—an act at once wholesome and blissfully violent, especially after a long winter cooped up together in the new cabin. It is a fine ending, true to the human condition, but it seems different in kind from the anagogical closure that has been detailed.

Now would be a fine time to claim that the closure used in this collection is typical of McDonald's work or that anagogical closure has become even more prevalent and important as his writing has progressed. Apparently closer to the truth, however, based on my reading of the dozen or so volumes McDonald has published since *Burning the Fence*, is that while he has not abandoned this technique, he does use it less often.[2] Why that is the case is a problem that must be addressed in a future essay, after a more thorough study of his canon. In a similar vein, given the intrinsically religious nature of readings open to anagogical interpretation, it would be worthwhile to see what role this kind of closure has played in the creation of what critics have called McDonald's "hardscrabble sublime."[3] But that topic too must be deferred to a future study.

In preparing this essay, I have often had in mind Robert Frost, who having said, "Every poem is a new metaphor inside or it is nothing" goes on to add, "[a]nd there is a sense in which all poems are the same old metaphor always" (786). Frost was, of course, free to claim

saint's privilege and leave that proclamation to rest without explanation. What he may have been sensing, I think, is that while poetry
is indeed metaphor, considered teleologically it directs us beyond
metaphor to a place where all things run together—to what such
faithful practitioners of the anagogical as Flannery O'Connor might
call "the Divine life and our participation in it" (Grimes 13). A more
extensive study might find that many contemporary poets, particularly people of faith, use methods of closure that succeed because
they lend themselves to anagogical interpretation. Once we become
comfortable with the concept, we realize that it is one of the things
that poets and readers of poetry have always sensed, more or less,
when they allow themselves to use good sense. For many readers,
the intimation of higher things is part of what brought them to poetry in the first place. We expect poets to help us see the divinity in
the details and to remind us that as readers we too participate in a divine design.

Perseverance in Walt Mcdonald's Poetry

Chris Willerton

Walt McDonald has always written about survival and faith, and memories—both real and imagined—have always been his source. I want to illuminate his concerns and his method by exploring the theme of perseverance in his poetry, drawing examples from several collections, especially *Counting Survivors*. All his collections share a similar subject matter, method, and worldview. His subject matter is the individual's confrontation with fortune: bad fortune, such as drought, disease, and war, and good fortune, such as returning from war to a happy marriage and healthy children. McDonald's favorite settings are West Texas and Vietnam, both famous for their possibilities of struggle. His method is the vignette told in a soliloquy or a dramatic monologue usually involving self, family members, or remembered friends. McDonald's worldview emphasizes that life must be redeemed by perseverance and insight. Perseverance is a common theme for writers of the American West and chroniclers of war, but not all base it on a religious foundation. In this respect, Mc-Donald deserves comparison with the Welsh poet and clergyman R. S. Thomas. Both poets study the mundane, reaching after God's perspective. McDonald uses religious allusions for the same reason he uses subjects from West Texas or the Vietnam War: his mind is furnished with them. They belong to his mental "regions," as he puts it ("Evidence" 173):

> All of my poems grow out of faith, whether set in my native
> West Texas or our other adopted home in the Rockies, in Air

Force cockpits, or Vietnam. None would be what they are without the habit of mind, the profession of faith I make daily. (175)

Especially in view of so confessional a statement, we need to observe a caveat about McDonald's method: the poems are not meant
as autobiography. He explains that each of his poems "is personal,
yes—but every poem is also a persona poem, a little fiction." He
transmutes his own experience: "I'm not there, frank and undis-
guised, in any poem. Experience is valuable for what it is; then the
writing takes over" (180).

To understand perseverance, let us begin with *Counting Survivors*,
which of all his collections examines the theme most thoroughly.
The book's cover photo is a crowd of names on the Vietnam Wall
monument. Its poems are spoken by survivors and about survivors
—survivors of the Vietnam War, of drought, of family disaster, of
bad decisions. Time and again, those who survive feel half-guilty for
having done so, or they have survived impaired. Based on this absolute candor about suffering and paradox, the book teaches acceptance and hard-won peace. The characters' hurts are never denied;
losses never go unacknowledged. But the trajectory of the collection
is from poems of grief, bafflement, and ugly paradox to poems of acceptance, humor, and kind irony. True, McDonald's other collections
also end with peace after struggle. This one, however, is especially
clear in delineating the crucial element of Christian perseverance.[1]

Why choose the term *perseverance* instead of *survival* or *endurance*?
Endure is used more often in English translations of the Bible than *persevere*, but perseverance is still the more accurate term where characters
have survived through determination or faith. Perseverance is active
and intentional whereas mere survival or endurance may be passive.
In biblical stories perseverance is usually heroic. Perseverance stands
out in the Apostle Paul's listing of his shipwrecks, beatings, abandon-
ments, and arrests (II Corinthians 11), and in his declaring that he has
"fought the good fight," has "finished the course" (II Timothy 4). He
has persevered in spite of harassment and privation. In *The Castle of Perseverance*, to persevere means to resist worldly pleasure and demonic
doubt; in *Pilgrim's Progress* or *The Faerie Queene*, it also means to persevere in a quest. In stories of martyrs, to persevere means to testify
for God despite the penalty of death. And in *Paradise Regained*, Milton praises Job for the "perseverance" that overcomes Satan's deeds
of "cruel malice" (I.148).

Perseverance is thus a pillar of the Christian heroic ideal. By contrast, survival is a more modest feat. A person may survive either because of perseverance or because of dumb luck, and his survival may
not be a thing to envy. McDonald's poems show us that, where survival has not been a matter of accident or fortune, it has depended on

perseverance. Scattered through these sixty-three poems of *Counting Survivors* are some forty biblical and religious allusions that link God to both luck and perseverance. Without these allusions, the poems' treatment of fate and character would be comparable only to the populist stoicism of John Steinbeck, Carl Sandburg, or Larry McMurtry. With these allusions, the poems resonate for the Christian reader. Like Ecclesiastes, Job, and the Book of Psalms, these poems trust that nothing is too harsh for God to hear. Every statement is permitted so that the believer's declaration of agony is as authentic as his declaration of faith.

This candor is a feature of all McDonald's war poems. "After the Fall of Saigon," for example, is a portrait of a haunted survivor, "a mad man aging hard," for whom "[e]ven good booze can't burn . . . out" the "fungus" of memory (*Counting Survivors* 3). "For Friends Missing in Action" is spoken by a survivor, wryly recalling his trainee days, when he and his friends "studied gauges and codes / like prayer beads, believing" that "those wings would hold us up" (6). "The Gleam of Silver Wings" follows, an elegy to a friend whose jet as it crashed seemed "a silver matchstick / tossed indifferently away" (7). In "For Dawes, on Takeoff," a young pilot dies merely because a mechanic misconnected the wires to his ailerons:

> They found his head
> stuck to his helmet.
> In trees downrange, they found his arms
> flung out from the body as if asking why.
> (*The Flying Dutchman* 48)

"Out of the Stone They Come" is spoken by a Vietnam War survivor. In it, he describes a painting of a middle-aged man like himself, standing before a war monument as ghosts of friends, eternally young, reach out from the granite. The painting belongs to the speaker's son, who is a soldier and has lost friends in the Persian Gulf War. Together the speaker and his son walk to the Vietnam Memorial Wall with his son. The names on the monument blur, and he sees only his son's reflection (*Counting Survivors* 16).

To survive, therefore, is both to grieve and to remain puzzled at the arbitrariness of war, the inexplicable selecting of some to die and some to live. One of the most astonishing poems in *Counting Survivors* is "What If I Didn't Die Outside Saigon." The speaker dreams of dying on a stretcher as a chopper lifts him from the battle. In his dream, he cries out to a cigar-chomping old officer that he wants to live for all the ordinary—and priceless—reasons: to see his wife and kids, to travel, to "[m]ake something of my life. Make love, / not war." The old officer thinks, blows smoke rings, and gives the young soldier back his life, ripping the killed-in-action tag from his chest. Shocked at his own resurrection, the speaker wakes suddenly. He finds himself an old man, surrounded in his bedroom with photos of grown children, his aging wife asleep beside him. The old officer was Death, with "a nicked machete / like a scythe strapped to his back" (8). The speaker realizes that to live to old age is as miraculous and as arbitrary as the Grim Reaper's sending one of his victims back from the dead.

McDonald's title poem "Counting Survivors" encapsulates the wonder and the pain of having outlived others and anchors this amazement in Christian observance and mystery:

> I'm stunned to see so many of us home.
> I drive downtown to shout hosanna quietly,
> pipe organ booming. The padded church bench
> shudders like a medevac on takeoff.
> Saigon falls often in my dreams. . . .
> I wish for Easter all year long.
> I watch parades from curbs
> and wonder how do survivors live?
> How do the dead arise? (34)

How do survivors live? McDonald's frequent answer is that they live by insight. The speaker in "Farms at Auction" watches a neighbor's farm sold off after three years of ruin by hailstorms. When the last storm had begun, he had watched "summer clouds a mile away, / bubbles a dozen churches prayed for," then envied his neighbor the rain that came to the neighbor's land but not his. When the hail began, he didn't hear it, "too busy cursing rain / to count my blessings." Only later did he pay attention to his good fortune. His farm had missed the rain but also the ruinous hail. Now, "loaded with luck," he watches his neighbor's property sold off to the bidders (40). The speaker doesn't even raise the question of justice. Clearly, the universe is not set up to distribute justice. Scripture may tell him that the rain falls on the just and unjust alike, but experience tells him that the rain falls where it pleases. To be the survivor—to have blessings to count, to have luck—is inexplicable. But attention is important; to appreciate being chosen is important.

When they are given no such insight, survivors know only dismay over the inexplicableness of fortune. In "The Weatherman Reports the Weather," the title character is rueful about his supposedly scientific role. In front of the camera, he does not report the two boys who died joy-riding during his last broadcast; he is not allowed to report "such things as finance / and behavior. Weather's a science: / it makes nothing happen" (60). Ironically, what he is allowed to say does not give much benefit: the "forecasts I knew were perfect" seem to "shift under my feet like sand." "I give it straight, no news, no predictions / on Super Bowls or children's fate, / not anyone's children, not yours, not mine" (61).

Balancing this call to pay attention is the call to interpret life carefully. That is, a survivor must read the signs but not overread them. The speaker in "The Signs of Prairie Rattlers" says,

> I've heard mad preachers claim this sand
> is like the Bible deserts. They quoted Moses
>
> with serpents impaled on poles. Watch signs,
> they warned with spitting tongues. . . .

Convinced that a rattler is a rattler, not an omen, the speaker puts his "faith in most home remedies—/ hard work and red-eye chili and homespun love." He cuts a hole in his wall "to save barn owls from cats. Our rafters are an ark / for owls" (*Counting Survivors* 33). Pragmatism and mercy, not a fancy eschatology, are guiding principles for survivors.

To read signs rightly—even the favorable signs—is to read them modestly. In "Grace and the Blood of Goats," the speaker and his wife are vacationing in a mountain cabin far from their familiar prairie. Gazing at the moon, he and his wife think of an Air Force friend who became an astronaut and walked upon it. They find themselves in a reverie:

> Crossing a log today, we stared at water tumbling fast.
> Don't look, I said, as if blind faith could save us.
>
> We confess everything takes luck, even a friend's
> jaunty steps on a moon we're staring at. Tonight,
> even if we call to it, peace, be still, the moon
> keeps bleaching before our eyes. We wait for grace
>
> in a world deserted, where the blood of goats
> can't save us. The babies we raised were worth it,
> but now we're alone, lost in a snow field at night
> in mountains. (63)

The poem ends like another moonlit poem, "Dover Beach," with a plea to be true to each other: "Tonight, we swear we'll worship flesh / and tongues with more patient ears. . . . We know / we won't change much, but anyway we swear" (64). But there is a difference. Matthew Arnold's melancholy couple make love their retreat from a harsh world and from the absence of God. McDonald's couple are older and wiser, accustomed to waiting for grace, accustomed to the arbitrary hardships and pleasures of human life in God's universe.

There are times, of course, when insight comes in a rush. One epiphany comes to an errant son in "In Times of Fever." His hard-drinking father had reformed after his wife had nearly died of fever. When the son comes home drunk one night and passes out in the front yard, his father lets him sleep and stays by him. The son wakes to unexpected grace: "When I awoke I found him / with me on the bottom step. I saw his hand come down / and flinched, and almost missed the blessing" (*Witching on Hardscrabble* 56). Exasperated hunters find an epiphany in the comic and powerful poem "Caught in a Squall Near Matador." Soaked and angry, they break into a sheep-herder's cabin and start a fire in the fireplace. They toss old magazines and maps into the fire but stop, surprised, at a calendar with

> a pastel maiden kneeling on a stone
> as if praying beside still water, knowing
> the shepherd whose hands find her
> will take her in and let her lie down
> at his table here in mesquite pastures. (27)

Their mood and perceptions change; they realize the blessings of home and marriage that wait for them after the storm has gone.

We turn now to some of McDonald's poems where vision is realized in action. These are poems of prayerful risk, couched in such metaphors as farming, flying, and fishing. To persevere in these things requires some sort of faith, some conviction (or at least a strong hunch) about things not seen. "Settling the Plains" says that the first settlers "planted / cottonseeds to prove they believed / in miracles." "Like Moses," they "called on God // to bless them all for doubting" (*Night Landings* 43). "Estacado" describes the speaker's Quaker great-grandparents who moved to West Texas expecting it to be "their promised land." They came "with nothing but a letter / to lead them." Even though the prairie "reminded them of bread without yeast, / the unleavened body of the Lord," they learned that "[t]he only milk here flowed in the cow / roped to their wagon, / their only honey, words in a book" (*After the Noise of Saigon* 14). "Luck of the Draw" makes irrigated farming a matter of luck and faith: water-witching "is prophecy, / and drilling a well, creation." The farmers pump water "up from nothing we've ever seen, / pouring our luck over fields." If the aquifer goes dry, they are certain that "nothing we know brings water out of stone," in contrast with Moses, who was promised that water would flow from the rock when he spoke to it. The speaker's conclusion about dry-land farming is that "Home is a casino / of chance and choice, / four arms that hold each other" (*Counting Survivors* 74). Even with this fatalism, a farmer's choice to search for water and drill down to it is an image of perseverance, not passive survival. "Witching on Hardscrabble" also makes water-witching an act of faith but one often futile. "Farming on dry land, a man keeps his witch-stick / handy. . . . Something will give a sign, and faith aside, / you go witching. . . ." The speaker mulls over his uncle's saying that "[i]f Zacchaeus / could see the Lord from a sycamore, . . . the same branch / ought to point me to the water of life" (*Rafting the Brazos* 76). Frustrated, he wonders whether his is the one place in Texas that won't yield water. In "Rigging the Windmill," the speaker completes "[a]nother well / witched with a willow stick. . . ." He loiters at the top, wondering "how many angels dance / in whirlwind, how many times / a pump goes around before breaking" (*Witching on Hardscrabble* 5). Even gardening can be a wry act of faith and an expectation of blessing. In "Weeding the Strawberry Garden," the speaker praises rain that is "as loud and steady as faith / if faith had sound." To a gardener, "[t]hat's prayer / in the garden, chopping the crust // with steel prongs" (*Blessings the Body Gave* 64). When this horticultural "prayer" is answered with a full crop, they share with neighbors, for they still have strawberry preserves from the previous year, "pressure-cooked," and, in the biblical phrase, "pressed down, / running over" (65).

Other Western activities provide emblems of prayerful risk. For example, "Midnight at Dillon" is humorous but direct in its Christian symbolism. As after the flood, cabins and homes lie beneath Dillon Reservoir, where "fish of all sizes breed like the days of Noah." The fishermen drop their lines, "true believers in lures and tobacco juice." They pass bourbon around "like communion, / the fellowship of the spirit of fishing / all that calls us from the sleep of this world." They fish, ready to feel

> the first hard whip of the line
> from under, to hold in our hands
> the wonder, the assurance
> of things not seen. (*Witching on Hardscrabble* 64)

In "Rodeo Fool," a monologue by a rodeo clown whose job is to rescue contestants, the speaker recounts how the spectators

> laugh at me and wave as if I'm some kind
> of saint, a fool holy enough to do what
> they'd like to do, nightly to save someone
> from death and make believe it's fun.
> Having seen him, they drive home
> believing death's a black bull
> mad and charging, all men are brave and cunning,
> that all fall down, get gored and trampled on,

all men are able to rise with the help
of clowns, able to look death in the eye,
to wear a clown's face, laughing, and walk again.
                              (*After the Noise of Saigon* 7)

The rodeo clown becomes a holy fool, wearing baggy pants, clown makeup, and cowboy boots as he imitates the risen Christ.

Flight is an obvious metaphor for prayerful risk, and McDonald's years as a pilot and instructor have given him hundreds of flight poems. "In unstable air / we find what dreams are made of," says the speaker of "Praying a Stall Won't Spin Us" (*The Flying Dutchman* 47). Flying in a storm has extra risk. The speaker in "First Solo in Thunderstorms" recalls that "[f]lying by dials, feet firm // on the rudders, I kept the stick / and throttle steady by faith." Clearly the struggle is more spiritual and emotional than physical:

At night, what can flesh do
but go on fighting panic,

believing storms like our lives
have to end, that wings never
level enough could hold me. . . . (*Night Landings* 16–7)

The speaker of "Taking Off in Winter" traces an even more literal connection between faith and flying. Taxiing before takeoff, he recalls his cowboy days, especially the Sunday services with

red hymnals of the Sacred Harp
swaying in our fists, our bowed legs
catching the first of the spirit,

the whole church of boots stomping
with new wine of the Sabbath,
like now, moving fast down a runway
and rising, lips healed
scorched eyes able to see. (*Rafting the Brazos* 18–9)

The faith in which perseverance is grounded shows plainly in "Faith Is a Radical Master" (*When Skies Are Not Cloudy*). In a living room, the speaker comforts a friend who has just been diagnosed with cancer:

Telephoned,

we've come to hold you. The ghost
who walked with mourners to Emmaus
hovers in this room. We are mere mortals,

all. We don't know anything but this.
Who knows this winter drought will last?
Who swears the last blind beggar's

doomed, no spittle for his lids?
Who calls down fire from heaven
and isn't seared? (43)

McDonald's most detailed exploration of faith may be "For God in
My Sorrows" in his 1998 collection, *Blessings the Body Gave*. Through
a meditation on the stars, which becomes a dialectic with himself,
the speaker reaches for the God behind them. He wants not the stars
"but beyond, whatever scattered them: *that* power":

Black night
has answers I don't want. But after stars collapse,
after all that mass snuffs out like a match, after whatever

Peter meant by the known world melting with fervent heat,
How much remains?

He wonders if blackness is what he really wants. What would he find
through the blackness, though—"The light that guided wise men? /
No, that's done and over, servant of the source I yearn for" (77). Nor
do the astronomers satisfy his yearning:

I believe

as I know my hand is here before me in the dark, my eyes
stretched wide—sun, moon and stars almost forgotten—
I feel faith inches away from my face, thumb and split claws

Cunningly made to hold a rope or grope along the wall at night
for a light switch. When I close my eyes, magically,
it's here. This, this is what I need, without lights or cities
man-made and dying, somehow to know I'm known. (78)

Perseverance and faith have their reward. For an emblem of this
reward and as a conclusion for this survey, we might consider
"Mesas I Never Took the Time to Climb," the concluding poem in
Counting Survivors. The speaker rides across his ranch as night falls,
seeing his house and the "starry skies / we pretend are diamonds."
He feels contentment with his trophies of perseverance—old boots,
old gloves, "that perfect slap of leather chaps." But the sight of a dying buzzard has made him pensive—"[w]ill it miss / the soaring, the
glide toward wide horizons?" Buzzards above him, attendants on
death, are "wheeling a slow blessing on flesh." An old survivor, the
speaker calmly begins to take stock, looking up toward the mesas he

has never bothered to ascend. He always took for granted that "[h]awks see no farther / than I could see from a mesa. The view is there, / if I want it." Soon, he decides, he will want it. He will discard earthly control and anxiety by cutting down his fences and riding to the top of a mesa he "never took the time to climb." Sending his gelding home, he will look down at his ranch the way the hawk or buzzard sees it, the way God sees it: "I'll look at these flat fields from far above, / the same parched sand and cactus after sundown, / night shining not with diamonds, but real stars." His old world will not have changed; sand and cactus will stay "the same"; but he will have moved to a place of vision and truth. Stars will not be pretended diamonds but "real stars" (79). The journey to the top of the mesa is a journey from the world of impressions and change into the world of truth and permanence. McDonald's homely image takes on the profundity of Paul's statement, "[f]or now we see through a glass, darkly; but then face to face: now I know in part; but then shall I know even as also I am known" (I Corinthians 13:12).

In volume after volume, McDonald and his reader earn the sense of peace in a poem like this one. After traveling through puzzled and painful vignettes of war, drought, and human ruin, not to mention the matter-of-fact accounts of unearned blessing and unearned disaster, they have not found peace casually. But they have found it. If luck has brought survival, perseverance has brought peace. In McDonald's splendid poetry, integrity consists in declaring the worst so that we may believe in the best and persevere.

Forms of Incarnation in the Recent Poetry of Walt McDonald

Helen Maxson

In his landmark book *Mimesis: The Representation of Reality in Western Literature*, Erich Auerbach traces strategies of literary realism through twenty eras extending from Homer to Marcel Proust. In the process, he describes the emergence in medieval Christian thought of the construct we think of as incarnation, defined by Auerbach as the blending in sublimity of the exalted and the ordinary:

> In antique theory, the sublime and elevated style was called *sermo gravis* or *sublimis;* the low style was *sermo remissus* or *humilis;* the two had to be kept strictly separated. In the world of Christianity, on the other hand, the two are merged, especially in Christ's Incarnation and Passion, which realize and combine *sublimis* and *humilitas* in overwhelming measure. (151).

Auerbach discusses Holy Scripture as an early manifestation of this union, explaining that it "had created an entirely new kind of sublimity, in which the everyday and the low were included, not excluded, so that, in style as in content, it directly connected the lowest with the highest" (154).

Holy Scripture enacted the principle of incarnation not only in its composition, but also in its role in Christian life: this most sacred collection of writings was seen as best "understood by all who are humble and filled with faith" (154). Just as God in human form gave mankind its highest gift, so on the meekest of readers does his Word have greatest impact.

In fact, much about the medieval world Auerbach describes illustrates this principle. His argument begins in the realm of literary aesthetics, exploring a twelfth-century Christmas play about Adam and Eve. The importance of its characters to human history makes the play's subject sublime, but its style is common. Elsewhere Auerbach brings his discussion to theology by examining Christ's incarnation, the residence of the divine in the fallen. At other points, he finds enactments of the principle in lifestyle, discussing a thirteenth-century letter from Francis of Assisi to another brother in his order urging him "not to leave the world behind—but to mingle with its torment and to endure evil with passionate devotion" (167). The dynamics of incarnation became a model for many forms of activity adhering to Christian beliefs in medieval life.

Of course, Auerbach is discussing one stage of a developing theme whose roots lie much earlier in the history of Christianity. *The Blackwell Encyclopedia of Modern Christian Thought* describes the process whereby it took hold. The God of the Hebrews had been predominantly a transcendent being, unwilling to be represented by worldly images. His nature would have made his incarnation in worldly forms unlikely. Similarly, Paul's letters refrain from incarnational theology, finding in Jesus a counterpart to Adam who succeeds—where Adam had failed—in resembling, but not embodying, God. However, in the Gospel of John the divine and the human merge: "the Word was made flesh" (1:14). John's assertion that "the Word was with God and the Word was God" sets up the paradoxical relationship of sameness and difference that has characterized the orthodox Christian view of incarnation for centuries. The Council of Nicea decreed in 325 that Jesus shares God's nature. The Council of Chalcedon went further in 451 to assert that Jesus Christ possesses both "a complete humanity and a complete divinity, and that they are united in his person 'without confusion, without change, without division, without separation.'" Here was the perfectly balanced union of man and God that Christians have traditionally ascribed to Jesus since that time (MacQuarrie 269–70).

Since its emergence, the principle of incarnation has lain at the heart of Christian thought and influenced centuries of literature. Contemporary literary critics and scholars trace it in writers ranging in time from Anselm through Robert Southwell to many recent writers like William Wordsworth, Robert Browning, Gerard Manley Hopkins, T. S. Eliot, C. S. Lewis, Wendell Berry, and Mikhail Bakhtin.[1] As a literary element, the principle of incarnation has given artistic form to the tenets of orthodox Christian faith. At the same time, it has reflected the thinking of many other religions which, in their own ways, assert union between the human and the divine. Finally, it has operated as a shaping principle in literary explorations of secular contexts. Just as Auerbach finds the principle of incarnation throughout medieval life, subsequent Western literature has depicted the ways in which it shapes and gives meaning to the world at large.

Varying as they move from one context to another, forms of literary incarnation define the cultures in which they appear and indicate the influence of a culture on the writing it produces. Scholar Myra Fehlen begins her book *American Incarnation: The Individual, the Nation, and the Continent* by locating the most important influences on the American identity in "the physical fact of the continent," explaining that "when the European settlers saw themselves as quickening a virgin land, the modern spirit completed its genesis by becoming flesh in the body of the American continent" (3–4). Fehlen goes on to trace this construct throughout American literature. Seeing in the land an embodiment of their identity, American writers participate in a tradition inherited through their own culture and through the larger Western culture of which America is a part.

True to this heritage, the poetry of Walt McDonald draws widely on the range of literary incarnations discussed here. As an American, McDonald finds in his native land metaphorical equivalents of human nature, experience, and culture. For him, the Texas prairie reflects and determines what we are. At the same time, he uses incarnation more broadly, letting it operate independent of the land, locating it in both spiritual and worldly contexts. The exalted and the common in McDonald's world often house each other, bringing some form of sublimity to most, if not all, aspects of life.

McDonald's sense of his own writing process reflects the incarnational nature of his vision. In a 1997 interview, McDonald described the generation of his poems as a process of discovery, seeing images and poems as gems hidden in lesser, more tentative writing:

> What keeps me going back to the keyboard day after day is a simple faith that words will show me the way. For a while, I feel totally ignorant; I have no idea what's coming. . . . For me, writing is an act of radical faith, like witching water. . . . After Vietnam, finding images like water in this suddenly fabulous desert where I live thrills and sustains me. Every day is grace. . . . Creative writing means *discovery* of poems we wouldn't have found if we hadn't begun to write. . . . Down here, under the pressure and heat of living are the images we need for making poems— some of them already diamonds. (interview with Fred Alsberg 6–7)

In McDonald's verse, much of what we want and need, elevated by its scarcity as well as by a spiritual or intangible nature, waits

diamondlike in some unlikely, obscuring, or even contradicting
context that, precisely because it is common, gives accessibility to
that which we seek. For this poet, much of experience consists in the
search and in the joy brought to us by what we find.

Each of McDonald's books conjures a distinct universe operating
according to its own laws. It is true that in theme, technique, and
phrasing, each book has much in common with the others. A few poems share titles with poems in other books. Still, by virtue of elements like juxtaposition, emphasis, and theme, each book offers a
unique perspective. Furthermore, internal consistencies and corre-
spondences give cohesion to each volume. McDonald's poems are
often clustered thematically, with some borrowing images or phrases
from elsewhere in the same volume and others paired as complementary opposites. Possessing its own character, each book adjusts
the principle of incarnation to serve its own themes. As the exalted
and the common change definition from book to book, the forms of
incarnation they create vary, speaking to both the breadth and the
consistency of McDonald's verse.

The medieval version of incarnation discussed by Auerbach involves the simultaneously divine and human nature that Christians
ascribe to Jesus Christ. In McDonald's verse, biblical references
abound, and the Christian understanding of incarnation finds confirmation at several points. In fact, one could argue that even those
poems that do not locate divinity in our midst involve Christian un-
dertones and implications. Still, McDonald is very much a student of
this world, saying of the Texas plains where life is hard and risky,

> I love this cactus land,
> the way it all says wait,
> the moon a headstone
> worshipped all night by coyotes
> seeking the highest knoll. (123)

There is religion here, but it has little to do with the Judeo-Christian
worship of God. In the same poem, titled "Plains and the Art of Writing" from *All That Matters,* the image of a snake moving over the
plains suggests the process of writing about them. The speaker describes snakes as

> excited by the scent of blood
> stirring at dusk,
> slowly uncoiling,
> tongues flick-flicking,
> long muscles flowing
> over the old, familiar sand. (123)

Detail by detail, McDonald's poems "flow over" the Texas plains, celebrating them and the earthly life of which they are a part. Of the kinds of incarnation they include, none is more powerful than those reflecting traditional Christian faith. At the same time, many locate great power in human experience on its own terms and bespeak McDonald's rich appreciation of the immediate world.

Four of McDonald's recent books illustrate his varying use of incarnation as a shaping principle and the varying degrees to which it includes the Christian sense of the term. The dynamics of incarnation in the books *All That Matters* and *Blessings the Body Gave* operate largely in the physical world. Even though aspects of the Judeo-Christian tradition inform both books, in neither is the spiritual a frequent component of the world portrayed. In *Counting Survivors*, the workings of incarnation are suggested by their absence, an absence that makes its own comment and becomes more conspicuous when the book is seen in light of the other three. In *Where Skies Are Not Cloudy*, however, McDonald clearly asserts his faith in the Christian sense of incarnation, depicting a world in which Christ's presence takes earthly forms that make him accessible to humanity.

I

All That Matters takes as a theme the biblical process of original creation, enlisting the work of incarnation on its behalf. Photographs printed along with these poems underscore the giving of form to worldly things. The final lines of the book summarize much of its contents, locating in the Texas landscape the paradox of making something from nothing. The plains portray "this scene in the desert / where we live, only brown earth and sky / and in between, all that matters" (135). If only "brown earth and sky" compose the scene, then "all that matters" resides in a void between them, a nothingness that human creation fills. It is this blank canvas that the book celebrates, the potential that lies within earthly effort and artistry. At some points, human artistry arranges disorderly materials rather than filling a void. Early lines of this poem focus, as McDonald often does, on the creative activity of the speaker's wife, who gathers from the surrounding landscape pigment for paint and objects for decorative arrangements. Every aspect of her life makes of the desert's potential a changing "scene," an evolving portrait expressing her values and standards of design:

> Even me, she polishes nightly with the roughest
> of kisses, giving up on nothing
> she's started, taking years and three children to
> paint over and over this scene in the desert. (135)

An artist for whom the people and the situations of her life provide the raw materials, she creates a reality that brings out their best, enacting her love as wife and mother.

The Vietnam War keeps a lower profile in this book than in McDonald's others, but it indirectly determines much about the landscape the poems describe and the creativity that the landscape demands. "After the Flight Home from Saigon" evokes a poem by an earlier poet in which another female artist shapes her world, serving in the history of American poetry as something of an archetype. McDonald's poem begins, "This is the rage for order on the plains, / barbed wires from post to post," (8) bringing to mind the phrase "Oh! Blessed rage for order" in Wallace Stevens's "The Idea of Order at Key West." The allusion humorously deflates the singing of Stevens's character, who "sang beyond the genius of the sea," to the stringing of barbed wire from post to post. At the same time, the cosmic dimensions of Stevens's poem bring significance to the compensatory orderliness McDonald ascribes to American soldiers after the fall of Saigon, confirming the power of human effort against a chaotic reality that would, if not defied, drown it out. Of course, shaping chaos and creating something from nothing are not the same process, but in the universe of this book, characterized by both the jungles of Vietnam and the plains of Texas, they play the same role, one becoming the other as McDonald's central theme moves from poem to poem. Both blend the desired and the status quo, the exalted and the common, into a new thing. It is interesting to note that biblical scholars have found both kinds of creation in Genesis; even though transcendence in *All That Matters* does not take a spiritual form, the poems reflect scriptural subtleties.[2]

The possibility of divine participation in human efforts recurs throughout the book, helping to determine the mode of incarnation informing it. Frequent images of desert nothingness make an eloquent backdrop for many explorations of that theme. In "Blue Skies," for example, one coyote

> with his heart
> on his tongue
> sniffs, sips a puddle
> of air. Nothing.
> A breath of wind
> would be enough,
> odor of coney, possum,
>
> . . . .
> even a turtle. Anything. (74)

But there is nothing. In the poem "Things about to Disappear," there is no water for twenty miles (121). A complaint in "Deductions from the Laws of Motion" summarizes the emptiness of the plains: "All roads lead away from here" (105).

Still, in this expanse of drought and absence, human effort pro-duces water and plenty repeatedly. In "Drying Up," for instance, "my brother with no choice changes oil in his engines, / tightens the nuts and in March starts them up / again. He waits. The wells suck deep. The water flows" (71). The sense of miracle is strong here as it is throughout the book. Furthermore, in some cases, the plenitude described contains ambiguities that raise the issue of source: is it di-vine or human? The opening poem, "Wind and Hardscrabble," de-scribes cattle that benefit from windmills:

> Parched, they wade still pastures
> shimmering in heat waves
> and muzzle deep in stock tanks
> filled and overflowing. (3)

The still pastures echo Psalm 23, conflating green pastures with still waters, interchanging the ever-desired water with dry land. The title of the collection's second work, "Starting a Pasture," extends the first poem's allusion, and its opening words again blend water and land, this time in an image echoing McDonald's experience in South-east Asia: "Flooded with sun, this ranch looks like a rice field, / a trick of optics" (4). Thus, opening with plenty, the book soon, though subtly, suggests drought. Miracle and mirage undermine each other in these images, and the two poems, like others in *All That Matters*, stop short of confirming their own suggestion that divine provi-dence helps us to provide for ourselves. Several poems liken human effort to divine creation, but the book leaves unresolved the question of divine participation in human endeavors, reproducing the uncer-tainty of characters in "Settling the Plains" who "planted / cotton-seed to prove they believed / in miracles" (61) and offering for comfort only an undefined power that may be obtained when the here and now imitates eternal patterns or when one believes in God.

Thus, human creativity, grit, and faith—in man and in God—are made known (or embodied) by the fruits of this world. Hopkins finds evidence of God in the dappled things of the earth. Similarly, McDonald gives form to human creativity in whatever takes shape between earth and sky—between, that is, the realms that God has made. A mode of creation as well as a mode of housing, incarnation in *All That Matters* fills the empty and arranges the chaotic to fit our needs. It is the same process by which a song, as Stevens put it, "[m]astered the night and portioned out the sea, / Fixing embla-zoned zones and fiery poles, / Arranging, deepening, enchanting night" (98).

II

The title of *Blessings the Body Gave* brings to mind the Christian dichotomy between body and spirit, with the religious connotations of "blessings" contributing to that effect. In fact, the spiritual, as conceived in Christian terms, appears in this book in such a way as to affirm faith in the Judeo-Christian God. However, as is the case in *All That Matters*, the spirit is not an emphatic presence here. The central dichotomy we find is not between body and soul, but between two kinds of blessings that the body gives, those representing the world and those enacting higher principles that transcend it. It is easier here than in *All That Matters* to connect life's higher blessings to Christian values, in part because the reader encounters the presence of the biblical God along with an explicit process of searching for him. Furthermore, the poems' complementary blessings extend the title's suggestion of the opposing traits perfectly balanced in the orthodox understanding of Jesus Christ. Still, things of the spirit here are distinctly upstaged by things of the physical world. It is largely within this world that the book's incarnational duality exerts its shaping power.

Even as the spirit is most often absent in this book, so are the particulars of the Texas landscape found in so much of McDonald's verse. In terms that do not reflect one locale, *Blessings the Body Gave* explores universal themes, one of which is the unification in our carnal nature of two opposing characteristics, each determining an aspect of our lives. On one hand, human beings act out the laws of animal life. In the practice of war, we live in packs, prey on each other, and suffer the loss to untimely death of those we love. One gruesome poem details a wildebeest's death in the jaws of a crocodile, an eloquent comment on our behavior in war (36). Another poem, "East of Eden," paints an image of our fallen world, replete with writhing snakes:

> Here by the lakes
> and shade of East Texas, dangerous
> mating in the shade of green magnolias
> when dogwoods blossom and azaleas bloom. (46)

It is "a dark garden of possibilities" in which "at ease / the heart hears itself, beating the old tattoo / of hunger and of hate" characterized by "macaws and cheetahs screaming, stray goats / and panthers leaping, light flashing on teeth." The lush vegetation of East Texas parallels here the jungles of Vietnam in which soldiers acquired persistent nightmares.

On the other hand, if *Blessings the Body Gave* begins in the "shade of East Texas" with violent death, it ends in the cactus of West Texas where an aging couple approaches a natural death together. The speaker in the penultimate poem of the book, "Where Buffalo Grass Grows Loud If We Listen," extols his marriage, describing himself and his wife as two loving "monogamous dinosaurs" in a world where partners change quickly (107). The book's last poem, "The Waltz We Were Born For," affirms human relationship as the state we were meant for, countering jungle brutality with loyalty and paired dance:

> What matters
> is timeless, dazzling devotion—not rain,
> not Eden gardenias, but cactus in drought,
> not just moons of deep sleep, not sunlight or stars,
> not the blue, but the darkness beyond. (109)

Though much of the book dwells on death and irretrievable loss, these lines suggest a life after death, a transcendence made real through love.

Still, when we love, we do not leave behind the immediate world. The book's title poem describes a week spent by an older couple in a mountain cabin, their love very much a blessing of the body:

> Her hands knew all the songs
> I needed, and she twisted distant stations off,
>
> Our last hours alone in the mountains.
> I leaned my rawhide chair to hold her,
> the pine logs popping sparks. She rubbed
> my flannel sleeves and we locked hands and rocked,
> the cabin cold unless we faced the fire. (98–9)

Each of these impulses—war and love, jungle and desert—is needed to define the other, bringing redemption to the low and definition to the high. In the scheme of this book, both are blessings of the body, bound together as complements that make us whole. Ever-present, they offer us a constant opportunity to act on one rather than the other, to choose love over "the old tattoo / of hunger and hate."

In the poem "The Child Abandoned on the Porch," the two impulses are juxtaposed and reflect a Christian perspective unusual in the book. On the one hand, we have the news report of a child abandoned by its mother; on the other, a couple to whom an infant they are adopting comes as the Christ child came to believing shepherds:

> The nurse must have swaddled babies
> a thousand times, but to us she was an angel

and we mere shepherds in from the cold.
There, near the gold-domed Denver capitol, star
on a highway map, there where they gathered taxes. . . .

In these parents a sense wells up that the child is miraculous:

. . . only that he
was the one, all of our luck in one boy,
and when we held him, he was,
he was the child in our arms. (51)

This moment constitutes the parents' own epiphany, pointing to the
Incarnation effected in Christ. Furthermore, the poem's association
between parenthood and Christ's way of life extends, though quietly, throughout the book. The final poem celebrates the "joyful
noise" of the speaker's playing children, evoking the gratitude of
Psalms 66 and 98 while linking the body's higher blessings once
again to God.

In "For God in My Sorrows," McDonald explores the highest form
of the partnership of high and low, the redemption of struggle as a
journey into God's presence. Going beyond biblical analogy, this
poem portrays divine presence. However, the speaker must resist
the temptation to use light to find it. Paradoxically, intimacy with
God comes through darkness:

. . . I try to ignore the stars, a billion witnesses
that I give myself to black skies, not even gravity holding
    me back,
cast into outer darkness, . . .

. . . .
. . . Is it blackness I seek,
after all, total loss, . . .

. . . .
. . . What, beyond wars and weapons, beyond stars,
what could I find? The light that guided wise men?
No, that's done and over, servant of the source I yearn for.

Astronomers call it no star at all, scoffing. I believe
as I know my hand is here before me in the dark, my eyes
stretched wide—sun, moon and stars almost forgotten—
I feel faith inches away from my face, thumb and split claws

cunningly made to hold a rope or grope along the wall at night
for a light switch. When I close my eyes, magically,
it's here. This, this is what I need, without lights or cities
man-made and dying, somehow to know I'm known. (77–8)

Here the circularity of knowing one is known establishes a communion with God, offering the speaker the comfort and intimacy that he
could find in a family but that death cannot interrupt or alter. Af-
firming the spirituality of a traditional Christian life, the poem
draws on the paradox of the *via negativa* to describe it. Even as it is
Satan's cunning, not Christ's inspiration, that prompts the searcher
to look for light, so it is the darkness incarnate in the body, not light,
that brings us what we need. As one scholar puts it, "the path of
God must follow the dark road of unknowing and inner suffering"
(McGinn 200). A function of the fallen, sublime experience becomes
an immediate part of life.

III

Among McDonald's recent books, the 1993 collection *Where Skies
Are Not Cloudy* makes divine presence and influence on the Texas
Plains most emphatic. The book's vision centers on incarnation as
Christians conceive of it, presenting a human form for God in a physical world, mingling high and low in transcendent experience. At
first glance, images in the book do not often seem to suggest the exalted. Furthermore, a frequent shifting of perspective between and
within poems—not surprising in a world offering the long view and
plenty of room in which to change one's stance—seems to thin out
any evidence of the eternal or absolute, apparently losing it in the
abundant space of alternatives. When one's reality can change so
easily, where does one locate within it what is constant?

It is precisely in these varying perspectives, however, and in the
routine details the poems depict that the true and the transcendent
reside. The poems assume many angles on biblical stories and principles, giving the initial impression that none has any authority and,
as a result, that this world contains no transcendent or eternal value.
But at certain points the flux ceases, having brought a poem's speaker
to genuine understanding. At these points a poem's diction may
change so as to confirm biblical truths that the poem evokes, or the
spiritual may emerge in convincing assertion. Either way, we know
that despite our initial perceptions we inhabit a Christ-centered
universe.

Whereas McDonald drew on the vision of Wallace Stevens in *All
That Matters,* in *Where Skies Are Not Cloudy* he shares the perspective
of a Christian master poet and forebear, T. S. Eliot. In *Four Quartets,*
our human endeavors to achieve perfect knowledge leave most of us
with only "hints and guesses"; nonetheless, in this poem's paradoxical universe, "the hint half guessed, the grit half understood, is

Incarnation." Eliot embraces misunderstanding as a path to understanding, saying that "We had the experience but missed the meaning, / And approach to the meaning restores the experience / in a
different form" (44). It is the journey toward knowledge, rather than
knowledge itself, that transforms; incarnation lies in the incomplete.

Elsewhere in *Four Quartets* we hear that "The sea has many
voices," and learn that they comprise a cacophony of generally un-
holy sounds. Still, amid them, one voice expresses the eternal:

> The tolling bell
> Measures time not our time, run by the unhurried
> Ground swell, a time
> Older than the time of chronometers . . .
>
> .   .   .   .
>
> And the ground swell, that is and was from the beginning,
> Clangs
> The bell. (36–7)

We know the groundswell here to be a divine presence that speaks
through one of the sea voices, the tolling bell. Later Eliot refers to
"the sea bell's / Perpetual angelus," referring to a devotion com-
memorating the Incarnation of Christ (43). The sea voices' inclusion
of the sublime in their number redeems them and points to a spiritual principle inherent in the poem's universe. Similarly, the varying
perspectives found in *Where Skies Are Not Cloudy*, even the uncon-
vincing ones, serve the purposes of incarnation, our imperfect un-
derstandings giving worldly form to truth. By extension, the poems
suggest that thinking of Christ often, even in idiosyncratic ways,
brings us moments when we see him clearly, experience his grace,
and are healed by him.

Many of the shifting perspectives in *Where Skies Are Not Cloudy*
emerge as part of the characterization process that brings the poems'
often quirky speakers to life. Others result from frequent and prominent literary allusions. The book's title, indicating that allusion functions here as both technique and theme, is lifted from the folk song
"Home on the Range." McDonald's speakers refer, either explicitly
or implicitly, to Humpty Dumpty; the Bible; the myth of Icarus;
Greek and Roman gods; poetry of Yeats, Frost, and Eliot; folk clichés
and songs. Furthermore, poetic allusions may bear an ironic relationship with their referents and with other aspects of the poems in
which they lie, and this irony adds to the number of perspectives we
find in the book. In "Sunday Morning Roundup," for example, the
speaker's unwitting reference to Psalm 23 deepens the hypocrisy
with which he justifies his absence from church even as it undercuts
his rationalizing (13). The speaker in "Frogs Croaking Their Love
Songs" seems to describe the philosophy underlying McDonald's

literary strategies: "We tell a prairie all we hope it means, / In-
venting corrals and barns" (8). The world in this poem seems reduced to perspective, with corrals and barns carrying no intrinsic
value of their own, serving only as inventions to express the wishes of
their builder. The speaker hears love songs in the croaking of frogs
and erases thousands of stars with each blink of his eyes. Momen-
tarily, it seems that the world is of his own making as he suggests,
not a reality independent of the viewer. By the same token, no one
point of view seems final in the book's patchwork of characterization and allusion.

The collection's biblical allusions, shaping elements of the incarnation it depicts, are caught up in this seeming relativism. Some distort the Bible. Others show both understanding and reverence but
fail to convey authority simply because so many have not done so.
Still, in the end, certain aspects of *Where Skies Are Not Cloudy* do give
authority to constant values that its shifting perspectives obscure. Its
structure is one literary feature that has this effect. Roughly halfway
through the book, several poems explore the nature and influence of
Jesus Christ in allusions that transcend perspective, forming something like a center around which the collection shifts and evoking the
first poem's appreciation of a circling windmill that changes the
desert to green pastures (3). Here we recognize the process of incarnation that the other poems, like Eliot's hints and guesses, or his ca-
cophonous sea voices, have carried out, offering us the worldly
forms which we need in order to find what is true. It is worthwhile to
look at these poems closely since, like spiritual things in a physical
context, the truth they portray takes subtle forms.

The poem "All Boys Are Humpty Dumpty" (38) reenacts in Texan
terms the story from Matthew 8:28–34 of Jesus' casting devils into a
herd of swine, which then careens madly down a cliff into the sea.
McDonald's version is the retrospective tale of a man who as a child
fell into a pigpen and was at the mercy of the pigs until one of his
brothers lifted him out. He recalls the

> . . . pigs fumbling
> and shoving me, a heart of shoats
>
> and me the cliff they charged.
> Thumped down in the dust and pig dung,
> I heard grunts and felt hot devil snouts
>
> rooting my face and crotch.
> I remember my brothers shouting,
> the whack of sticks casting out demons,

> pigs squealing and stumbling
> in sunlight and dust
> and someone lifting me. (38)

The speaker's point of view "from below" radically alters our experience of the biblical narrative. Furthermore, the title of the poem
seems to lower the biblical to the level of an inconsequential nursery
rhyme about a smashed egg that cannot be reassembled. Initially,
there appears to be no hope of redemption here. Still, the notion of a
fall from grace is clearly part of the story, as is the notion of a
brother's performing the saving function of Christ. What is more, the
poem's diction changes in the last three lines from the earthy to the
transcendent, passing through an intermediate stage of sunlight and
dust as the boy is lifted from dung into safety. A colloquial speaker
would probably refer to someone's lifting him *up*, but this speaker
who is simply "lifted" moves simultaneously into unwitting lyricism and into the spiritual and emotional relief that a physical lifting
up can only suggest as metaphor. In its final stylistic grace, the poem
leaves behind the jolting, squealing, and stumbling of the pigs, along
with the conflicting perspectives that undermine many of the book's
apparent messages; in their stead, it creates a transcendent state af-
firming the power of Christ to save.

   One page closer to the book's center, the poem "Macho" traces
much the same journey. A hunter who associates hunting with the
need, which Adam incurs through the Fall, to labor for one's living,
the speaker distorts the biblical story somewhat by having Adam assume the posture of the serpent:

> This is how it is some days,
>
> crawl on your belly like a snake,
> taking nothing home but dust,
> picking burrs from your shirt,
>
> Hard work like love, labor we live on
> after sundown.

The poem's references to Genesis are many. At the same time, the
poem takes the sun's power as a theme: it is possibly the sun glinting
off the hunter's rifle that alerts a deer to his presence. In his frustration, the hunter tries to bring the sun down to size by questioning
its traditional associations with divinity: "What if the sun / was
never a god, a burning bush, / a chariot?" This mixing of religious
traditions—the sun god Helius crossing the sky in a chariot and the
Old Testament God speaking from a burning bush—privileges neither, placing them together on one plane. Nothing is sacred here. In

the uneven rhythm of the next sentence and in the incongruity of its images there is no suggestion of the transcendent, only the irritation of a man who mocks the sun's power with demeaning names: "Could it be swamp gas, / boots, perpetual stutter?" However, later in the poem, his naming ultimately picks up a momentum that leads him into more lyrical language:

> Or the rich man's tongue in torment
>
> With only the moon's eclipse
> Like a finger dipped in water to cool it?
> More like a man after all? (39)

In devaluing the sun, the speaker ultimately associates it with man, ironically suggesting both Christ's human form and the exalted being it embodied. Furthermore, his reference to the parable of Lazarus and the rich man (Luke 16:19–31) reinforces our sense that divine influence is at play in his thoughts. Jesus tells the story of the rich man who, unkind to the beggar Lazarus, goes to the torments of hell where his tongue burns; he begs Father Abraham to allow Lazarus, who is now in heaven, to dip his finger in water to cool his tongue. In his allusion, McDonald's hunter "deflates" the machismo of the sun into the burning that punishes arrogance, transforming himself unawares from a resentful complainer into a witness of God's sovereignty. It is true that the hunter's blindness is not resolved. He speaks better than he knows, and God's power seems circumscribed by the speaker's limited understanding. However, the lyricism expressing that power transcends limitation. The relief for which the rich man yearns is edged in the silver of the moon and cooling water. As the speaker's inspiration produces its final question—"More like a man after all?"—his simple words smooth the ugly staccato of gas and boots and stutter into the simple grace of truth.

At the middle of the book, we find "Faith Is a Radical Master," a dense palimpsest which conflates three New Testament scenes with a West Texas vignette in which Christ's healing power plays an explicit role. In this poem, the Christian perspective is not one among many; it is the only one, making it not perspective at all but simply reality. Christian faith informs the story from several angles that confirm each other and focus the poem's implications clearly:

> We touch you one by one and mumble,
> words stumbling on our tongues,
> stunned in your blurred living room
>
> hours after your lab report:
> a little lump, a mass of bulged,
> malignant cells. Telephoned

We've come to hold you. The ghost
who walked with mourners to Emmaus
hovers in this room. We are mere mortals,

all. We don't know anything but this.
Who knows this winter drought will last?
Who swears the last blind beggar's

doomed, no spittle for his lids?
Who calls down fire from heaven
and isn't seared? (43)

At the center of this poem lies a reference to the resurrected Christ
walking with two disciples to Emmaus (Luke 24:13). The poem re-
plays that scene with two differences: first, McDonald's modern disciples know as they walk who their companion is; second, he is not
physically among them. Experiencing his presence is a function not
of knowledge, but of faith. We thus learn that we must take faith as
our master when the Master in whom we have faith seems absent.

One illness that faith eradicates is, of course, doubt, the curing of
which is a major theme of "Faith Is a Radical Master." In Luke, the
journey to Emmaus is followed by the scene in which the disciples
come to know with whom they have walked. They feel Christ's
wounds, grasp the reality of his resurrection and, like Thomas in
John 20:25–7, grow stronger in their faith. In McDonald's poem, the
friends touch the cancer victim one by one and come to know the
ghost who hovers in the room. McDonald's metaphor for the consequences of doubt, the life-threatening nature of cancer, gives special
impetus to the development of faith; in his version of the touching of
Christ's wounds, overcoming doubt is urgent work.

The scene suggests the presence of the Holy Ghost, a means of val-
idating faith, with two allusions to Pentecost, one of which evokes as
well Elijah's contest with the prophets of Baal. At the beginning, the
friends are stunned by the diagnosis of cancer, "words stumbling on
[their] tongues." At the end, they are seared by the fire that has come
down from heaven. In this image, the spiritual power that comes to
the apostles in "cloven tongues like as of fire" (Acts 2:3) is infused
with that of the "fire of the Lord [that] fell" at Elijah's bidding, reminding the children of Israel that "The Lord, he is the God" (I Kings
18:38–9). The poem's speaker asks questions prompted by inspiration and faith. There is no need here for lyrical diction to signal unwitting knowledge of the divine, since the characters' conscious
faith finds its way into their ordinary speech. Unlike the questions at
the end of "Macho," those at the end of this poem are meant to express the hope that faith permits. They assert that as mere mortals

we do not know that the worst will come to pass or that Christ no longer heals; our blindness bestows possibility, not dubiousness. Along with hope, the poem's last question offers knowledge that if Christ does heal us, it will hurt. Here, the poem extends the metaphor of its title, putting forth the idea that faith as a radical master has much the same effect as does a radical mastectomy, excising sicknesses like sin and doubt or, in the poem's parallel metaphor, searing them away. We think of Christ as the "refiner's fire" (Malachi 3:2) that will purify us, and as the "consuming fire" (Hebrews 12:29) whom we must serve with fear. We think of Eliot's "intolerable shirt of flame / Which human power cannot remove" but which was designed by Love (57). We think of his image of Christ as a surgeon:

> The wounded surgeon plies the steel
> That questions the distempered part;
> Beneath the bleeding hands we feel
> The sharp compassion of the healer's art
> Resolving the enigma of the fever chart. (29)

McDonald's allusions reach deep into the tradition of Christian imagery, each one confirming our sense that for the poet they speak the truth. Faith in God's Comforter sustains the comforting friends and the cancer victim of "Faith Is a Radical Master," and in all of the poem's biblical allusions, West Texas merges with the Holy Land. The Resurrection of Christ is a fact of life here, and the unreliable perspectives of the book dissolve in the clear vision that sees the plains in his light.

IV

Since incarnation characteristically informs McDonald's vision, its absence in the 1995 book *Counting Survivors* is conspicuous. Dominated by the nightmares of returned soldiers, including their guilt at surviving, and focusing as well on the premature death of loved ones, the book conjures a world that seems flat and devoid of elevated or transcendent components. The behavior of an entire culture bespeaks distress. In "The Hairpin Curve at Durango," truck drivers selfishly hog the center of the road on hairpin turns. In "Uncle Jerry and the Velvet Dog," a wife whose husband's post-war pain undermines his promises to her punches a velvet dog he bought her and tries to shove it into a dumpster. Snakes and buzzards appear frequently. Life here incorporates much from the jungle world portrayed in *Blessings the Body Gave,* alleviated by only the vaguest suggestions of that book's devotion, love, creativity, or nurturance.

In the title poem of *Counting Survivors*, returned soldiers have suffered an ironic spiritual death:

> . . . Most friends I knew
> are back in body. . . .
> . . . .
> I wish for Easter all year long.
> I watch parades from curbs
> and wonder how do survivors live?
> how do the dead arise? (34)

There is no indication in this poem that Easter will come. A photograph of the Vietnam Wall Memorial introduces each section of poems, circumscribing all experience within that of war. In a number
of poems, and in a number of ways, people are reduced to names
like those on the Wall. Life unfolds in consistently diminished or
limited terms.

Repeatedly, poems in this book dispel myths, beliefs, and imaginary constructs that might otherwise relieve the facts of pain, loss,
and grief. The final poem ends with the speaker's intent to climb a
mesa he has never climbed in order to "look at these flat fields from
far above, / the same parched sand and cactus after sundown, /
night shining not with diamonds, but real stars" (79). The tone here
approaches the inspirational, suggesting a new beginning. Still, seeing stars as stars rather than as diamonds underscores the book's de-
bunking of myths that might otherwise give meaning to life or
sustenance to those who live. In "Charts," the speaker comments on
the inability of constellations, imaginary pictures inscribed in the
stars, to chart a human course, ending with a supplication for divine
guidance:

> . . . Father of light,
> we can't dread outer darkness where burning stars
> hurtle outward, a gallery of myths,
> but beg more light in this created world. (60)

These lines address God, but the poem gives no sense that an answer
will come. With the words, "We're not alone," "Neighbors Miles
Away" invites the reader to think of God but goes on to explain,
"When we drive flat roads to town, / neighbors miles away look up
and wave" (49), a tribute to Texan friendliness but not to divine companionship. These vast, empty plains seem analogous to the book's
vast, unpopulated skies, mentioned frequently, in which stars are
neither diamonds nor constellations and in which there is little evidence of God. In another poem, the speaker and his wife are sitting
together on a porch swing in the evening, and the repeated phrase,

"We're not alone," is explained in the line, "We hear a scream squeezed out by talons" (52). The transcendent seems evolved for the sole purpose of declaring it mythological, uncertain, or missing. In its place we find the violent natural forces that define this world.

Still, the various forms of incarnation one finds in McDonald's work as a whole encourage us to regard its absence in this book as one more variation on a theme. In this poet's vision, the principle of incarnation survives its own lapses. Taken together, the four books discussed here reflect the capacity of life to offer redemption, pointing overtly to that potential when it is not fulfilled. The Christian elements of McDonald's thought help us consider instances of this failure as products of our own choices or of divine reticence that we cannot understand rather than as contradictions of more hopeful perspectives. There is a suggestion of abiding promise when, in the lines cited earlier, "this cactus land / . . . all says wait." Merging emptiness and plenitude, pain and joy, selfishness and love, the wide expanses of world and experience in McDonald's verse embody their own transcendence. Seen in this larger frame, even their driest deserts connote fertility; their darkest struggles, meaning and hope.

VI. In McDonald's Own Words

An Interview with Walt McDonald

Phyllis Bridges

Walt McDonald is among the most admired of all writers from the Southwest. His nineteen collections of poetry have won many awards, and his workshops for writers have been in high demand. Walt McDonald is a native of Lubbock, Texas, where he is the Paul Whitfield Horn Professor of English and poet-in-residence at Texas Tech University. Dr. McDonald was Poet Laureate of Texas in 2001. Prior to his appointment to the faculty at Texas Tech, he was a member of the faculty of the United States Air Force Academy. He served as a pilot in the Air Force before his work in teaching. Walt McDonald and his wife Carol have been married over forty years. They have three children and seven grandchildren.

April 2000

Phyllis Bridges (PB):

When did you first begin to write poetry?

Walt McDonald (WM):

I came to poetry late, as a middle-aged Air Force pilot. After some of my friends went off to Vietnam, and one was shot down, then another, I felt a need to say something to them, or about them.

I was writing fiction in those years, and I turned to poems when nothing else worked; my first stumbling attempts were like letters to the dead, or to someone unable to hear, like a poem I wrote for my little daughter, when I got my own orders for over-seas.

PB: Was there some special moment or event that led you to begin writing?

WM: Probably, but I don't remember. I think I backed into writing, curious about a character and a situation I thought of, in graduate school. It was fun, like a hobby, and I wrote some other stories before going to Iowa's Writers' Workshop a few years later.

PB: What were the subjects of your earliest works?

WM: In poems: flying, Vietnam, good friends, and family. Those are still some of the regions I keep prowling—again, part of what I am. Tennyson's *Ulysses* says, "I am a part of all I've met."

PB: In what ways did your education at Texas Tech and the University of Iowa prepare you for your life as a poet and teacher? How early in your life did you know that you wanted to be a poet?

WM: I came to poetry late. Before Vietnam, I had tried nothing but fiction. In the 1960s I studied fiction writing under R. V. Cassill and Vance Bourjaily at the University of Iowa. I flew on weekends, on active duty in the Air Force—an odd, double life. At Iowa, I didn't have sense enough to even want to take a poetry workshop, so I'm always playing catch-up.

In 1977, after a sixth attempt at writing novels, I turned to poems with the energy I once poured into fiction—stumbling apprentice work, but finding a few poems before 1983 which made me think someday, maybe.

PB: Do you remember when and where your work was first published?

WM: My first dozen poems and stories, strung out over a half dozen years starting in 1967, were in journals including *New Campus Review, Prairie Schooner, Descant*, and *South Dakota Review*.

PB: How did you feel seeing your name and work in print for the first time?

WM: It meant nothing. Some of my best friends were in or soon going to Vietnam, and those early poems and stories seemed utterly insignificant. Like whatever I write now, those early attempts were only part of what I did, what I could do. Oh, I'm as vulnerable to the vanity of human wishes as Solomon was, often "desiring this man's art and that man's scope," as Shakespeare said. But I take heart from Paul's advice: "Whatever you do, work at it with all your heart, as working for the Lord."

PB: What would you say were the major literary influences on you in your student days? In your military service? In your teaching career?

WM: Decades ago, in college, someone told me that T. S. Eliot was *the* poet; so when I began trying to write poems, I assumed that was the way it was done, and I struggled along under a yoke of literary allusion. My crude understanding of the art was to blame.

In the Air Force, I was lucky to know a lot of heroes, and several of those were also writers. I learned to admire writing and writers, more from those men than from all other experiences up until then.

Reading widely in contemporary poetry gave me the excitement by the mid-1970s to get started toward how I write now.

PB: Which writers did you particularly admire or learn from? Any that you decided to avoid?

WM: Decades ago—and still, and probably even more, now—I admired and thrilled to the best of James Dickey, Richard Hugo, James Wright, Denise Levertov, Theodore Roethke—and other poets with strong imagery and stories and sense of driving rhythm and powerful, compelling sounds.

Earlier writers I admired even before trying to write poems were Frost and Whitman; Hemingway and Faulkner; Tennyson (especially such poems as *Ulysses*) and Robert Browning; John Donne and Yeats and Hopkins; Edna St. Vincent Millay and Wallace Stevens; Joseph Heller and Thomas Wolfe. In the last two decades, I've discovered with wonder hundreds of other amazing poets. What a rich time to be alive and reading. I served as poetry editor for the Texas Tech University Press for twenty years and read voraciously and loved every month.

Writers I avoid are ones whose poems or stories bore me. The old saying applies, laughable as it is: "Read great books; there isn't enough time to read good books." The catch is that I have to read what strikes me as good and as boring to find the "great," but I don't usually keep going back to works that leave me cold. Another old saying: "there's no accounting for taste." So I'm probably often wrong. And, inconsistent as I am, sometimes I've gone back to some from years ago and felt amazed to discover how much better they are than I thought! I was just too dumb to spot the spark, my first time through.

PB: Who are the contemporary writers of poetry or fiction that you most admire?

WM: Dozens, hundreds. Among poets of the last couple of decades, more than half of my favorites are women; for example, check the books of poems I published as poetry editor of the Texas Tech University Press. Some of my favorite poets are Texans.

PB: How have you managed to combine the demands of teaching and the discipline of writing at the same time? You have a very substantial body of work published. The Walt McDonald canon is about the size of the Emily Dickinson body of work, I believe. In the evolution of this impressive publication record, have there been times of great productivity and times of silence? Could you describe the pattern of your composition—mentioning times or circumstances of high productivity and times of little or no publication?

WM: As a teacher, I learned long ago to go with the ebb and flow of semesters. When I'm teaching, I belong to my students. Wiser writers than I am warned me that writing and teaching creative writing draw on the same sources of energy; for a time, I denied that. But I think they're right.

   As a writer, I found years ago that I need a chunk of time before trying to start new poems—at least four uninterrupted hours; I can work gladly revising if I have only thirty minutes before shutting down and hurrying to class or a meeting, so I revise and rewrite continually. But I try spooking up first drafts only on weekends, holidays, and when I take a semester or summer off. Those large, swift chunks of time give me enough first drafts to stay busy during the pressure cooker of teaching.

   Do I wish I had more time to write? Yes. Am I frustrated that I don't? No. Every day's a gift, and I try to lie down at night, knowing that nothing else I could have written will last, that what matters is faith, not works. I go to the book for assurance that working with words is all right, even a good thing to do; "whatever your hand finds to do, do it with all your might."

   I like what John Berryman wrote, after his conversion: "Father Hopkins said the only true literary critic is Christ. Let me lie down exhausted, content with that." (#10 of "Eleven Addresses to the Lord")

PB: Is the Vietnam era of your life still part of the subject matter for recent poems, and will it be part of future compositions?

WM: Flying, and a war I went to briefly, are two of about five regions that I keep prowling; they're my background, part of what I am. Since 1970, I have never set out to write a flying poem, though, or a West Texas poem. I agree with the truism that the poems we want to write are already there, inside us—the regions we own, or that own us.

A friend told me he can't stop writing about the war and wishes he could—but war poems keep coming. I never went through what he did, but I can't squeeze off the flow, either—although I never intend to write about Vietnam or the guilt of surviving. Since coming back, I have never intended to write poems about a locale, a person, or an experience of any kind.

I'm open to anything, when I'm trying to find a poem—an image, a phrase, a word. Usually, a trickle of words will come that intrigues me, and I plunk them into the keyboard as fast as my fingers can go. All poems are little fictions, and most often they take hours of hard work, but sometimes one comes suddenly, like a gift. Happy poems—upbeat, affirmative—have come during times of crisis; and haunted poems, the darker glimpses, have come on some days when I was giddy or even just staying alive, when nothing particularly good or ill was happening to me.

I don't write with an idea or a plot in mind. I simply don't write that way. I never know if I'll be writing about hunting or holding a grandchild high overhead until I'm into a first draft. I never know what will come of those first words, or if anything will. If a first draft surprises me, I'll work on it again and again, through dozens of drafts. But after Vietnam, that's the way every poem I've published has begun.

PB: You write often of the Southwest—the experiences of hard-scrabble farm life. Could you comment on your personal experience in the Southwest? What locales and traditions have informed your poetry of the Southwest?

WM: I was born and raised in Lubbock, and the Llano Estacado (the Staked Plains, a region of flat farmland, west of the caprock) is part of the West Texas region I keep prowling through poem after poem. The Breaks, east and southeast of here, keep cropping up in my poems, as much as Lubbock cotton does. They were part of me from earliest memory, on trips to Abilene, where my father's father lived. A Lubbock boy older than Buddy Holly, I knew nothing but flat horizons and wide skies, except on those frequent trips through the wind country on the way to Abilene, and I loved it—the stones and boulders, the mesas, arroyos and coyotes, the hawks, and always the buzzards.

Accepting my native region into my poems has been the best thing for me, as a writer. For years, I had not considered this world to be my home. But I let down my bucket in a plains region doomed to dry up and found all sorts of water, all sorts of poems, even if I could live to write for forty years in this suddenly fabulous desert.

PB: You write with such authenticity about family life, of love, and children and grandchildren, and friendships within family. Could you comment on how these themes of family connection and images of lasting affection have come to characterize your poetry?

WM: What a wonderful thing to say, Phyllis. Last year, another friend remarked that "Love, especially love of family, seems particularly pervasive in your works," and asked, "Are you also a 'love poet' of sorts?" I answered gladly that if any label fits, I would more gladly wear that than any others. I love flying, a matter of life or death; but a good story or poem gives pleasures I find nowhere else. But not nearly as much joy as holding hands with my wife in the park or bending down to lift one of my granddaughters above my head and feel her hug my neck. I know the difference between a poem and a person. Life is grass, stunningly brief—but abundant in so many ways. Living as long as we have brings heartache and loss, but how joyful to us are the continual surprises of friendships and family.

PB: You have recently published a new book at the Texas Tech University Press called *Whatever the Wind Delivers*. It combines your poetry with photographs from the Southwest Collection at Tech. I believe you received the Western Heritage Award from the National Cowboy Hall of Fame for this work. What do you think it is that makes the myth of the Southwest so appealing to persons all over the world? Why has the experience of the Great American Southwest become so significant?

WM: Yes, that book received the fourth award from the National Cowboy Hall of Fame, so I'm amazed, and grateful to so many. I never set out intending to receive such a gift, but those four Wranglers on our mantel testify to the gift of being born.

The pervasive influence of the cowboy on American culture is a concept I never heard until I was twenty, but it was in my bones from the start like calcium from mother's milk. Born to this culture, who hasn't been touched by the myth of the cowboy?

What does it mean to grow up, as so many of us did, "loving the cowboy ways"? Apparently, the influence of the cowboy on American culture reaches from Alaska to Alabama, from spaghetti westerns to German novels set oddly on the Llano Estacado, the Staked Plains of West Texas where I was born. Texas born. What does that mean? Baptized with a pinch of dust from the banks of the Brazos? Instead of getting a quarter from the tooth fairy, branded like cattle with a Lone Star? It must mean something. Last year in Trinidad, Colorado, parked next to a family in a big car with Alabama plates, I saw a five-year-old boy pouting, tagging along behind his grandfather. Bored, the boy kicked a pebble, looked around and stopped, and stared at our front license plate. "Grandpa!" he shouted, tugging the old man's sleeve. "They're from TEXAS!"—as if NOW he was SEEING something!

I remember my father's old spurs and a pair of chaps so stiff the leather was brittle as old parchment. I was born hearing about cowboys and cattle, sandstorms and blue northers that drove the livestock to barbed wire fences where they froze. When my mother married my father, he was a working cowboy with five borrowed dollars in his pocket, and he took her in a borrowed buggy out to the ranch to a shack near the bunkhouse, and the foreman's wife was her only female friend for years. A cowboy who had eaten more trail dust than I had walked on, my daddy despised dime novels that prattled and paraded cowboys as heroes, gunslingers, with nifty codes of honor like King Arthur's knights. My daddy's middle name was Arthur, and he told me sometimes why he disliked fiction—so fake, nothing at all like the cowboys he bunked with, the foreman he worked for.

Over the years, I challenged and probably pushed him away with questions about the old days; and he told me, grudgingly, without venom, about hard work and boredom and little pay. I was relieved to hear about the squalor and boredom, of course, for I envied his years of freedom on horseback and secretly feared that his stories would be even more heroic than novels which I devoured, trapped in a dusty town called Lubbock on the plains.

I grew up in Texas during World War II, and cowboys and pilots were my heroes. I ran across a thousand acres of ranchland pocked with prairie-dog holes, flying models of P-51 Mustangs and British Spitfires. I left Texas and became a pilot, and years later I turned to poems in middle age when I had to stop flying.

Now, cowboys and flying combine in my poems no one would ever call "cowboy poetry." But without the pervasive influence of the cowboy on American culture, I doubt that I would have done more than that first, stumbling book of war poems. Memories of cowboys and flying keep coming back—sometimes when I least expect them. And when memories come, warped and set free by imagination, I write, and sometimes get a poem that says what I didn't even know I needed to say. Without the influence of cowboys, without my father's brittle chaps and my own first pair of spurs, I would never have found most poems I've come to.

PB: You have a new collection of poetry entitled *All Occasions* just out from the University of Notre Dame Press in the fall of 2000. What can we see in this new collection?

WM: In this book, I didn't "intend" to include more poems than usual that show an obviously Christian habit of mind; but now I think it has more. If the healing mystery of faith is more pronounced in the last decade or so, and therefore in this book, maybe it's because I have more of a feeling of grace, lately; for example, "Faith Is a Radical Master"—the poem that ends my 1999 book (*Whatever the Wind Delivers*). You probably recognize that the title comes from a sermon by John Donne: "All occasions invite his mercies, and all times are his seasons" (LXXX Sermons, 3, preached on Christmas Day, 1624).

I feel like Paul in Romans 7:14–25, completely dependent on grace. All of my poems grow out of faith, whether set in my native West Texas or our other adopted home in the Rockies, in Air Force cockpits, or Vietnam. None would be what they are without the habits of mind, the profession of faith I make daily.

If I've done more poems in recent years with obvious ardor and affirmation of faith, it's probably because I'm able to accept the grace that I had felt for decades I had to earn. Lately, texts I read for decades begin to make sense. "Throw all your worries on him, for he cares for you" (I Peter 5).

The sixty-five poems in *All Occasions* are about a boy who later flies as an Air Force pilot, marries a woman so lovely and loving he's stunned, goes home after a war and discovers with friends and family what John Donne meant in one Christmas sermon: "All occasions invite his mercies, and all times are his seasons." The poems celebrate the wonder and need of all occasions, the heartache and longing and joy of being alone or loved—in war, in a cockpit at forty thousand feet, riding the range on a mustang, or in the arms of family. Father Hopkins, in "Carrion Comfort," wrote, "That night, that year / of now done darkness I wretch lay wrestling with (my God!) my God." In part 2 of *All Occasions*, "When Rockets Fell Like Stars," the writer feels this in Vietnam, and discovers over swift decades how deeply he needs friends and family and God. Always, even after flying "to Saigon and back," the book's about the risks and joys of marriage and raising babies in a dangerous world, where love is our hope and only grace saves: "I'm stunned that a woman can be this lovely / at sixty …. / I see her eyes, the shadows / of her face, think flecks of silver in her hair. / It hasn't rained in months, but I'm healed / wholly by her touch, amazed each time / she lifts my gnarled, stiff knuckles to her lips" ("The Midas Touch in Texas," *All Occasions* 14).

PB: You have published one book of fiction. Do you think that you will work in fiction in the future?

WM: No. Now, as it has been for years, when I sit down to write, I'm thinking poems.

PB: Do you have plans for additional collections of poetry? What are you working on now?

WM: Always, something's brewing. This stuff is fun to do, or I wouldn't do it. Two books in the works, but I don't know if they'll see print. A failed novelist and a boy of the soil, I like corrals. I write a line at a time, poem at a time, but continually I'm herding and culling, heading for home. This summer, I'm taking off from teaching and hope for three months to write.

Someone claimed that writers are writers only when they are writing, and I believe that. Therefore, no more summer school for me; I miss the money, but time is quicksilver. Every spring and summer, I write as much as I can, and by August, I'm exhausted, but restored.

PB: Of your many, many honors, which has been the most meaningful to you?

WM: Every one's a gift, grace, unmerited favor. Weeks ago, after I heard the stunning news about the fourth Wrangler Award from the National Cowboy Hall of Fame, and the Lifetime Achievement Award from the Texas Institute of Letters, I was both happy and embarrassed to have such riches. I told Carol, I don't deserve so much. I don't deserve anything. She wrapped her arms around my neck, looked at me with those eyes I love, and said, "It's okay, Walt." That's the most meaningful one, that touch of my wife's human grace, that hint of mercy, which is finally all I'll need.

PB: What is your favorite word in the English language?

WM: Lord—with the connotation of where it comes from into modern English—"bread-keeper." It stuns me to think that the Lord who said He is the bread of life born in a "manger" (in French, "to eat") is our Lord. Favorite human word? "Carol," of course. Aren't words fun? Aren't we lucky to use and play with and savor them?

PB: What is your favorite way to spend a day?

WM: Whatever I'm doing. That's easy to say, but ALMOST true. Again, every day is grace, and at my age, every breath's a blessing. It may not always be so. All is well. All is well. Some days, I don't feel that; but I believe.

PB: You have been very generous with your time and talent over the years in helping writers who are evolving. I know that you have conducted programs at over 125 major colleges and universities. It is obvious that the students and creative writers who attend these workshops gain enormously from their association with you. What benefit do *you* get from conducting workshops and courses for aspiring creative writers?

WM: One of the pleasures I enjoy as a writer who teaches is watching students discover with delight some of the best poems they've ever read or written. That's why I got into this work to begin with. As a young pilot, when I applied to teach English at the Air Force Academy, all I wanted to do was hang around some of the best-used language in the world, some of the most moving, exciting words I'd ever heard—and to share them with others.

I feel lucky that for a little while, before the golden bowl breaks and the silver cord snaps, I get to hang around words and see what happens—my students' words, and words that spin off my own fingertips. We've all seen students make amazing discoveries in words. As teachers, we get to be there when it happens. What writer doesn't want to move us to tears or chills or hugs or laughter? What writing teacher doesn't want to pass along a thrill like that?

Notes

Walt McDonald, Poet of the Southwest

1. In his introduction to an anthology of Texas poetry published in the late 1970s, the editor Paul Ruffin chooses not to put it mildly: "Compared to her fiction and non-fiction prose . . . the body of noteworthy poetry produced in the state before the middle of this century is paltry indeed" (xiii). Ruffin asserts that in this respect Texas is like "other states of the South and Southwest" and goes on to announce that the "primary explanation" for the lack of good poetry in Texas is due to three "influences": "a predominantly Southern background, a frontier mentality, and a fundamentalist morality" (xiii).

2. See, for instance, *Signature of the Sun: Southwest Verse, 1900–1950; Southwestern Anthology of Verse, 1945: Poets of the Southwest;* and *The Friendly Shore: Poems from the Southwest Writers Conference.* A number of anthologies of Southwestern poetry were published during the 1930s, *The Golden Stallion* and *The Southwest Scene,* for example. *New Voices of the Southwest* contains poems by a handful of recognizable names: Mary Austin, Witter Bynner, Robinson Jeffers, Haniel Long, Yvor Winters, and Stark Young. With regard to those writers and to my point about the previous lack of a strong poet to associate with the Southwest, I think we have to ask, are Mary Austin and Stark Young primarily poets? Are Witter Bynner, Robinson Jeffers, and Yvor Winters Southwestern poets? And how strong a poet is Haniel Long?

3. See, for instance, Lawrence's "Autumn at Taos," "Eagle in New Mexico," "Men in New Mexico," "The Red Wolf," and "Mountain Lion."

4. See Williams's "The Sparrow" and especially "The Desert Music," the latter a poem in which he not only recoils at the Southwest's (in this case El Paso's) seediness but swings to the other side of the spectrum as well, gushing, for example, over its "color! Isn't it / wonderful!" (91–2).

"Dark Pearls": An Introduction to Walter McDonald's Poetic Journey of Faith

1. The phrases "Man's mounting spirit" and "scanted in a dull cage" come from Hopkins's "The Caged Skylark," a sonnet that succinctly summarizes a variety of themes important to McDonald, including the struggle between flesh and spirit, the emergence of music through suffering, and the paradoxical freedom of being "flesh-bound."

2. Examinations of McDonald as a war poet do acknowledge the considerable range of the poet's interests. For example, Vince Gotera, in *Radical Visions: Poetry by Vietnam Veterans,* writes: "It is patently unfair to McDonald

to brand him as only a Vietnam-veteran poet. In *Night Landings*, for example, only five of forty-two poems expressly mention Vietnam. In *After the Noise of Saigon*, only seven of forty-nine poems are even remotely about Vietnam. In *The Flying Dutchman*, only two of forty-five poems touch on Vietnam in some direct way . . ." (89–90). Gotera concludes that McDonald is a marvelous poet, "both because of and despite Vietnam" (90). Philip Beidler counts McDonald as one of six Vietnam War poets who have gone on "to become significant poets of their American generation as well; he is one of the few who, even as they continue to speak [the war's] memory, now trace out in addition the patterns of its broader mythic configuring within our life and culture at large" (*Rewriting America* 146).

3. Curiously, critical assessments, such as those by Gotera, Beidler, and Wright, are generally silent about the religious themes in McDonald's work.

4. Given the stark subject matter of so many of McDonald's poems, some readers may be surprised by the claim that McDonald's poetry reflects deep spiritual sensitivity; yet McDonald suggests in various interviews and in his unpublished essay "Deliverance: The Amazing, Simple Mystery" that spiritual concerns have always animated his poetic work. He further adds, in the interview published in *Christianity and Literature*, "If the healing mystery of faith is more pronounced in the last decade or so . . . maybe it's because I have more of a feeling of grace, lately" (xx).

5. Though easily misunderstood, the term "Christian tragedy" might well be applied to McDonald's vision. His work takes full account of the evils that are visited upon humankind, though he remains aware of redemptive possibilities. He is in line with Louis A. Ruprecht's view of the tragic: "'Tragedy shows us pain and brings us pleasure in the process.' Which is to say that suffering teaches, and *that* is the tragic in tragedy. *You never gain something but that you lose something*" (*Tragic Posture and Tragic Vision* 97). McDonald is preeminently a poet of loss who realizes gain through loss.

6. His work has appeared in virtually every major U.S. literary journal, including *Atlantic Monthly, Poetry, New York Review of Books, American Scholar, Sewanee Review, Southern Review, The Nation, Kenyon Review, American Poetry Review, Antioch Review, New Criterion,* and *The Georgia Review*. Critical studies of McDonald's work appear in Vince Gotera, *Radical Visions: Poetry by Vietnam Veterans;* Philip D. Beidler, *Rewriting America: Vietnam Authors in Their Generation,* 1991; Ronald Baughman, *"Walter McDonald," Dictionary of Literary Biography: American Writers of the Vietnam Way.* Documentary Series, Vol. 9, 1992; and Charlotte M. Wright, *"Walter McDonald," Dictionary of Literary Biography: American Poets Since World War I.* Second Series, Vol. 105, 1991. It is worth noting that McDonald not only has received numerous honors for his poetry, but he is also an award-winning fiction writer (for *A Band of Brothers: Stories from Vietnam*), and he is a distinguished professor, receiving the Council for the Advancement and Support of Education's Texas Professor of the Year Award in 1992.

7. As his essay, "Deliverance: The Amazing, Simple Mystery" makes plain, McDonald has been considerably affected by James Dickey's novels and poetry, and in his response to Dickey's prose and poetry one can perceive McDonald's peculiar brand of Christian stoicism. McDonald responds to one of Dickey's most remarkable poems called "Falling," which is based

upon a newspaper account of a young female flight attendant who falls from a commercial aircraft. Dickey imagines the young woman struggling, thinking, and praying as she falls to her death. In his response to "Falling," in a poem called "In Dickey Country," McDonald expresses what might be viewed as a personal credo: "We're all drowning with others / and all we can do is try to save someone. . . . We're all seeking 'deliverance'":

> Having done
> All we can do, kneeling down by our hacked,
> Glittering graves, under pressure,
> Or in amazing armor we put on
> When we begin living forever, falling
> In the dark without a parachute, calling
> With our last few feet of breath for God. (*Blessings the Body Gave* 72)

8. The final question paraphrases St. Paul: "But someone will ask, 'How are the dead raised?'" (I Corinthians 15:35 NRSV).

9. Apophatic theology is "[b]oth a way of talking about God and a method of approaching God by looking beyond all created categories of sensation and thought to the God who can in no way be conceptualized. . . . Apophatic theology moves toward God by asserting that he is not, in fact, any of the things he is called. This movement is from the physical creation through the intelligible to a union with God in the divine darkness which lies beyond concept" (*Westminster Dictionary of Christian Theology* 32). "For God in My Sorrows" appears to support Nicholas of Cusa's opinion on the unknowability of God (such as expressed in *De docta ignorantia*). Nicholas emphasized that the wise person knows the limits of his learning, in particular his inability to fathom Infinite Being. Knowing God involves a "learned ignorance," that is *"docta ignoranta."* "[T]he limits of knowing are acknowledged as the threshold of the reality of the unknown" (Pacini 207). McDonald's search for God similarly leads him to faith in the "darkness" beyond the visible heavens. Compare Henry Vaughn's "The Night" which expresses the view that faith is most luminous in the gloom:

> There is in God (some say)
> A deep, but dazzling darkness; as men here
> Say it is late and dusky, because they
>   See not all clear;
> O for that night! Where I in him
> Might live invisible and dim. (397)

Intimations of Higher Matters: Anagogical Closure in Walter McDonald's *Burning the Fence*

1. Even given the tremendous amount of energy spent doing theory in recent years, much work remains to be done concerning how poems— especially in free verse—work. One of the most extensive studies that touches on this subject is Bahti's *Ends of the Lyric*, which argues for chiasmus as the figure which has given the essential structure to lyric poems. Also well worth reading is Golding's "Openness, Closure, and Recent American

Poetry"; Golding is insightful concerning Williams/Olson-influenced "open form" poetry, particularly in relation to Language poetry and the New Formalism. More common by far are applied studies in this area, and in fact most "how to" books on poetry writing have a section on last lines. More thorough than most such discussions, partly at least because of its heavy use of Smith, is Elton Glaser's "Entrances and Exits: Three Key Positions in the Poem."

2. My preliminary work indicates that during the 1980s this kind of ending was most prevalent in McDonald's work (particularly in *Witching on Hardscrabble, The Flying Dutchman,* and *Rafting the Brazos*) and that during the 1990s (especially *Where Skies Are Not Cloudy* and *Counting Survivors*), the phenomenon is relatively rare. If that is the case, it is all the more interesting that "The Waltz We Were Born For," the final poem in McDonald's collection, *Blessings the Body Gave,* ends with what seems to me a stunning anagoge. This topic, however, demands more study, not only of McDonald's growing canon but also of contemporary poetics generally.

3. In a 1986 interview with McDonald, Christopher Wood mentions the closeness between the sublime and the gruesome in McDonald's literary landscape. Ten years later, Michael Hobbs refers to the "hardscrabble sublime" that McDonald's poems celebrate. I find the religious suggestion of the term to be at home in the same ideational space that anagogical closure seems to inhabit.

Perseverance in Walt McDonald's Poetry

1. "Perseverance" here denotes a biblical ideal, not "perseverance of the saints" as defined in Article 17 of the Westminster Confession:

> They, whom God hath accepted in His Beloved, effectually called, and sanctified by His Spirit, can neither totally, nor finally, fall away from the state of grace: but shall certainly persevere therein to the end, and be eternally saved. . . . This perseverance of the saints depends not upon their own free will, but upon the immutability of the decree of election . . . upon the efficacy of the merit and intercession of Jesus Christ; the abiding of the Spirit, and of the seed of God within them; and the nature of the covenant of grace; from all which ariseth also the certainty and infallibility thereof.

As the poems show, McDonald is no Calvinist. (For the record, he worshipped in Churches of Christ most of his life and later with the Disciples of Christ. He now attends a Baptist church.) He uses *perseverance* in its original sense (*OED*: "persistence in a course of action, purpose, or state; steadfast pursuit of an aim" and so forth). His conception of Christian perseverance is easily traced to such scriptures as Matthew 10:22, 24:12–3; Mark 13:13; Ephesians 6:18; II Timothy 4:6–7; Hebrews 12:1; and James 1:12, 5:10–1.

Forms of Incarnation in the Recent Poetry of Walter McDonald

1. See, respectively, studies by Brown, Carballo, Haney, Kass, Lichtmann, Servotte, Werge, Lang, and Lock.

2. See Breuggemann regarding chapter 1 of Genesis:

The relation of verses 1 and 2 is not obvious. Verse 1 suggests God began with nothing. Verse 2 makes clear there was an exciting chaos. . . . The very ambiguity of *creation from nothing* and *creation from chaos* is a rich expository possibility. We need not choose between them, even as the text does not. Both permit important theological information. The former asserts the majestic and exclusive power of God. The latter lets us affirm that even the way life is can be claimed by God (cf. Isaiah 45:18–9). Perhaps for good reason, this text refuses to decide between them. By the double focus on the power of God and on the use made of chaos, the text affirms the difference between God and creature and the binding that also marks them (cf. John 1:15). (29–30)

Works Cited

Transcending Hardscrabble:
The Evolving Vision of Walt McDonald

Browne, Sir Thomas. *Religio Medici. The Norton Anthology of English Literature*. Ed. M. H. Abrams, et al. New York: Norton, 1979. 1678.

McDonald, Walt. *All Occasions*. Notre Dame: Notre Dame University Press, 2000.

———. *Blessings the Body Gave*. Columbus: Ohio State University Press, 1998.

McDonald, Walter. *After the Noise of Saigon*. Amherst: University of Massachusetts Press, 1988.

———. *Anything Anything*. Berkeley: L'Epervier Press, 1980.

———. *The Digs in Escondido Canyon*. Lubbock: Texas Tech University Press, 1991.

———. *The Flying Dutchman*. Columbus: Ohio State University Press, 1987.

———. *Night Landings*. New York: Harper & Row, 1989.

———. *Witching on Hardscrabble*. Peoria: Spoon River Poetry Press, 1985.

Moore, Marianne. "He 'Digesteth Harde Yron'." *The Norton Anthology of Modern Poetry*. 1st ed. Ed. E. Richard Ellman and Robert O'Clair. New York: Norton, 1973. 430.

All His Hands Can Do: The Poetry of Walt McDonald

McDonald, Walt. *All Occasions*. Notre Dame: University of Notre Dame Press, 2000.

———. *Blessings the Body Gave*. Columbus: Ohio State University Press, 1998.

McDonald, Walter. *After the Noise of Saigon*. Amherst: University of Massachusetts Press, 1988.

———. *Anything Anything*. Berkeley: L'Epervier Press, 1980.

———. *Rafting the Brazos*. Denton: University of North Texas Press, 1988.

———. *Where Skies Are Not Cloudy*. Denton: University of North Texas Press, 1993.

Domestic Tranquillity and National Defense:
The Personal History of Walt McDonald

McDonald, Walt. *All Occasions*. Notre Dame: Notre Dame University Press, 2000.

McDonald, Walter. *"Caliban in Blue" and Other Poems*. Lubbock: Texas Tech University Press, 1976.

Reclaiming the Homefront:
Walt McDonald's Peacekeeping Soldiers

McDonald, Walter. *All That Matters: The Texas Plains in Photographs and Poems*. Photographs of the Southwest Collection selected by Janet M. Neugebauer. Lubbock: Texas Tech University Press, 1992.
———. *Burning the Fence*. Lubbock: Texas Tech University Press, 1981.
———. *"Caliban in Blue" and Other Poems*. Lubbock: Texas Tech University Press, 1976.
———. *Counting Survivors*. Pittsburgh: University of Pittsburgh Press, 1995.
———. *Rafting the Brazos*. Denton: University of North Texas Press, 1988.
———. *Witching on Hardscrabble*. Peoria: Spoon River Poetry Press, 1985.

McDonald's *A Band of Brothers*: A Plea for a Deeper Understanding

McDonald, Walter. *A Band of Brothers: Stories from Vietnam*. Lubbock: Texas Tech University Press, 1989.

Walt McDonald's Beautiful Wasteland

Baughman, Ronald. "Walter McDonald." *American Writers of the Vietnam War*. Dictionary of Literary Biography Documentary Series Vol. 9. Detroit: Gale, 1992. 215–74.
Eliot, T. S. *The Waste Land and Other Poems*. New York: Harcourt Brace Janovich, 1962. 31.
McDonald, Walt. Interview with Chris Ellery. *Concho River Review* 10.1 (1996): 31–49.
———. Letter to the author. May, 1997.
McDonald, Walter. *Anything Anything*. Berkeley: L'Epervier Press, 1980.
———. *Counting Survivors*. Pittsburgh: University of Pittsburgh Press, 1995.
———. *The Digs in Escondido Canyon*. Lubbock: Texas Tech University Press, 1991.
———. *The Flying Dutchman*. Columbus: Ohio State University Press, 1987.
———. *Where Skies Are Not Cloudy*. Denton: University of North Texas Press, 1993.
———. *Witching on Hardscrabble*. Peoria: Spoon River Poetry Press, 1985.
Stevens, Wallace. *The Collected Poems of Wallace Stevens*. New York: Vintage Books, 1990. 467.
Woods, Christopher. "An Interview: Walter McDonald." *Touchstone* 10.3 (1985): 3–12.

Unignored Plunder: The Texas Poems of Walt McDonald

Karr, Mary. *Abacus*. Middletown: Wesleyan University Press, 1987.
———. *The Devil's Tour*. New York: New Directions, 1993.
———. *The Liar's Club*. New York: Viking, 1995.
McDonald, Walt. *Whatever the Wind Delivers: Celebrating West Texas and the Near Southwest*. Photographs of the Southwest Collection selected by Janet M. Neugebauer. Lubbock: Texas Tech University Press, 1999.
McDonald, Walter. "After a Week in the Rockies." *Manoa* 2 (1990): 11.

————. *All That Matters: The Texas Plains in Photographs and Poems*. Photographs of the Southwest Collection selected by Janet Neugebauer. Lubbock: Texas Tech University Press, 1992.

————. *Anything Anything*. Berkeley: L'Epervier Press, 1980.

————. *Burning the Fence*. Lubbock: Texas Tech University Press, 1981.

————. *"Caliban in Blue" and Other Poems*. Lubbock: Texas Tech University Press, 1976.

————. "Colonel Mackenzie Maps the Llano Estacado." *The Texas Review* 10 (1989): 55.

————. *Counting Survivors*. Pittsburgh: University of Pittsburgh Press, 1995.

————. *Night Landings*. New York: Harper & Row, 1989.

————. *One Thing Leads to Another*. New Braunfels: Cedar Rock Press, 1978.

————. *Rafting the Brazos*. Denton: University of North Texas Press, 1988.

————. *Where Skies Are Not Cloudy*. Denton: University of North Texas Press, 1993.

Patterson, Frank Allen, ed. *The Student's Milton*. New York: Appleton-Century-Crofts, 1961.

Ramke, Bin. *The Difference Between Night and Day*. New Haven: Yale University Press, 1978.

————. *White Monkeys*. Athens: University of Georgia Press, 1981.

An Uneasy Truce:
Wildness and Domesticity in the Poems of Walt McDonald

McDonald, Walt. *Blessings the Body Gave*. Columbus: Ohio State University Press, 1998.

McDonald, Walter. *Counting Survivors*. Pittsburgh: University of Pittsburgh Press, 1993.

————. *The Digs in Escondido Canyon*. Lubbock: Texas Tech University Press, 1991.

————. *Where Skies Are Not Cloudy*. Denton: University of North Texas Press, 1993.

Walt McDonald, Poet of the Southwest

Auden, W. H. "Robert Frost." *The Dyer's Hand*. New York: Vintage, 1989.

Botkin, B. A., ed. *The Southwest Scene: An Anthology of Regional Verse*. Oklahoma City: Economy, 1931.

Bushby, D. Maitland, ed. *The Golden Stallion: An Anthology of Poems Concerning the Southwest and Written by Representative Southwestern Poets*. Dallas: Southwest, 1930.

Bynner, Witter. *Selected Poems*. Ed. James Kraft. New York: Farrar, Straus and Giroux, 1978.

Frost, Robert. *A Boy's Will*. New York: Henry Holt, 1913.

————. *The Complete Poems of Robert Frost*. New York: Holt, Rinehart and Winston, 1961.

———— *North of Boston*. New York: Henry Holt, 1913.

Greer, Hilton Ross, and Florence Elberta Barns, eds. *New Voices of the Southwest*. Dallas: Tardy, 1934.

Jewett, Sarah Orne. *The Country of the Pointed Firs*. Boston: Houghton Mifflin, 1910.

Kemp, John C. *Robert Frost and New England: The Poet as Regionalist*. Princeton: Princeton University Press, 1979.

Lawrence, D. H. *D. H. Lawrence and New Mexico*. Ed. Keith Sagar. Salt Lake City: Gibbs M. Smith, 1982.

Major, Mabel, and T. M. Pearce, eds. *Signature of the Sun: Southwest Verse, 1900–1950*. Albuquerque: University of New Mexico Press, 1950.

Maxson, Helen F. "Forms of Incarnation in the Recent Poetry of Walter McDonald." *Christianity and Literature* 49.2 (2000): 225–44.

McDonald, Walt. *Blessings the Body Gave*. Columbus: Ohio State University Press, 1998.

McDonald, Walter. *Anything Anything*. Berkeley: L'Epervier Press, 1980.

———. *The Flying Dutchman*. Columbus: Ohio State University Press, 1987.

———. Interview. "Evidence of Grace." By Darryl Tippens. *Christianity and Literature* 49.2 (2000): 173–87.

Ruffin, Paul, ed. *The Texas Anthology*. Huntsville, TX: Sam Houston State University Press, 1979.

Stevens, Pearle Moore, ed. *Southwestern Anthology of Verse, 1945: Poets of the Southwest*. San Antonio: Naylor, 1945.

Tippens, Darryl L. "'Dark Pearls': An Introduction to Walter McDonald's Poetic Journey of Faith." *Christianity and Literature* 49.2 (2000): 189–203.

Williams, Loring. Foreword. *The Friendly Shore: Poems from the Southwest Writers' Conference*. Ed. Katherine Evans and J. Meredith Tatton. San Antonio: Naylor, 1955.

Williams, William Carlos. *The Collected Poems of William Carlos Williams, Vol. II, 1939–1962*. New York: New Directions, 1988.

Poetry to Trespass For

McDonald, Walt. *Whatever the Wind Delivers: Celebrating West Texas and the Near Southwest*. Photographs of the Southwest Collection selected by Janet M. Neugebauer. Lubbock: Texas Tech University Press, 1999.

McDonald, Walter. *All That Matters: The Texas Plains in Photographs and Poems*. Photographs of the Southwest Collection selected by Janet M. Neugebauer. Lubbock: Texas Tech University Press, 1992.

Walt McDonald's Poetry: Images of Man's Acceptance of His Place in Time

Durrell, Lawrence. *A Key to Modern British Poetry*. Norman: University of Oklahoma Press, 1952.

McDonald, Walter. *Anything Anything*. Berkeley: L'Epevier Press, 1980.

———. Big Country Writing Workshop Presentation. Abilene Christian University. Abilene. 11 Feb. 1989.——. *Burning the Fence*. Lubbock: Texas Tech University Press, 1981.

———. *"Caliban in Blue" and Other Poems*. Lubbock: Texas Tech University Press, 1976.

———. *Night Landings*. New York: Harper & Row, 1989.

———. *Witching on Hardscrabble*. Peoria: Spoon River Poetry Press, 1985.

———. *Working Against Time*. Walnut Creek: Calliope Press, 1981.

Angel and Mirage:
Concerns of Imagination in Walt McDonald and Wallace Stevens

Auden, W. H. *Collected Poems*. Ed. Edward Mendelson. New York: Random House, 1976.

McDonald, Walt. *All Occasions*. Notre Dame: University of Notre Dame Press, 2000.

———. *Blessings the Body Gave*. Columbus: Ohio State University Press, 1998.

McDonald, Walter. *After the Noise of Saigon*. Amherst: University of Massachusetts Press, 1988.

———. *All That Matters: The Texas Plains in Photographs and Poems*. Photographs of the Southwest Collection Selected by Janet M. Neugebauer. Lubbock: Texas Tech University Press, 1992.

———. *Counting Survivors*. Pittsburgh: University of Pittsburgh Press, 1995.

———. Interview. "Evidence of Grace." By Darryl Tippens. *Christianity and Literature* 49.2 (2000): 173–87.

———. *Rafting the Brazos*. Denton: University of North Texas Press, 1988.

———. *Where Skies Are Not Cloudy*. Denton: University of North Texas Press, 1993.

Stevens, Wallace. *Collected Poetry and Prose*. Library of America, 1997.

How to Spin Rightly: Walt McDonald's Vision of the Artist

Hopper, Kippra D. "A Poet Among Us." *Vistas: Texas Tech Research* Spring 1993: 28–31.

McDonald, Walt. *All Occasions*. Notre Dame: University of Notre Dame Press, 2000.

———. *Blessings the Body Gave*. Columbus: Ohio State University Press, 1998.

McDonald, Walter. *All That Matters: The Texas Plains in Photographs and Poems*. Photographs of the Southwest Collections selected by Janet M. Neugebauer. Lubbock: Texas Tech University Press, 1992.

———. *Anything Anything*. Berkeley: L'Epervier Press, 1980.

———. *"Caliban in Blue" and Other Poems*. Lubbock: Texas Tech University Press, 1976.

———. *Counting Survivors*. Pittsburgh: University of Pittsburgh Press, 1995.

———. *The Flying Dutchman*. Columbus: Ohio State University Press, 1987.

———. *Rafting the Brazos*. Denton: University of North Texas Press, 1988.

———. *Where Skies Are Not Cloudy*. Denton: University of North Texas Press, 1993.

———. *Witching on Hardscrabble*. Peoria: Spoon River Poetry Press, 1985.

———. *Working Against Time*. Walnut Creek: Calliope Press, 1981.

"Dark Pearls":
An Introduction to Walt McDonald's Poetic Journey of Faith

Allen, C. Leonard. Letter to the author. 14 July 1999.

Baughman, Ronald. "Walter McDonald." *American Writers of the Vietnam War*. Dictionary of Literary Biography Documentary Series Vol. 9. Detroit: Gale, 1992. 215–74.

Beidler, Philip D. "Poets After Our War." *Rewriting America: Vietnam Authors and Their Generation.* Athens: University of Georgia Press, 1991. 145–205.

Browne, Sir Thomas. *The Major Works.* Ed. C. A. Patrides. Harmondsworth: Penguin, 1977.

Dillard, Annie. *Pilgrim at Tinker Creek.* New York: Harper & Row, 1974.

Gordon, Mary. "Getting Here from There: A Writer's Reflections on a Religious Past." *Spiritual Quests: The Art and Craft of Religious Writing.* Ed. William Zinsser. New York: Book-of-the-Month, 1988. 25–53.

Gotera, Vince. "Walter McDonald: After the (Machine) Noise of Saigon." *Radical Visions: Poetry by Vietnam Veterans.* Athens: University of Georgia Press, 1994. 80–90.

Hopkins, Gerard Manley. "The Caged Skylark." *The Poems of Gerard Manley Hopkins.* Ed. W. H. Gardner and N. H. MacKenzie. London: Oxford University Press, 1982. 70–1.

McDonald, Walt. *Blessings the Body Gave.* Columbus: Ohio State University Press, 1998.

McDonald, Walter. *After the Noise of Saigon.* Amherst: University of Massachusetts Press, 1988.

———. *Burning the Fence.* Lubbock: Texas Tech University Press, 1981.

———. *"Caliban in Blue" and Other Poems.* Lubbock: Texas Tech University Press, 1976.

———. *Counting Survivors.* Pittsburgh: University of Pittsburgh Press, 1995.

———. "Deliverance: The Amazing, Simple Mystery." Unpublished essay, 1997.

———. *The Flying Dutchman.* Columbus: Ohio State University Press, 1987.

———. Interview. "Evidence of Grace." By Darryl Tippens. *Christianity and Literature* 49.2 (2000): 173–87.

———. *Night Landings.* New York: Harper & Row, 1989.

"McDonald, Walter (Robert)." *Contemporary Authors.* Gale Literary Database 30 June 1999 <http://www.galenet.com>.

Myers, Jack. "A Declension of Tools." Rev. of *"Caliban in Blue" and Other Poems*, by Walter McDonald. *Southwest Review* 62.1 (1997): 94–6.

O'Connor, Frank. "The Lonely Voice." *Short Story Theories.* Ed. Charles E. May. Athens: Ohio University Press, 1987. 83–93.

Pacini, David S. "Reading the Holy Writ: The Locus of Modern Spirituality." *Christian Spirituality: Post-Reformation and Modern.* Ed. Louis Dupre and Don E. Saliers. New York: Crossroads, 1989. 174–210.

Ruprecht, Louis A., Jr. *Tragic Posture and Tragic Vision: Against the Modern Failure of Nerve.* New York: Continuum, 1994.

Steiner, George. *Real Presences.* Chicago: University of Chicago Press, 1989.

Vaughan, Henry. "The Night." *George Herbert and Henry Vaughn.* Ed. Louis L. Martz. London: Oxford University Press, 1986. 395–7.

Wright, Charlotte M. "Walter McDonald." *American Poets Since World War II.* Dictionary of Literary Biography Ser. 2 Vol. 105. Gale, 1991. 158–63.

Intimations of Higher Matters:
Anagogical Closure in Walter McDonald's *Burning the Fence*

Bahti, Timothy. *Ends of the Lyric: Directions and Consequences in Western Poetry*. Baltimore: Johns Hopkins University Press, 1996.

Dante. "The Banquet." *Critical Theory Since Plato*. Ed. Hazard Adams. New York: Harcourt Brace Jovanovich, 1971. 121.

Frost, Robert. "The Constant Symbol." *Collected Poems, Prose, and Plays*. New York: Library of America, 1995. 786–91.

Golding, Alan. "Openness, Closure, and Recent American Poetry." *Arizona Quarterly* 47.2 (1991): 77–91.

Glaser, Elton. "Entrances and Exits: Three Key Positions in the Poem." *North Dakota Quarterly* 62.4 (1994–95): 34–59.

Grimes, Ronald L. "Anagogy and Ritualization: Baptism in Flannery O'Connor's *The Violent Bear It Away*." *Religion and Literature* 21.1 (1989): 9–26.

Hobbs, Michael. "Walter McDonald." *Updating the Literary West*. Ed. Thomas J. Lyon, et al. Fort Worth: Texas Christian University Press, 1997. 608–16.

McDonald, Walter. *Blessings the Body Gave*. Columbus: Ohio State University Press, 1998.

———. *Burning the Fence*. Lubbock: Texas Tech University Press, 1981.

———. *Counting Survivors*. Pittsburgh: University of Pittsburgh Press, 1995.

———. *The Flying Dutchman*. Columbus: Ohio State University Press, 1987.

———. Interview with Christopher Woods. *RE: Artes Liberales* 13.1 (1986): 1–6.

———. *Rafting the Brazos*. Denton: University of North Texas Press, 1988.

———. *Where Skies Are Not Cloudy*. Denton: University of North Texas Press, 1993.

———. *Witching on Hardscrabble*. Peoria: Spoon River Poetry, 1985.

Myers, Jack, and Michael Simms. *Longman Dictionary of Poetic Terms*. New York: Longman, 1989.

Rico, Gabrielle Luser. *Writing the Natural Way*. San Francisco: Tarcher, 1983.

Smith, Barbara Herrnstein. *Poetic Closure: A Study of How Poems End*. Chicago: University of Chicago Press, 1968.

Perseverance in Walt McDonald's Poetry

McDonald, Walt. *Blessings the Body Gave*. Columbus: Ohio State University Press, 1998.

McDonald, Walter. *After the Noise of Saigon*. Amherst: University of Massachusetts Press, 1988.

———. *All That Matters: The Texas Plains in Photographs and Poems*. Photographs of the Southwest Collection Selected by Janet M. Neugebauer. Lubbock: Texas Tech University Press, 1992.

———. *Counting Survivors*. Pittsburgh: University of Pittsburgh Press, 1995.

———. Interview. "Evidence of Grace." By Darryl Tippens. *Christianity and Literature* 49.2 (2000): 173–87.

———. *The Flying Dutchman*. Columbus: Ohio State University Press, 1987.

———. *Night Landings*. New York: Harper & Row, 1989.

———. *Rafting the Brazos*. Denton: University of North Texas Press, 1988.

———. *Where Skies Are Not Cloudy*. Denton: University of North Texas Press, 1993.

———. *Witching on Hardscrabble*. Peoria: Spoon River Poetry Press, 1985.

Forms of Incarnation in the Recent Poetry of Walter McDonald

Auerbach, Erich. *Mimesis: The Representation of Reality in Western Literature*. Princeton: Princeton University Press, 1953.

Breuggemann, Walter. *Genesis: Interpretation: A Bible Commentary for Teaching and Preaching*. Atlanta: John Knox, 1982.

Brown, Montague. "Anselm's Argument for the Necessity of the Incarnation." *Proceedings of the Patristic, Mediaeval, and Renaissance Conference*. Villanova: Augustinian Historical Institute, Villanova University, 1992–93. 39–52.

Carballo, Robert. "The Incarnation as Paradox and Conceit in Robert Southwell's Poetry." *American Benedictine Review* 43 (1992): 223–32.

Eliot, T. S. *Four Quartets*. New York: Harcourt, 1971.

Fehlen, Myra. *American Incarnation: The Individual, The Nation, and The Continent*. Cambridge: Harvard University Press, 1986.

Haney, David P. "Incarnation and the Autobiographical Exit: Wordsworth's *The Prelude*, Books IX–XIII (1805)." *Studies in Romanticism* 29 (1990): 523–54.

Kass, Thomas G. "Incarnational Tension in Robert Browning's 'Karshish.'" *American Benedictine Review* 44 (1993): 236–48.

Lang, John. "'Close Mystery': Wendell Berry's Poetry of Incarnation." *Renascence* 35 (1983): 258–68.

Lichtmann, Maria R. "The Incarnational Aesthetic of Gerard Manley Hopkins." *Religion and Literature* 23.1 (1991): 37–50.

Lock, Charles. "Carnival and Incarnation: Bakhtin and Orthodox Theology." *Literature and Theology* 5.1 (1991): 68–82.

MacQuarrie, John. "Incarnation." *The Blackwell Encyclopedia of Modern Christian Thought*. 1993.

McDonald, Walt. *Blessings the Body Gave*. Columbus: Ohio State University Press, 1998.

McDonald, Walter. *All That Matters: The Texas Plains in Photographs and Poems*. Photographs from the Southwest Collection Selected by Janet M. Neugebauer. Lubbock: Texas Tech University Press, 1992.

———. *Counting Survivors*. Pittsburgh: University of Pittsburgh Press, 1995.

———. Interview with Fred Alsberg. *Westview* 17.2 (1998): 1–11.

———. *Where Skies Are Not Cloudy*. Denton: University of North Texas Press, 1993.

McGinn, Bernard. "The English Mystics." *Christian Spirituality: High Middle Ages and Reformation*. Ed. Jill Raitt. New York: Crossroad, 1988.

Servotte, Herman. "The Poetry of Paradox: 'Incarnation' in T. S. Eliot's *Four Quartets*." *English Studies* 72 (1991): 377–85.

Stevens, Wallace. *The Palm at the End of the Mind*. Ed. Holly Stevens. New York: Random, 1972.

Werge, Thomas. "Sanctifying the Literal: Images and Incarnation in *Miracles*." *Word and Story in C. S. Lewis*. Ed. Peter J. Schakel and Charles A. Huttar. Columbia: University of Missouri Press, 1991. 76–85.

Works by Walt McDonald

Books

McDonald, Walt. *All Occasions.* Notre Dame: University of Notre Dame Press, 2000.

——. *Blessings the Body Gave.* Columbus: Ohio State University Press, 1998.

——. *Whatever the Wind Delivers: Celebrating West Texas and the Near Southwest.* Photographs from the Southwest Collection selected by Janet M. Neugebauer. Lubbock: Texas Tech University Press, 1999.

McDonald, Walter. *After the Noise of Saigon.* Amherst: University of Massachusetts Press, 1988.

——. *All That Matters: The Texas Plains in Photographs and Poems.* Photographs from the Southwest Collection selected by Janet M. Neugebauer. Lubbock: Texas Tech University Press, 1992.

——. *Anything Anything.* Berkeley: L'Epervier Press, 1980.

——. *A Band of Brothers: Stories from Vietnam.* Lubbock: Texas Tech University Press, 1989.

——. *Burning the Fence.* Lubbock: Texas Tech University Press, 1981.

——. *"Caliban in Blue" and Other Poems.* Lubbock: Texas Tech University Press, 1976.

——. *Counting Survivors.* Pittsburgh: University of Pittsburgh Press, 1995.

——. *The Digs in Escondido Canyon.* Lubbock: Texas Tech University Press, 1991.

——. *The Flying Dutchman.* Columbus: Ohio State University Press, 1987.

——. *Night Landings.* New York: Harper & Row, 1989.

——. *One Thing Leads to Another.* New Braunfels: Cedar Rock, 1978.

——. *Rafting the Brazos.* Denton: University of North Texas Press, 1988.

——. *Splitting Wood for Winter.* Denton: University of North Texas Press, 1988.

——. *Where Skies Are Not Cloudy.* Denton: University of North Texas Press, 1993.

——. *Witching on Hardscrabble.* Peoria: Spoon River Poetry Press, 1985.

——. *Working Against Time.* Walnut Creek: Calliope Press, 1981.

Edited Works

McDonald, Walter, and Frederick T. Kiley, eds. *A* Catch-22 *Casebook.* New York: Crowell, 1973.

——, and James P. White, eds. *Texas Stories and Poems.* Dallas: Texas Center for Writers, 1978.

Works about Walt Mcdonald

Interviews

Alsberg, Fred. *Westview* 17.2 (1998): 1–11.

Ellery, Chris. *Concho River Review* 10.1 (1996): 31–49.

Stone, Robin. "I Give Myself to the Only Territories I Have." *The Kenyon Collegian* 122.17 (1995): 10.

Tippens, Darryl. "Evidence of Grace." *Christianity and Literature* Winter 2000: 173–87.

Woods, Christopher. *Re: Artes Liberales* 13.1 (1986): 1–6.

———. *Touchstone* 10.3 (1985): 3–12.

Criticism

Rev. of *After the Noise of Saigon*, by Walter McDonald. *Blue Light Review* 12 (1989): 47.

Rev. of *After the Noise of Saigon*, by Walter McDonald. *English Studies* 71.1 (1990): 62.

Rev. of *After the Noise of Saigon*, by Walter McDonald. *The Virginia Quarterly Review* 65.1 (1989): 27.

Rev. of *All That Matters*, by Walter McDonald. *Publishers Weekly*. 7 Sept. 1992: 53.

"Anthology Appeals to Collective History of Texans." *Midland Reporter-Telegram* 16 Jan. 2000: B8.

Rev. of *A Band of Brothers*, by Walter McDonald. *Cite AB* 2 July 1990: 19–20.

Rev. of *A Band of Brothers*, by Walter McDonald. *Shalom: Jewish Peace Letter* 23.3 (1991): 7.

Rev. of *A Band of Brothers*, by Walter McDonald. *Texas Journal* 12.2 (1990): 61.

Barker, Wendy. "A Deep-Felt Need for What Can Keep Us Human." *Texas Books in Review* 9 (1990): 6–7.

Barnett, Michael. "*Counting Survivors*." *Southwestern American Literature* Spring 1995: 140–41.

Basile, Joseph Lawrence. Rev. of *Caliban in Blue*, by Walter McDonald. *South Dakota Review* Winter 1976–7: 89.

Baughman, Ronald. "Walter McDonald." *American Writers of the Vietnam War*. Dictionary of Literary Biography Documentary Series Vol. 9. Detroit: Gale, 1992. 215–74.

Beidler, Philip D. *Rewriting America: Vietnam Authors in Their Generation*. Athens: University of Georgia Press, 1991.

Bradley, Jerry. Rev. of *Caliban in Blue,* by Walter McDonald. *New Mexico Humanities Review* Sept. 1978: 62.

Breeden, David. Rev. of *All That Matters,* by Walt McDonald. *Texas Writers' Newsletter* Spring 1993: 7.

Rev. of *Burning the Fence,* by Walter McDonald. *Choice.* Dec. 1981: 507.

Butcher, Grace. Rev. of *Anything Anything,* by Walt McDonald. *Hiram Poetry Review* Fall/Winter 1981: 46–7.

———. Rev. of *Counting Survivors,* by Walter McDonald. *Hiram Poetry Review* 58/59 (1995–96): 79–81.

Catherwood, Michael. "About 'The Last Pitched Battle on the Plains.'" *Plainsongs* 17.1 (1996): 36.

Chappell, Fred. Rev. of *Anything Anything,* by Walter McDonald. *Greensboro Daily News/Record* 18 Jan. 1981: B5.

Collins, Robert. Rev. of *Counting Survivors,* by Walter McDonald. *Birmingham Poetry Review* 14 (1996): 43–6.

Cramer, Steven. Rev. of *Night Landings,* by Walter McDonald. *Poetry* 156.2 (1990): 100–02.

Cuba, Nan. Rev. of *The Digs in Escondido Canyon,* by Walter McDonald. *Texas Books in Review* 12.3 (1992): 6.

Davis, Robert Murray. Rev. of *A Band of Brothers,* by Walter McDonald. *New Mexico Humanities Review* 34 (1991): 150–1.

Davis, William Virgil. Rev. of *Anything Anything,* by Walter McDonald. *Texas Writers' Newsletter* Apr. 1981: 13–5.

Rev. of *The Digs in Escondido Canyon,* by Walter McDonald. *Borderlands: Texas Poetry Review* Spring 1993: 88.

Rev. of *The Digs in Escondido Canyon,* by Walter McDonald. *Kliatt* 26.2 Feb. 1992): 12.

Rev. of *The Digs in Escondido Canyon,* by Walter McDonald. *The Missouri Review* 15.2 (1992): 213–4.

Dodd, Bill. Rev. of *Witching on Hardscrabble,* by Walter McDonald. *Puerto del Sol* 22.2 (1987): 182–6.

Durham, Daniel. Rev. of *Blessings the Body Gave,* by Walter McDonald. *Lubbock Magazine* Apr. 1999: 16–9.

Ehrhart, W. D. "Soldier-Poets of the Vietnam War." *The Virginia Quarterly Review* 63.2 (1987): 246–65.

Fairchild, B. H. "McDonald's Prize Poems Show a World of Form and Meaning." *Texas Books in Review* 8.3 (1988): 4–5.

Filkins, Peter. Rev. of *Witching on Hardscrabble,* by Walter McDonald. *The Hiram Poetry Review* 41 (1986–7): 50–3.

Flores, Dan. Rev. of *All That Matters,* by Walter McDonald. *Panhandle-Plains Historical Review* 66 (1993): 73–4.

Rev. of *The Flying Dutchman,* by Walter McDonald. *The South Florida Poetry Review* 5.3 (1988): 49.

Flynn, Robert. Foreword. *A Band of Brothers: Stories from Vietnam,* by Walter McDonald. Texas Tech University Press, 1989. xi–xvi.

Frank, Robert. "Walter McDonald: Poet of Sight and Insight." *Poet Lore* Winter 1986: 220–6.

Gaskin, Bob. Rev. of *Anything Anything,* by Walter McDonald. *Cedar Rock* Winter 1981: 22.

Gilman, Owen W., Jr. *Vietnam and the Southern Imagination*. Jackson: University Press of Mississippi, 1992.

Goluboff, Benjamin. "Strategies of Allusion in Poetry of the Vietnam War." *Journal of American Culture* 16.3 (1993): 16–7.

Gotera, Vince. *Radical Visions: Poetry by Vietnam Veterans*. Athens: University of Georgia Press, 1994.

———. "Vietnam Souvenirs: Poems by Veterans." *North Coast Journal* Nov. 1990: 22–3.

Gwynn, R. S. Rev. of *The Flying Dutchman*, by Walter McDonald. Dictionary of Literary Biography 1987 Yearbook. Detroit: Gale, 1987. 184.

———. Rev. of *Witching on Hardscrabble*, by Walter McDonald. *Concho River Review* 1.1 (1987): 75–81.

Haines, John. Rev. of *Counting Survivors*, by Walter McDonald. *The Hudson Review* Winter 1996: 667–8.

Heinzelman, Kurt. "The Year in Poetry, 1988." *The Massachusetts Review* Spring 1989: 137, 149–52.

Henderson, Archibald. Rev. of *Anything Anything*, by Walter McDonald. *The South Central Bulletin* Spring/Summer 1982: 25.

———. Rev. of *One Thing Leads to Another*, by Walter McDonald. *The South Central Bulletin* Fall 1979: 116.

Hoggard, James. Rev. of *Burning the Fence*, by Walter McDonald. *Dallas Times Herald* 3 Jan. 1982: G4.

———. "Generous Voices." *The Texas Observer* 17 Sept. 1993: 17.

———. "The Glide Will Hold You." Rev. of *Night Landings*, by Walter McDonald. *The Texas Observer* 19 May 1989: 19.

———. "Home to West Texas." Rev. of *After the Noise of Saigon*, by Walter McDonald. *The Texas Observer* 14 Oct. 1988: 19.

———. Rev. of *Witching on Hardscrabble*, by Walter McDonald. *The Dallas Morning News* 30 Mar. 1986: C9.

Hopper, Kippra. "A Poet Among Us." *Vistas* Spring 1993: 28–31.

Hudgins, Andrew. "From First Books to Collected Poems." *The Hudson Review* 4 (1989): 737–44.

Jones, Roger. Rev. of *One Thing Leads to Another*, by Walter McDonald. *The Texas Review* Spring 1980: 127–8.

———. Rev. of *Witching on Hardscrabble*, by Walter McDonald. *Review of Texas Books* 1.1 (1986): 7.

Kennelly, Laura. Rev. of *Counting Survivors*, by Walter McDonald. *The Texas Writers' Newsletter* Fall 1995: 11–2.

Kerns, William. "McDonald's Poetry Digs in Area's Soul." *Lubbock Avalanche-Journal* 8 Nov. 1992: D1+.

Kinzie, Mary. "A Generation of Silver." *The American Poetry Review* 10 (1981): 13–20.

Landess, Thomas. Rev. of *Caliban in Blue*, by Walter McDonald. *The Dallas Free Gazette* 27 Oct. 1976: 6.

Leepson, Mark. "The Words Just Keep on Coming: Vietnam War Poetry." *The VVA Veteran* May 1996: 35–6.

Littledog, Pat. "Buzzards and Light." *The Texas Observer* 14 July 1995: 13.

McCarron, William E. Rev. of *After the Noise of Saigon*, by Walter McDonald. *Concho River Review* 2.2 (1988): 4–5.

————. "Names and Allusions in *A Band of Brothers.*" *The Round Table* 10 (1998): 4–5.

Mewshaw, Michael. Rev. of *Caliban in Blue,* by Walter McDonald. *Texas Monthly* Dec. 1976: 132.

Middleton, David E. Rev. of *Witching on Hardscrabble,* by Walter McDonald. *South Central Review* 4.1 (1987): 155–8.

Milligan, Bryce. Rev. of *Rafting the Brazos,* by Walter McDonald. *Dallas Morning News* 29 Oct. 1989: C8+.

Mills, Ralph J., Jr. Rev. of *The Flying Dutchman,* by Walter McDonald. *Tar River Poetry* 27.2 (1988): 53–5.

Myers, Jack. "A Declension of Tools." *Southwest Review* 62.1 (1977): 94–6.

Oliphant, Dave. Rev. of *Anything Anything,* by Walter McDonald. *The Pawn Review* 4 (1981): 90–7.

————. "Poems and Pictures Document the 'Open Plains.'" *Texas Books in Review* 12.4 (1992): 20–1.

————. "Three Texas Poets." *The Texas Observer* 27 March 1992: 18.

————. "Unignored Plunder: The Texas Poems of Walter McDonald." *Concho River Review* 10.1 (1996): 50–62.

Pike, Douglas. "*Counting Survivors.*" *Indochina Chronology* 12 (1997): 12.

Popelka, LaVerne. "Time in Walter McDonald's Poetry." Thesis. Abilene Christian University, 1989.

"Profile." *Texas Techsan Magazine* 45.1 (1992): 3, 15.

Pughe, Bronwyn G. Rev. of *The Flying Dutchman,* by Walter McDonald. *Cutbank* 29/30 (1988): 121.

Rev. of *Rafting the Brazos,* by Walter McDonald. *Amarillo Sunday News-Globe* 15 Apr. 1990: D8.

Rev. of *Rafting the Brazos,* by Walter McDonald. *Center for Texas Studies: Focus on Texas* 9 (1988–89): 1.

Rev. of *Rafting the Brazos,* by Walter McDonald. *Houston Chronicle* 30 Apr. 1989: 21.

Rev. of *Rafting the Brazos,* by Walter McDonald. *North San Antonio Times* 1 June 1989: 10.

Rev. of *Rafting the Brazos,* by Walter McDonald. *Publishers Weekly.* 24 Feb. 1989.

Rasco, Barbara. Rev. of *Anything Anything,* by Walter McDonald. *English in Texas* Fall 1981: 20–1.

Reynolds, Clay. Rev. of *A Band of Brothers,* by Walter McDonald. *Review of Texas Books* 4.4 (1990): 3.

Ringnalda, Don. *Fighting and Writing the Vietnam War.* Jackson: University Press of Mississippi, 1994.

Rogers, Bill M. Rev. of *One Thing Leads to Another,* by Walter McDonald. *English in Texas* Fall 1979: 8.

Ruffin, Paul. Rev. of *A Band of Brothers,* by Walter McDonald. *The Texas Review* Fall/Winter 1989: 139.

————. "*Where Skies Are Not Cloudy.*" *The Texas Review* Fall/Winter 1993: 111.

Sale, Richard B. "Poems Recount One Survivor's Journey." *Texas Books in Review* 15.4 (1995): 12–3.

Sanderson, James B. Rev. of *A Band of Brothers,* by Walter McDonald. *Concho River Review* Fall 1990: 96–7.

Schultz, Lee. "*All That Matters.*" *Western American Literature* 29.3 (1994): 283–4.

———. "Essay Review of *Counting Survivors* and of Robert S. McNamara's *In Retrospect: The Tragedy and Lessons of Viet Nam.*" *Western America Literature* 30.4 (1995): 427–32.

Schwetman, John. Rev. of *Caliban in Blue,* by Walter McDonald. *Sam Houston Literary Review* Dec. 1976: 49–50.

Shevin, David. "'Who Won the War You Were In?' Is Asked Again." *San Francisco People's Daily World* 4 Aug. 1990: 23.

Smith, Lorrie. "'After Our War': Poets of the Vietnam Generation." *Poetry Wales* June 1989: 7–11.

Speer, Laurel. Rev. of *Anything Anything,* by Walter McDonald. *The Small Press Review* July 1981: 1.

Stitt, Peter. Rev. of *The Flying Dutchman,* by Walter McDonald. *Poetry* June 1988: 169–71.

Sweetman, Charles P. "*All That Matters* Is a Rare Gift." *Texas Books in Review* 13.4 (1993): 18.

Swetman, Glen R. Rev. of *Caliban in Blue,* by Walter McDonald. *The South Central Bulletin* Spring 1978: 23–4.

Vaughan, Alden T. and Virginia Mason Vaughan. *Shakespeare's Caliban: A Cultural History.* Cambridge: Cambridge University Press, 1991, 1993.

West, Kathleen. "Landscapes of the West." *25th Anniversary Issue.* Spec. issue of *Puerto del Sol* (1988): 292–5.

Wolfe, Peter. Rev. of *Caliban in Blue,* by Walter McDonald. *St. Louis Globe Democrat* 16–17 Oct. 1976: "Books" page.

Wood, Susan. Rev. of *Caliban in Blue,* by Walter McDonald. *Texas Books in Review* 1977: 12.

Wright, Charlotte M. "Walter McDonald." *American Poets Since World War II.* Dictionary of Literary Biography Ser. 2 Vol. 105. Gale, 1991. 158–63.

Zarzyski, Paul. Rev. of *Witching on Hardscrabble,* by Walter McDonald. *Cutbank* 27/28 (1987): 124–6.

Zigal, Thomas. "Prizes for A Plains Poet." *The Dallas Morning News* 10 Apr. 1988: C14.

Contributors' Notes

Jerry Bradley is Dean of Graduate Studies and Associate Vice-President for Research at Lamar University. The author of four books, he is past president of the Texas Association of Creative Writing Teachers and the Southwest/Texas Popular Culture Association. He received the Scholar-Teacher of the Year Award from the Texas College English Association in 2000. A member of the Texas Institute of Letters, he has published in *Modern Poetry Studies, Poetry Magazine, Dark Horse Review,* and *New England Review.* He is poetry editor of *Concho River Review.*

Phyllis Bridges is Professor of English at Texas Woman's University. She earned her B.A. from West Texas State University, her M.A. from West Texas State University, and her Ph.D. from Texas Tech University; she has done postgraduate study at the University of Oklahoma; Universidad de Valencia, Spain; Huntington Library; and the Library of Congress. Named a Distinguished Alumna in English at Texas Tech, she has served as president of the Southwest/Texas Popular Culture Association and is on the board of the Texas Folklore Society.

Dan Flores currently teaches at the University of Montana in Missoula as A. B. Hammond Professor of Western American History. He specializes in the history of the West and American environmental history; among his books are *Jefferson and Southwestern Exploration* (1984), *Caprock Canyonlands* (1990), *Horizontal Yellow* (1999), and *The Natural West* (2001).

Michael Hobbs is Associate Professor of English at Northwest Missouri State University. He received his Ph.D. from the University of North Texas. He published a chapter on Walt McDonald in *Updating the Literary West* and also has published articles in *The Wallace Stevens Journal, Southwestern American Literature, Western American Literature, American Literary Realism, Studies in Short Fiction,* and the *Henry James Review.*

Andrew Hudgins is Professor of English at Ohio State University. He received his M.F.A. from the University of Iowa in 1983. His publications include *Saints and Strangers, After The Lost War: A Narrative, The Never-Ending: New Poems,* and *The Glass Hammer: A Southern Childhood;* poems in *American Poetry Review, The New Yorker, The Hudson Review, Poetry* and other journals; his short stories have appeared in *The Southern Review, The Missouri Review,* and other journals; his personal essays have been published in *Contemporary Authors: Autobiography Series, The Oxford American, The Hudson Review, The Southern Review, The American Scholar,* and *The Washington Post Magazine.* He is the recipient of the Witter Bynner Award of the American Academy and Institute of Arts and Letters, has been a finalist for the Pulitzer Prize for *Saints and Strangers,* and a finalist for the National Book Award for *After the*

Lost War. He is also the recipient of The Poet's Prize for *After the Lost War*, the Haines Prize for poetry from the Fellowship of Southern Writers, The Taft Distinguished Faculty Award, the Ohioiana Award for lifetime contributions to poetry in Ohio, and two NEA fellowships.

William Jolliff is Professor of English at George Fox University. He has published a chapbook of poems entitled *Whatever Was Ripe*, which won the 1998 Bright Hill Press competition; he also has published poems in journals including *Southern Poetry Review, Literature and Belief*, and *Quarterly West;* other of his scholarly writings have appeared in *Appalachian Heritage* and *The Explicator;* he has edited and written the introduction for *The Poetry of John Greenleaf Whittier: A Reader's Edition* (2000).

April Lindner is Assistant Professor of English at Saint Joseph's University in Philadelphia. She received her Ph.D. from the University of Cincinnati and her M.F.A. from Sarah Lawrence College; her criticism has appeared in *Paintbrush, The Chattahoochee Review*, and *Critique;* her poems have been published in various journals, including *Prairie Schooner, The Spoon River Quarterly, The Greensboro Review, The Cincinnati Poetry Review,* and *Peregrine*. Boise State University Press's Western Writers Series has published her booklets, *Dana Gioia* and *New Formalist Poets of the American West*. Her collection of poetry, *Skin,* won the 2001 Walt McDonald Poetry Prize and is forthcoming from Texas Tech University Press.

Helen Maxson is Professor of English at Southwestern Oklahoma State University. She received her Ph.D. from Cornell University in 1987, her M.A. from Middlebury College in 1977, and her B.A. from Middlebury College in 1971. She has published essays in *The Midwest Quarterly, Dialogue, Westview, Nineteenth-Century Prose, Christianity and Literature*, and *The Journal of Comparative Literature and Aesthetics.*

Nick Norwood is Assistant Professor of English at McMurry University in Abilene, Texas. He received his Ph.D. from Arizona State University in 1998 with a dissertation on Southwestern Literature of and about the 1940s and '50s; his poems have appeared in various journals, including *The Paris Review, Southwest Review, Western Humanities Review, Red River Review, Concho River Review, Pleiades,* and *Ekphrasis;* his manuscript, *A Palace for the Heart*, was a finalist for the Vassar Miller Prize and a semifinalist for the Verse Prize. His first manuscript, *The Soft Blare,* will appear in the Andrew Hudgins Poetry Series from River City Press in the spring of 2003.

Dave Oliphant is a lecturer at the University of Texas at Austin. He received his Ph.D. from Northern Illinois University in 1975, his M.A. from the University of Texas at Austin in 1966, and his B.A. from Lamar University in Beaumont, Texas, in 1963. His publications include *Texan Jazz; Roundup: An Anthology of Texas Poets, 1973–1998* (editor); *Figures of Speech: Poems by Enrique Lihn* (translator); and *Memories of Texas Towns & Cities.*

LaVerne Popelka received her M.A. from Abilene Christian University; her master's thesis was entitled *Time in the Poetry of Walter McDonald.*

Clay Reynolds is Professor of Aesthetic Studies and Studies in Literature at the University of Texas at Dallas. He received his Ph.D. from the University of Tulsa in 1979. His book publications include *Monuments, Players, Twenty Questions: Answers for the Aspiring Writer, Franklin's Crossing, Taking Stock: A Larry McMurtry Casebook, Agatite, Stage Left: The Development of the American Social Theater in the Thirties*, and *The Vigil.*

Barbara Rodman received her Ph.D. from the University of Denver; she is Director of Creative Writing at the University of North Texas. She has published short fiction in a variety of journals, including *The Denver Quarterly, Colorado Review, The Forum, Creative Woman,* and *New Mexico Humanities Review.* She is Fiction Editor of the *American Literary Review.*

Henry Taylor received his M.A. from Hollins College. His third collection of poems, *The Flying Change,* received the 1986 Pulitzer Prize in Poetry. His first two books, *The Horse Show at Midnight* and *An Afternoon of Pocket Billiards,* have been reprinted as one volume. His most recent collection of poems is *Brief Candles: 101 Clerihews. Understanding Fiction: Poems 1986–96* appeared in 1996. He has received Fellowships in Creative Writing from the National Endowment for the Arts (1978 and 1986), a Research Grant from the National Endowment for the Humanities (1980–81), the Witter Bynner Prize of the American Academy and Institute of Arts and Letters (1984), and the Golden Crane Award of the Washington Chapter of the American Literary Translators Association (1989).

Darryl Tippens received his B.A. from Oklahoma Christian University in 1968, his M.A. from Louisiana State University in 1971, and his Ph.D. from Louisiana State University in 1973. Since January 2001, he has been Provost at Pepperdine University. From 1996 to 2000 he was the James W. Culp Distinguished Professor of English at Abilene Christian University.

William Wenthe received his Ph.D. from the University of Virginia. A specialist in modern British and American poetry, he is Associate Professor of English at Texas Tech University. He has published poems in such journals as *Poetry, The Georgia Review, Ironwood, Southern Humanities Review, Cimarron Review,* and *TriQuarterly.* His books of poems are *Birds of Hoboken* and *Not Till We Are Lost* (forthcoming from LSU Press). He has won fellowships from the National Endowment for the Arts and the Texas Commission on the Arts, and a Pushcart Prize.

Janice Whittington received her B.A. from the University of Wyoming, her M.A. from Texas Tech University, and her Ph.D. from Texas Tech University. Her collection of poems, *Into a Thousand Mouths,* winner of the Walt McDonald First Book Award, was published by Texas Tech University Press in 1998. Her chapbook *Does My Father Dream of Sons?* was published by the University of West Florida Press in 1990.

Chris Willerton is currently Professor of English and Director of the Honors Program at Abilene Christian University. He received his B.A. from Texas Christian University in 1969, his M.A. from the University of North Carolina in 1970, and his Ph.D. from the University of North Carolina at Chapel Hill in 1979. His articles have appeared in *The National Honors Report, Sparks That Leap: Essays on Faith and Learning, Dictionary of Literary Biography,* and *Currents in Electronic Literacy;* his poems have appeared in *Texas in Poetry, Christianity and Literature, Kansas Quarterly, Borderlands,* and *Southern Poetry Review.*

Index

acceptance, 8, 96, 144
adoption, 127, 170, 203–4
affirmation, 30, 63, 65, 75–6
"After a Week in the Rockies," 85
"After the Fall of Saigon," 75, 187
"After the Fires We Once Called
    Vietnam," 166
"After the Flight Home from Saigon,"
    137, 200
"After the Monsoon," 117
"After the Noise of Saigon," 21–2
After the Noise of Saigon, 2, 4–6, 8–10,
    21–2, 89–91, 136–9, 141–3, 166–9, 190,
    192
"After the Rains of Saigon," 43–4
"After Years in the Mountains," 45, 85
aging, 38, 45, 47
"All Boys Are Humpty Dumpty," 207–8
Allen, C. Leonard, 167
Allen, Terry, 112
All Occasions, 10–13, 17–19, 23, 25–6,
    31–6, 145–6, 159, 172, 222–3
"All That Aches and Blesses," 47, 166–7
*All That Matters: The Texas Plains in Pho-
    tographs and Poems*, 41, 113–114, 137,
    159–160, 199–202, 205
allusions, literary, 20, 84, 138, 153,
    200–01, 206; biblical, 10, 11, 106, 173,
    185, 187, 198, 207–8, 211
ambiguity, 21, 74
animals, 21, 71, 89, 92, 94, 135, 219; bull,
    10, 84, 95–6; buzzards, 79, 89; calf, 96;
    cattle, 34, 92–3, 135; coyotes, 2, 27,
    135; dog, 21, 24, 97, 135; eagles, 2,

94–5; elk, 94; hawks, 34, 30, 71, 89, 96,
    135; hummingbirds, 12–13; rabbits,
    96, 135–6; snakes, 2, 71, 92, 135
"An Old Dog's Winter Nights," 22–3
Anselm, 196
Anything Anything, 2–3, 19–21, 62–3,
    105–6, 126–30, 152–4
Arnold, Matthew, 22, 189
art/the artist, 72, 89–90, 152–60, 199
"At the Dawn with the Blinds Raised,"
    12–13
"At the Stone Café," 88–9
Auden, W. H., 109, 111, 139, 147
Auerbach, Erich, 195–8
awards, McDonald's, 30, 92, 100, 165,
    221, 224

background, McDonald's, 216, 220, 222
Bakhtin, Mikhail, 196
balance, 98; fatherly pride with the dark
    side, 19; humor and pathos, 23; imag-
    ination and reality, 140, 145–7; in
    treating the region, 107–9; joy with
    violence, 5; of truth and distortion,
    23, 136
Bamboo Bed, The, 48
A Band of Brothers, 48–59; as a picaresque
    novel, 53, 56; Colonel Tydings, 53–7;
    irony in character's actions, 56;
    DEROS (Date of Earliest Return from
    Overseas), 54–5; Lieutenant Mosley
    (Little Moose), 53–7; minor charac-
    ters, 54–6; SNOW (Successfully

Numbered Observations on War), 53,
    56–7; themes in, 51
"The Barn on the Brazos," 82–3
Beamon, Bob, 17, 27
Behlen, Charles, 87
"Before the War," 72
Berryman, John, 11, 219
Berry, Wendell, 196
"Between the Moon and Me," 5–6
"Billy Bastard and the Centipede," 124
birds as emblems of domestic life, 42
"Black Granite Burns Like Ice," 72–4, 77
"Black Wings Wheeling," 4
Blades, Joe, 49
blessings, 11, 25, 40, 190, 202
"Blessings the Body Gave," 145, 203
Blessings the Body Gave, 9–10, 22, 24–7,
    93–5, 108–9, 144–5, 158, 163, 170–2,
    174, 191, 193, 199, 202–5, 211
"Bloodlines," 127–8
"Blue Skies," 200
Bosnia, 27, 37
Bourjaily, Vance, 217
"A Brief History of Glass," 152–4
Browne, Sir Thomas, 162, 164
Browning, Robert, 196, 218
"Bull," 139
"Burning the Fence," 132–3, 180
Burning the Fence, 45–6, 62, 85, 87, 122–7,
    129, 132–3, 175–84
Bush, Laura, 114
Butler, Robert Olen, 52
Bynner, Witter, 101

"Cabin," 183
"A Cabin, Even a Cave," 94–5
Caliban in Blue, 19, 30–2, 46, 62, 64, 82,
    122–3, 128, 131–2, 148–52, 162–3
"Caliban on Spinning," 131, 148–52
Candide, 34
Caputo, Phillip, 51
"Carrion Comfort," 223
Cassill, R. V., 217
The Castle of Perseverance, 186
"Cataracts," 26
"Caught in a Squall Near Matador," 190

characters, 37, 38, 87, 134
"Charts," 41, 212
"The Child Abandoned on the Porch,"
    203
children, 38, 93; as agents of mercy, 170
"The Children of Saigon," 43, 89
"Chili at the Rattlesnake Roundup," 2
"Chocolate," 33
Christian, 104; dichotomy, 202; dimen-
    sions, 165; faith, 185–94; symbolism,
    191; vision, 10
Christ-like figures, 10
"Claiming Kin," 182
closure. See endings
"Colonel Mackenzie Maps the Llano
    Estacado," 86
Colorado, 38, 103, 122, 148
comic, 68, 93, 190 (See also humor)
companionship, 72
comparisons, 32, 39
Conrad, Joseph, 30
contrasts, childhood and adulthood, 126;
    human and animal, 139; purpose and
    effort, 44; Texas and the mountains,
    32; Texas and Vietnam, 31
"Counting Survivors," 74–5, 87, 168–9,
    188, 212
Counting Survivors, 41, 46–7, 72, 74–9,
    83–4, 86–90, 92–9, 139–40, 144–5,
    151–2, 155–7, 162, 164, 166, 168–70,
    185–90, 193–4, 211–12
country-western songs, 23–4, 82, 90
cowboy, influence of, 221–2
"Coyotes and Dogs," 88
"Crashes Real and Imagined," 138
Crawford, Max, 112
Creeley, Robert, 20

Dante, 178–9
death, acceptance of, 26; as motif, 39, 40,
    45, 69, 122–33, 157
"Deductions from the Laws of Motion,"
    201
Delveccio, John M., 51
departures, 34, 46–7, 123

Desert Storm, 27, 58
devotion, search for, 9
"Diamonds in the Carnegie Museum,"
    145–6
Dickey, James, 21, 168, 218
Dickinson, Emily, 16, 147, 219
diction, 83, 150–153, 155, 157, 208
"The Digs at Escondido," 39–40, 70
The Digs in Escondido Canyon, 5, 93
domesticity, 41–2, 93; and national
    defense, 30–6
Donne, John, 10, 218, 223
"Drying Up," 201
duality, of humans, 164; soldier and
    family man, 31
Durrell, Lawrence, 125
"The Dust We Are Made Of," 172–4

early work, McDonald's, 30, 62, 72
"East of Eden," 202
"Ejecting from Jets," 38–39
elegiac aspect, 70, 72, 166, 187
Eliot, T. S., 9, 63, 73–4, 139, 165, 196,
    205–7, 211, 218
Ellery, Chris, 63
Ely, Joe, 112
"Embarkations," 46
endings, anagogical, 175–84; literal,
    182–3
endurance, 129, 131, 166
epigraphs, 11, 19
epiphanies, 35, 122, 190, 204
"Especially at Night," 21
"Estacado," 5, 116, 190
"Evolution," 181

"Facing It," 18–19
The Faerie Queen, 186
faith, 8–9, 11–12, 36, 40, 83–4, 142;
    McDonald's journey of, 195–213
"Faith Is a Radical Master," 12, 192–3,
    209–11
familiar ground, McDonald's, 17
"Faraway Places," 46, 122–3
"Farms at Auction," 188

father/daughter, 123, 127
father/son, 2–3, 6–7, 19, 25–7, 44–7, 69,
    75–6, 122–3, 126–7, 131–2
"Fathers and Sons," 26–7, 131–2
"Father's Mail-Order Rifles," 46
Faulkner, William, 19, 87, 102–3, 218
fear, 6, 21, 128
Fehlen, Myra, 197
female, power of, 44; voices, 38, 44
"Fences," 42
"Finding My Father's Hands in
    Midlife," 45–6, 132
"First Blood," 124–5, 182
"The First Hard Thunder of Another
    Dawn," 117
"The First Months Home," 22
"First Solo," 44, 180
"First Solo in Thunderstorms," 40
fishing, 66–68
flying, 33, 39, 44, 89, 131, 148–51, 180,
    192, 217–9, 222
"The Flying Dutchman," 106–7
The Flying Dutchman, 4, 7–8, 22–3, 67–9,
    106–7, 158, 164, 187
Flynn, Robert, 57–8
"The Food Pickers of Saigon," 89
"For Dawes, on Takeoff," 187
"For Friends Missing in Action," 6, 39,
    187
forgiveness, 45
"For God in My Sorrows," 144, 170, 172,
    193, 204–5
Francis of Assisi, 196
"Frogs Croaking Their Love Songs,"
    206–7
Frost, Robert, 22, 79, 84, 97, 101–2, 104,
    106–10, 134, 183–4, 206, 218

gallery of figures/characters, 37
"Getting It Done," 158, 164
Gilmore, Jimmie Dale, 112
"The Girl in the Mackinaw and Panties,"
    20, 87, 128
"Giving Time," 129
"The Gleam of Silver Wings," 187
"The Goats of Summer," 93

"Going Home," 129–30, 163, 180
"The Golden Bowl," 42
"Goliath, Night Before Battle," 106
Gordon, Mary, 173
grace, 144–5
"Grace and the Blood of Goats," 76–7, 144–5, 166, 189
Gray, Anthony, 51

Haley, J. Evetts, 112
"The Hairpin Curve at Durango," 211
"The Hammer," 82, 132
Hancock, Butch, 112
hardscrabble, 2, 4, 17, 69, 76, 79, 82
"Harvest," 97–8
Heller, Joseph, 53, 56, 218
hell motif, 86
Hemingway, Ernest, 5, 7, 30, 125, 128, 218
Herbert, George, 165
Hershey, John, 53
"High Plains Drifter," 116–7
"His Side of It," 156
Hogue, Alexander, 112
Holly, Buddy, 112, 220
Homer, 30, 195
Hopkins, Gerard Manley, 10–11, 163, 196, 201, 218, 219, 223
hostile world, 5–6, 11
Hugo, Richard, 80, 101, 134, 218
human, attempts to stave off the inevitable, 180; position in the land, 136; situation, 107; struggle to keep order, 97; urge toward wildness, 96
humor, 24, 64, 67, 68, 86, 90, 191, 200 (See also comic)
hunting, 21
husband/wife, 8–9, 38, 40–2, 44–5, 64–5, 73, 76–8, 94, 144–5, 156–9, 189, 203

imagery, 44, 65, 89, 105, 109, 122, 218; animal, 128; wasteland, 69–74
images, 43, 73, 103, 149, 151–2, 154–5; ease with, 23; of beauty, 73
incarnation, forms of, 195–213
influences, 30, 218–9

initiation, 126–7
innocence, loss of, 3, 122
insight, 90
"Instant Replay," 32
"In the Alchemist's Household," 33, 159
"In the Rare Acquisitions Room," 154–5
"In Times of Fear," 190
irony, 3, 35, 39, 64, 68, 71, 75, 83, 100, 104, 107, 123, 128, 133, 144, 173, 182, 186, 188–9
"I Still Can't Say the Word," 25–6, 34

Jarrell, Randall, 30
Jewett, Sarah Orne, 102
Jones, James, 53
Joyce, James, 30
"The Jungles of Da Lat," 128
Justice, Donald, 64, 103–4
juxtapositon, humor and pathos, 23; sincerity and posturing, 24; death and tender moments, 38–39; life and death, 43; war and domesticity, 43

Karr, Mary, 80–83, 89
Kelton, Elmer, 112
Kemp, John C., 101–2, 104, 107
Kennedy, John, assassination of, 48
"Killing Nothing But Time," 32, 36
Korean War, 49, 57
Kostadinova, Stefka, 17
Kunitz, Stanley, 30

"Lake Solon," 130
Land of 1000 Elephants, 48
landscape, 82, 85, 97–9, 109–10, 111–19, 134–6, 148, 150–1, 157, 159, 200; as ground for imagination, 1, 103, 136; as microcosm of postmodern world, 63; as outer/inner terrain, 38, 72; as screen, 99; poetry, 118; to increase tension, 106–7
language, 4, 10, 62, 65–7, 69–70, 108–9, 131, 148–60; honesty of, 35; of gospels, 10, 12; self-referential, 65–6, 69; sexual, 178–9

"The Last Saloon in Lubbock," 88, 118
Lawrence, D. H., 109
"Learning How in the Southwest,"
    108–9, 170
"Learning to Live with Nightmares," 43
"Learning to Live with Sandstorms," 118
Levertov, Denise, 218
Lewis, Carl, 27
Lewis, C. S., 196
"The Lifeguard," 133
"Life with Father," 46
line breaks, 150, 152–3, 158
literary influences, 30
"Living on Buried Water," 136–7
"Living on Open Plains," 131
"Living on the Plains," 41
"Llano Estacado," 129
"Loading a Shotgun," 2
love, of family, 7, 32, 38, 221; mutual, 41,
    44; marital, 7, 11, 32, 38; power to
    heal, 40, 42
Lowell, Amy, 101
loyalty, 6
"Luck of the Draw," 47, 190

machismo, lack of, 38, 40
"Macho," 129, 208–10
"Making a Living," 3
"Making Time," 30
"Manna International" 169
"Marching Through Georgia," 33
Mailer, Norman, 48, 53
marriage, embrace, 45
"Marriage," 40
Maxson, Helen F., 103
McMurtry, Larry, 112, 187
"The Meaning of Flat Fields," 98–9
"Measuring Time," 180–1
"Memento Mori," 157
memory, 7, 38, 45, 70, 72, 222
"Mending the Fence," 97–8
"Mesas I Never Took the Time to
    Climb," 75, 77–9, 151–2, 193–4
metaphors/metaphoric language, 7, 12,
    105, 109, 146–7, 148, 159–60, 179–80,
    190, 192, 197, 211

meter, 24; McDonald's irregular, 17
Michener, James, 48
"The Midas Touch in Texas," 33
"The Middle Years," 8–9
"Midnight at Dillon," 64, 66–7, 191
Millay, Edna St. Vincent, 218
Milton, John, 84, 86
"Mirror Images," 155
monologue, dramatic, 106, 185
Momaday, N. Scott, 101
Moore, Marianne, 10
"Morning in Texas," 124–6, 176–8, 181
Morris, John Miller, 112
"My Brother and the Golden Gloves," 46
"My Brother in Summer," 105
"My Father Quits Another Job," 6–7
Myers, Jack 164; and Michael Simms,
    177
mystery, 64, 79, 188

nature, beauties of, 11, 143–5
"Nearing the End of a Century," 141–4
"The Neighbor," 133
"Neighbors Miles Away," 116, 212–3
Neugebauer, Janet M., 113–14, 116–7
"Never in My Life," 45
Neitzsche, Friedrich, 166
"Night at Cam Ranh Bay," 46
"Night Before My Father Went to War,"
    46
"Night Landings," 38–9
Night Landings, 4, 38–41, 43–4, 46, 89,
    131–2, 166–7, 190, 192
"Nights at the Hi-D-Ho," 118
"Nights in the San Juans," 41–2
"Night Skiing on Lake Buchanan," 64–6
"No Matter Where We've Been," 71–2
nostalgia, 33–4

O'Brien, Tim, 52
O'Connor, Flannery, 184
O'Connor, Frank, 168
O'Keeffe, Georgia, 112
"Old Pets," 93–4, 99
One Thing Leads to Another, 84, 87

"On Planting My First Tree Since
    Vietnam," 82
"On Teaching David to Shoot," 2–3, 19,
    126–7
order, man's need for, 5
"Out of the Stone They Came," 75–6

paradox, 66, 168; bleak/affirmative, 64;
    Christian, 163, 165; faith/doubt, 169;
    intimacy through darkness, 204;
    terror/beauty, 70; of atmosphere in
    poems, 107; passive/active, 35;
    unlikely voices and backgrounds, 37;
    what saves can destroy, 2
"The Party," 122–3
peacekeeping soldiers, 37–47
persistence/endurance, 105
personas, 2, 7, 33, 75–6, 103, 105; consis-
    tent, 106, 151–2
perspectives, 89; shifting, 205–7
perseverance, 76–7, 185–94
"Picasso and the Art of Angels," 90, 154
Pilgrim's Progress, 186
"Plains and the Art of Writing," 159–60,
    198
plain style, 35, 107
Plato, 146
"Plowing Through Ashes," 183
poems, as little fictions, 219; as
    metaphors, 168, 184; with shared
    titles, 84, 198
poetry, imaginative force of, 139; of high
    seriousness, 83
Pound, Ezra, 101
point of view, 18, 19, 95, 150
Powell, Mike, 27
"Principles of Flight," 39
"Progeny," 132
Proust, Marcel, 195
pursuits of men as metaphors, 47

"Rafting the Brazos," 124–5
Rafting the Brazos, 23–4, 42, 83, 135–6,
    139, 143–4, 154–6, 191–2

Ramke, Bin, 80–3, 89
ranching, 23, 95, 97
"Rattler," 117
"Reading Ecclesiastes at Sixty," 36
"Reasons for Taking Risks," 166
Reaugh, Frank, 112
redemption, 108–9, 139, 168, 170, 173
regional poet, McDonald as, 92, 100–10;
    as more than regionalist, 100–10, 164
"Releasing the Hawk in August," 96
religious, belief, 143; meaning, 142;
    poetry, 140–1
"Rembrandt and the Art of Mercy,"
    89–90, 155–6
remembering fallen comrades, 6
resurrection, 169
returning veteran, 107
revisiting themes, 84
rhyme, 25
Rico, Gabrielle, 178
"Riding Herd," 95, 99
"Rigging the Windmill," 191
"Rig Sitting," 90, 91
risk, 7, 20, 65–6, 148–50, 156–9, 198
Robinson, Edwin Arlington, 101
"Rocket Attack," 25
"The Rodeo Fool," 10, 191–2
Roethke, Theodore, 181, 218
Rogers, Pattiann, 92

Sandburg, Carl, 187
"Saying the Blessing," 46
"Scout Arapaho," 127
"Seining for Carp," 68–9
"Settling the Plains," 84, 190, 201
sensual details, 89
"Setting Out Oaks in Winter," 83
Shakespeare, William, 30, 163, 217
"Signs and Warnings," 20–1
"The Signs of Prairie Rattlers," 98–9, 189
Smith, Barbara Herrnstein, 175, 177
"Someday," 83
"The Songs of Country Girls," 23
"The Songs We Fought For," 23–4
sounds, 83, 89, 151–2, 155, 218

Southwell, Robert, 196
spiritual, belief, 138; progress, 8; search,
    10; sustenance, 136
"Splitting the Wood for Winter," 44
"Stalls in All Weather," 92–4, 96
"Starting a Pasture," 116
"Steeples and Deep Wells," 84–5
Stegner, Wallace, 112
Steinbeck, John, 187
Steiner, George, 164
Stevens, Wallace, 78, 89, 91, 134–47, 200,
    205, 218
Stevenson, Robert Louis, 18
Strand, Mark, 20
"The String of the Visible," 139
suffering as construct, 168
"Sunday Morning Roundup," 206
"The Summer Before the War," 72
survivors/surviving, 25, 34, 74, 87, 89,
    106–7, 186–91; guilt of, 186; ques-
    tioning how to, 7
"Sweet Nothings," 5
symbolism, 12, 68, 123; undercutting, 98
synechdoche, 108
syntax, 18, 35, 176

"Taking Each Breath," 41
"Taking Off in Winter," 192
"The Tap of Angry Reins," 83–4
"Teaching Our Sons Old Chores," 46
Tennyson, Alfred, 218
"Ten O'Clock Scholar," 129
tension, between, dead and living, 106;
    humans and nature, 97; wild and
    domestic, 92, 95, 97
"That Child Abandoned on the Porch,"
    170
"That Silence When a Mountain Lion
    Attacks," 31–2
"Things About to Disappear," 200
themes in McDonald's poetry, 30, 164;
    revisiting, 84
Thomas, Dylan, 22, 133
Thomas, R. S., 185
"A Thousand Miles of Stars," 35

time, images of, 122–33, 181
Tippens, Darryl L., 100
"To Derek, Still in West Texas," 87
tone, 3, 5, 34, 64, 71–2, 78, 94; bitter, 23
"Tornado Alley," 179
"To the Tribe," 33
transcendence, 78–9, 203
tropes, 136
Tuan, Yi–Fu, 112
"Turning Their Shimmer into Wells," 118

The Ugly American, 48
"Uncle Jerry and the Velvet Dog," 211
"Uncle Phillip and the Endless Names,"
    87
"Under Blue Skies," 96
"University Library," 179–80
Uris, Leon, 53
verticality in McDonald's poetry, 136
Vietnam, 2,11, 17, 27, 32, 42–43, 48–59,
    72, 75, 82–3, 100, 103–4, 106, 122–3,
    137, 141, 163, 187, 200, 202, 217, 219
    223; as literary war, 49; fiction, 48–53,
    58–9; themes in fiction, 51–3; memo-
    rial wall, 46, 72–3, 75–76, 87, 168,
    186–7, 212; post-war anxieties, 22
violence, 4–5, 21, 36, 39
voice, 4, 63; consistency of, 34, 106;
    female, 38
"Voices on Jukebox Wax," 24–5

Wagoner, David, 134
Walt/Walter, 22
"The Waltz We Were Born For," 9–10,
    158, 203
war, 2, 6, 25, 31, 37, 187
"War Games," 6
"War in the Persian Gulf," 89
wasteland, beautiful, 62–79
"Watching Dawn on Padre Island,"
    12–13, 36
"The Weatherman Reports the Weather,"
    139, 188–9
Webb, Walter Prescott, 112

"Weeding the Strawberry Garden," 191
Whatever the Wind Delivers: Celebrating
   West Texas and the Near Southwest, 30,
   88–9, 92, 113–19, 221, 223
"What If I Didn't Die Outside Saigon,"
   187–8
"When Children Think You Can Do
   Anything," 4
"When Rockets Fell Like Stars," 223
"When the Children Have Gone," 47,
   77–8, 94
"When the Wind Dies," 64–6, 78
"Where Buffalo Grass Grows Loud If We
   Listen," 203
"Where Seldom Is Heard," 117
"Where Skies Are Not Cloudy," 25, 154
Where Skies Are Not Cloudy, 24, 71–4,
   82–5, 89–90, 96, 138–9, 192, 199,
   205–10
"Wildcatting," 40–1, 91
"The Wild Swans of Da Lat," 42–3
Wilkinson, Andy, 112
Williams, William Carlos, 90, 109, 134,
   165
"Wind and Hardscrabble," 201
"The Winter Our Grandson Turned Thir-
   teen," 13
"Wishing for More Than Thunder,"
   139–40
"Witching," 44

"Witching on Canvas," 156–7
"Witching on Hardscrabble," 191
Witching on Hardscrabble, 1–4, 39, 63–8,
   72, 125, 132–3, 157, 190–1
"With Derek in the Dunes," 62–3, 65
"With Mercy for All," 170
"With My Father in Winter," 69–70, 72,
   74
"With Steve at Lake Raven," 46, 122–4
"The Witness of Dry Plains," 135–6
Wolfe, Thomas, 218
"A Woman Acquainted with the Night,"
   7–8
women, 47; as antidotes to solitariness,
   33; as stay against chaos, 33; healing
   touch of, 33
Wordsworth, William, 196
work, amount of, McDonald's, 16
"Working Against Time," 130–1
Working Against Time, 129–31, 155
World War I, 48
"World War I Soldiers," 181
World War II, 18, 27, 48–9, 51, 137, 153–4
Wouk, Herman, 52–3
Wright, James, 101, 218
writing poetry, 34, 67, 99, 148–60, 216–25

Yeats, W. B., 206, 218